METHODIST AND PIETIST

KINGSWOOD BOOKS

Rex D. Matthews, Director
Candler School of Theology, Emory University

EDITORIAL ADVISORY BOARD

Ted Campbell
Perkins School of Theology, Southern Methodist University

Joel B. Green
Fuller Theological Seminary

Richard P. Heitzenrater
The Divinity School, Duke University

Henry Knight III
Saint Paul School of Theology

Mary Elizabeth Moore
School of Theology, Boston University

F. Douglas Powe Jr.
Saint Paul School of Theology

Sam Powell
Point Loma Nazarene University

Jason E. Vickers
United Theological Seminary

Karen B. Westerfield Tucker
School of Theology, Boston University

Sondra Wheeler
Wesley Theological Seminary

M. Kathryn Armistead, *ex officio*
Abingdon Press

Neil Alexander, *ex officio*
Abingdon Press

METHODIST AND PIETIST

Retrieving the Evangelical United Brethren Tradition

Edited by
J. Steven O'Malley
and Jason E. Vickers

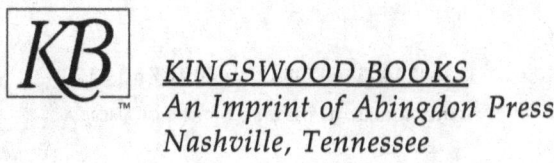

KINGSWOOD BOOKS
An Imprint of Abingdon Press
Nashville, Tennessee

METHODIST AND PIETIST
RETRIEVING THE EVANGELICAL UNITED BRETHREN TRADITION

Copyright © 2011 by Abingdon Press

All rights reserved.

No part of this work may be reproduced or transmitted in any form or by any means, electronic or mechanical, including photocopying and recording, or by any information storage or retrieval system, except as may be expressly permitted by the 1976 Copyright Act or in writing from the publisher. Requests for permission should be addressed to Abingdon Press, P.O. Box 801, 201 Eighth Avenue South, Nashville, TN 37202-0801, or e-mailed to permissions@umpublishing.org.

This book is printed on acid-free paper.

Library of Congress Cataloging-in-Publication Data

Methodist and Pietist : retrieving the Evangelical United Brethren tradition / edited by J. Steven O'Malley & Jason E. Vickers.
   p. cm.
Includes bibliographical references (p.   ) and index.
ISBN 978-1-4267-1435-1 (book - pbk./trade pbk. : alk. paper)
1. Evangelical United Brethren Church. I. O'Malley, J. Steven (John Steven), 1942- II. Vickers, Jason E.
BX7556.R48 2011
289.9—dc22

2010037751

Scripture quotations, unless noted otherwise, are from the New Revised Standard Version of the Bible, copyright 1989, Division of Christian Education of the National Council of the Churches of Christ in the United States of America. Used by permission. All rights reserved.

Scripture quotations noted KJV are from the King James or Authorized Version of the Bible.

Scripture quotations noted NIV are from the Holy Bible, NEW INTERNATIONAL VERSION®. Copyright © 1973, 1978, 1984 by International Bible Society. All rights reserved throughout the world. Used by permission of International Bible Society.

Scripture quotations noted RSV are from the Revised Standard Version of the Bible, copyright 1952 [2nd edition, 1971] by the Division of Christian Education of the National Council of the Churches of Christ in the United States of America. Used by permission. All rights reserved.

Contents

INTRODUCTION—J. STEVEN O'MALLEY AND JASON E. VICKERS . . VII

PART ONE—HISTORY

    1. THE PIETIST BACKGROUND OF THE EVANGELICAL UNITED BRETHREN CHURCH—K. JAMES STEIN 3

    2. MARTIN BOEHM, PHILIP WILLIAM OTTERBEIN, AND THE UNITED BRETHREN IN CHRIST—SCOTT KISKER 19

    3. JACOB ALBRIGHT AND THE EVANGELICAL ASSOCIATION— KENNETH E. ROWE 37

PART TWO—DOCTRINE AND THEOLOGY

    4. THE THEOLOGICAL HERITAGE OF PIETISM— J. STEVEN O'MALLEY 57

    5. DOCTRINE AND THEOLOGY IN THE CHURCH OF THE UNITED BRETHREN IN CHRIST—TYRON INBODY 75

    6. DOCTRINE AND THEOLOGY IN THE EVANGELICAL ASSOCIATION/CHURCH—WILLIAM NAUMANN 93

    7. THE CONFESSION OF FAITH: A THEOLOGICAL COMMENTARY—JASON E. VICKERS 109

CONTENTS

PART THREE—POLITY AND PRACTICES

    8. EPISCOPACY AND ORDINATION—JAMES E. KIRBY ... 139

    9. THE PRACTICE OF LITURGY AND SACRAMENTS IN THE EVANGELICAL UNITED BRETHREN TRADITION—
KENDALL KANE MCCABE 149

    10. THE PRACTICE OF MISSION AND EVANGELISM: THE MISSION TO GERMANY—ULRIKE SCHULER 163

    11. "TRUE HOLINESS" AS SOCIAL PRACTICE IN THE EVANGELICAL AND UNITED BRETHREN TRADITIONS: A LEGACY FOR SUCCESSOR DENOMINATIONS—
WENDY J. DEICHMANN EDWARDS 179

    12. WOMEN IN THE PIETIST HERITAGE OF METHODISM—
PAUL W. CHILCOTE 191

AFTERWORD—THE EVANGELICAL UNITED BRETHREN TRADITION AND THE FUTURE OF UNITED METHODISM—
WILLIAM J. ABRAHAM 215

APPENDIX—EVANGELICAL UNITED BRETHREN WOMEN'S TIMELINE—PAUL W. CHILCOTE 227

NOTES 231

CONTRIBUTORS 277

INDEX 281

INTRODUCTION

In 2008, United Methodists commemorated the fortieth anniversary of the merger between The Methodist Church and The Evangelical United Brethren Church (EUB) to form The United Methodist Church. Amid the conferences and special reporting that took place in conjunction with the anniversary, three observations concerning United Methodism's EUB heritage surfaced again and again. First, awareness of United Methodism's EUB heritage is largely a function of geography. In those regions where The EUB Church was strongest (most notably the upper Midwest), many United Methodists have an appreciation for their EUB heritage either because they are former EUB members or because they have worshiped and worked alongside former EUB members across the years. By contrast, in those regions in which the EUB was largely absent (most notably the southern and western regions), knowledge of and appreciation for the EUB tradition are almost altogether lacking.

Second, former EUB members as well as persons who were on the "Methodist side" of the merger frequently noted that, as a general rule, United Methodists have not adequately appreciated the richness and vitality of their EUB heritage. Following the merger, many former Methodists went about business as usual, assuming that former EUB members would preserve and promote their heritage in appropriate venues and on appropriate occasions. At one level, this is readily understandable. After all, many former Methodists knew very little about the EUB tradition. In these circumstances, surely it was best to leave the promotion and

Introduction

interpretation of all things EUB to those who had personal knowledge of the tradition.

This brings us directly to the third and most important observation. Participants in the commemorations of the fortieth anniversary of The United Methodist Church noted repeatedly that the number of former EUB members is now rapidly dwindling. Moreover, many of those who remain have entered or will soon enter retirement from active ministry. Indeed, it is only a matter of time before the ranks of United Methodist clergy will be devoid of anyone with a personal knowledge of The EUB Church and its traditions.

In the wake of this last observation, the editors of this volume agreed that the time was ripe to produce a volume that would assist present and future United Methodist clergy in discovering and appreciating the richness and vitality of their EUB heritage. Having said this, we readily acknowledge that all traditions are not destined to be remembered. In some cases, traditions fade from memory because they lack the sort of vitality and distinctiveness that makes traditions worth remembering in the first place. In other cases, vital and distinct traditions fade from memory because an insufficient number of people are willing to do the sorts of things necessary to keep those traditions alive.

We believe that a careful reading of this volume will demonstrate that the EUB heritage does not belong in the former category. On the contrary, we believe that we have a tradition that is full of rich conceptual and practical resources awaiting rediscovery and implementation in United Methodism today. We believe that, if taken seriously, the EUB heritage can be a source of renewal and revitalization in United Methodist doctrine and theology, polity and liturgy, evangelism and mission, and in social ethics and action.

The greater danger, it seems to us, is that the EUB tradition will fall into the second category, if it has not done so already. With this concern in mind, we have organized this volume into three sections corresponding to the courses in United Methodist history, doctrine, and polity that are required for ordination in The United Methodist Church. The chapters in these sections are intended to cover the essentials and to accentuate the distinctive contributions of the EUB heritage to United Methodism. It is our sincere hope that United Methodist history, doctrine, and polity instructors will aid in the work of keeping the EUB heritage alive by recommending or requiring future generations of United Methodist clergy to read the sections that correspond to the courses that they teach.

Finally, by way of introduction, we would like to say a word about the contributors to this volume. When the time came to put together a list of prospective contributors, we agreed that it was important to include both former EUB members and former Methodists. On the one hand, we wanted to take advantage of the wealth of personal knowledge possessed by former EUB members, some of whom had recently retired from long teaching careers in United Methodist colleges and seminaries. On the other hand, we also felt strongly that former Methodist contributors would provide a critical perspective that would prevent the kind of interpretive overreach that can happen when authors are too close to their subject. To our delight, leading historians, theologians, and practitioners were quick to accept our invitation to contribute to the volume, often commenting that such a volume was long overdue and imminently useful. Suffice it to say, it has been our pleasure to work with them all. They have more than delivered the goods.

The chapters for this volume were based upon papers presented at the Fortieth Anniversary Conference of the United Methodist Church, which was convened by the Center for the Evangelical United Brethren Heritage and the Commission on Archives and History of the United Methodists Church at United Theological Seminary in 2008. This material is presented here with our thanks to the Center.

The Editors
All Saints' Day, 2009

PART ONE
History

CHAPTER 1

THE PIETIST BACKGROUND OF THE EVANGELICAL UNITED BRETHREN CHURCH

K. James Stein

To discern Pietism's influence in the creation of The Evangelical United Brethren Church, we must first come to grips with the nature or meaning of Pietism itself. Most scholars agree that defining and describing Pietism are not easy. For example, Ernest Stoeffler began his book *The Rise of Evangelical Pietism* with this discouraging sentence: "One of the least understood movements in the history of Christianity has undoubtedly been that of Pietism."[1] Similarly, when Carter Lindberg raised the questions about what Pietism, piety, and a pious person really are, he immediately concluded: "Here we jump with both feet into that vast swamp of Pietist studies. The scholars of Pietism give us many and sometimes conflicting maps for traversing this swamp."[2] Keeping in mind that there is a vast scholarly debate about the nature and meaning of Pietism, we can begin to get our bearings by attending to the origins and aims of this important movement in the history of Christianity.

THE ORIGINS AND AIMS OF EARLY PIETISM

Despite the scholarly debate about the nature and meaning of Pietism, there is general agreement among scholars that Pietism originated as a renewal movement within Protestantism. This view has much to commend it. For example, Philipp Jakob Spener (1635–1705), whom I like to call "the Pietist Patriarch," was accused by his orthodox Lutheran detractors of being dissatisfied with Martin Luther's Reformation. To be sure, Spener denied being discontented with what Luther had done in the previous century. He even praised the good that had emerged in the Reformation. However, he also believed that Christians must go beyond and improve the Reformation.[3] Indeed, early Pietists like Spener frequently saw their seventeenth-century movement as being "the second phase of the Reformation."[4]

A later example of Pietist dissatisfaction with the Reformation can be found in early American Methodism. Bishop Francis Asbury's *Journal* entry of April 28–29, 1775, recounts having dinner with William Otterbein and Benedict Schwope and reports their intention to make proposals to the German Reformed synod "to lay a plan for the reformation of the Dutch congregations."[5]

These examples suggest an obvious question. Why were early Pietists dissatisfied with the Reformation churches of their day? Although many Pietists publicly acknowledged their gratitude for the theological foundations provided by Martin Luther, Ulrich Zwingli, and John Calvin, they clearly felt that the churches founded by these major sixteenth-century Reformers were lacking in their time. But what precisely did they lack? To answer this question we need to familiarize ourselves with additional background developments.

Shortly after Martin Luther's death in 1546, internal theological battles threatened to divide the German Lutheran branch of Protestantism. In the wake of this threat, the adoption of the Formula of Concord in 1577 and the publication of the *Book of Concord* in 1580 provided a theological center around which Luther's followers could rally. This led, however, to a strong creedal ethos within Lutheranism so that, by the seventeenth century, many Lutherans came to view churchmanship largely in terms of adherence to creeds and living an outwardly acceptable moral life. To a degree this also occurred in Calvinism.

Spener, who helped revive catechetical instruction and confirmation in German Lutheranism, recounted how when he was ministering in Frankfurt, an intelligent foreigner, who was passing through the city, visited his catechetical classes and remarked that such instruction went only into the children's heads, but how could they "bring the head into the heart?"[6]

Pietism was and is "heart religion." It seeks not to change basic Protestant doctrines, but to enable the gospel that the doctrines carry to arouse an affective and not just an intellectual response in Christian believers.[7] Indeed, many early Pietists believed that in their failure to engage the affections, Reformation churches failed to provide believers with what they needed most to survive the wider social and political realities of their day. Hence, Karl Heussi explains the origins of Pietism as follows:

> German Pietism is a partial appearance of a great interconfessional movement, which was aroused in the seventeenth century through the great economic and political vibrations and the stiffness of orthodox church life. It had its parallels in Catholic mysticism and Jansenism, in English Puritanism and Quakerism of the seventeenth century, and in English Methodism of the eighteenth century.[8]

Heussi clearly associates the rise of Pietism with the horrors of the Thirty Years' War (1618–48) and the inability of entrenched Protestant orthodoxy to address the spiritual needs of European Protestants. Yet a deeply spiritual movement swept across early seventeenth-century Europe embracing not only Roman Catholic and Protestant but also Jewish believers. Pietism seems to have emerged within this devotional and less formal religious atmosphere that antedated it. Indeed, one can see this explicitly in the work of Johann Arndt (1555–1621), whom many regard as the father of Pietism. Arndt was a Lutheran pastor advocating the mystical union existing between Christ and believers, and his major work, *Wahres Christenthum* (*True Christianity*), beautifully weds Lutheran doctrine with Roman Catholic mysticism. His chief aim is to help people see that a living faith involves trusting God, uniting oneself with God, wishing for nothing except God, and doing all of this through Jesus Christ.[9] For Arndt, true Christianity is a "living faith whose fruit is a godly, active life."[10]

In the light of its origins and aims, many scholars view Pietism as a spiritual movement seeking to inculcate conversion and a sanctification ethic. For example, Stoeffler defines Pietism as "the major manifestation of the experiential tradition within post-Reformation Protestantism."[11] Similarly, Edward Farley recognizes in Pietism "an exclusive concern with warmness of heart and religious emotions."[12] Donald Bloesch casts the net wider, saying, "The post-Reformation spiritual movements known as Pietism, Puritanism and Evangelicalism all sought to recover the centrality and priority of Christian commitment and devotion."[13]

On another front, Dale Brown, whose book *Understanding Pietism* is one of the best analyses of the movement, points to the problem of subjectivity in Pietism. Brown views Pietism's moralism as minimizing the doctrine of justification by grace, and he sees Pietism's religious empiricism as lessening the importance of revelation and tradition.[14] These concerns notwithstanding, Brown acknowledges that Pietists found great meaning in accenting the inner life of the individual Christian.

In my work, I have often defined Pietism as a movement in seventeenth- and eighteenth-century Lutheranism and Calvinism that sought to reform the church, not with creedal or institutional change, but with spiritual renewal in terms of personal religious commitment and holy living. Of course, like any succinct definition, this one only scratches the surface of the origins, aims, and nature of Pietism. Indeed, there are important aspects of Pietism that we have not yet discussed.

ADDITIONAL ASPECTS OF EARLY PIETISM

One additional aspect of Pietism worth noting is its relationship to the *Aufklärung* (the Enlightenment). Both Pietism and the Enlightenment, albeit from different perspectives and for different reasons, fought the predominant Lutheran and Calvinist orthodoxies of the time. Both resisted intellectual dogmatism—the Pietists with their plea for Christian experience and the Enlightenment with its appeal to reason. Both stressed individual rights and inner development. Similarly, some see in Pietism's chiliasm, its expectation of Christ's thousand-year reign on the earth, a parallel to Enlightenment optimism with regard to human self-improvement. Likewise, the perfectionist tendencies of some Pietists in ethical and spiritual matters can be seen as supporting the aims of the Enlightenment.[15]

Despite these similarities and confluences, the jury is still out as far as the coalescence of Pietism and the Enlightenment is concerned. For example, some have argued that it was not Pietism's inwardness but the extreme intellectualism of orthodoxy that paved the way for the Age of Reason.[16] Moreover, some eighteenth-century Pietists considered rationalism as an enemy to be confronted. Thus if Pietism and the Enlightenment shared some common concerns, it is far from clear that there was an alliance between them.

A second important aspect of Pietism worth noting is its durability. Emerging in the seventeenth century, Pietism abides today. Manfred Kohl declares, "Pietism is to be understood not merely, or even primarily as a movement in modern church history from about 1675 to about 1750, but even more important, as a force within the stream of Protestantism to the present day."[17] Indeed, I saw this firsthand when, during my sabbatical in 1970–71, I met with Pietist members of the Landeskirche in Tübingen, Germany. At a Pietist men's group one evening, I watched as the full-time director of the pietistic programs led a devotional. This particular Pietist group had its own building, youth work, men's group, women's organization, prayer meetings, and social outreach. To be sure, most members attended Sunday services regularly at the local state church congregation. Yet while remaining in the state church, they were a lively "church within a church," following their own Lutheran Pietist theology.

Though small in number, today's German Pietists still believe that Pietism has much to offer the church's ministry. For example, in the year 2000, a group of young Pietist scholars published a series of articles concerning Spener's relevance for issues facing the twenty-first-century church. One scholar, Peter Steinacker, maintained that, for Spener, true Christianity consisted not in an outwardly good moral life, but in spiritual formation so that love for God and neighbor can take living form within believers. Steinacker sought to apply this "true inheritance" to contemporary church life, pleading for increased church-run kindergartens and a greater place for contemporary worship in order to reach people more effectively with the gospel.[18]

STRENGTHS AND WEAKNESSES OF EARLY PIETISM

Like any movement, early Pietism had its weaknesses. Occasionally, early Pietists exhibited self-righteousness by refusing to receive the Lord's Supper with persons they deemed unconverted. Early Pietists can also be viewed as undermining church unity, as some Pietist small groups separated from the Lutheran and Calvinist state churches in which they originated. Further, some regard as problematic the occasional emotional excesses in early Pietism. Finally, early Pietism is sometimes criticized for depriving people of the pleasures of life, such as attending the opera, dancing, and card playing, and for demanding a legalistic Sabbatarianism.

There were also strengths in early Pietism. For example, Gary Sattler affirmatively referred to the "Pietist Trinity" as being "God's glory, neighbor's good, and one's own holiness."[19] In addition, Pietism has been credited with awakening "many thousands of souls."[20] This resulted from Pietism's stress on the *Wiedergeburt* (the new birth) and *Erneuerung* (renewal or sanctification), its emphasis on daily Christian living in word and deed, its gathering of renewed persons into conventicles that promoted Christian fellowship, and its resultant increase of the laity's involvement in the life of the church.

Many early Pietists also stressed the amelioration of social ills and the importance of education. The Pietist foundations encouraged and made possible by Spener and creatively and forcefully led by August Hermann Francke (1663–1727) at Halle in Brandenburg in the early eighteenth century set a high standard for popular education, care for orphans and widows, publication and distribution of inexpensive Bibles and devotional literature, and foreign missions. Indeed, the high quality of the theological education at Halle University caused Lutheran congregations in

Europe and in colonial America to seek Halle graduates as their pastors. Equally telling is the fact that the Prussian King Frederick Wilhelm I chose many Pietists to be Prussian army chaplains. For that matter, the cooperation between Francke and King Frederick IV of Denmark resulted in the founding of the successful Danish-Halle mission in Tranquebar, India, in 1705. Thus, in 1715, the New England Congregationalist pastor Cotton Mather (1663–1728), who maintained a correspondence with Francke, could exclaim, "The world begins to feel a warmth from the fire of God which thus flames in the heart of Germany, beginning to extend into many regions; the whole world will ere long be sensible of it."[21]

THE PIETIST HERITAGE OF THE EVANGELICAL UNITED BRETHREN CHURCH

There can be little doubt concerning Pietism's influence on the movements that eventually formed The Evangelical United Brethren Church, namely, the United Brethren in Christ and The Evangelical Association. Most tellingly, the founders of each of these predecessor denominations had personal Pietist connections. For example, Martin Boehm (1725–1812), the cofounder of the United Brethren in Christ, had a grandfather who was persecuted in his native Switzerland for his adherence to Pietism. When Boehm's grandfather arrived in America, he joined the Mennonites, who later disapproved of his grandson Martin's conversion experience while plowing on his Pennsylvania farm. Apparently, the experience had "too Pietist" a ring to it.[22]

Martin Boehm's partner in founding the United Brethren in Christ, Philip William Otterbein (1726–1813), was the product of a Reformed parsonage in the German state of Nassau. Together with his five brothers, Otterbein followed his father into the ministry of the Reformed Church. The brothers were educated at Herborn Academy, where Professors Johann Henry Schramm and Valentine Arnold, both Pietists, sought to arouse *thätiges christenthum* (active Christianity) in their students. Indeed, J. Steven O'Malley has shown that by the time the Otterbein brothers studied at Herborn Academy, it had "become the veritable center of Reformed Pietism."[23]

Arriving in America in 1752 as a Reformed Church missionary, Philip William Otterbein began a Pietist-oriented pastoral career in several parishes. At the Lancaster parish, he experienced a growing religious assurance.[24] At Tulpehocken, he instituted prayer meetings. But the most significant event happened during his York pastorate. In 1767, Otterbein attended a *grosse Versammlung* (a big meeting) at Long's barn near Lancaster. The sermon at this meeting so moved Otterbein that he hugged Martin Boehm, the little Mennonite preacher, uttering the words, "Wir sind Brüder" ("We are brothers"). This event precipitated the founding of one of the first new denominations in North America. Beginning in 1800, Otterbein and Boehm began holding annual conferences of the like-minded preachers associated with them. They referred to themselves as *unpartheiische* (unsectarian or nondenominational)—manifesting Pietism's penchant for placing mission above denominational affiliation.[25]

Philip William Otterbein's Pietist heritage can also be seen in his brothers' theological publications. Among these works were Georg Otterbein's three large volumes of sermons on the Heidelberg Catechism—the creedal formulation of German Calvinism. These sermons were aimed against the rationalists and moralists of the time. On another front, there were Johann Daniel Otterbein's published sermons against radical and separatist Pietists. During his thirty-nine-and-one-half-year pastorate of an independent German Reformed Church in Baltimore, Philip Otterbein worked to circulate these volumes in the new world.[26]

Also indicative of his Pietism are Philip William Otterbein's extant writings. Though few in number, one of these works is a sermon titled "The Salvation-Bringing Incarnation and Glorious Victory of Jesus Christ over the Devil and Death." In this sermon, Otterbein urges that the indwelling of Christ in believers is essential to the Christian life, saying, "If there is no Christ in us, there is also no Christ for us."[27] His Pietist point is only too clear. Justification without sanctification means little.

The Pietist roots of The Evangelical Association are as readily discernible as those of the United Brethren in Christ. A Pennsylvania farmer and tile maker, Jacob Albright (1759–1808), founded The Evangelical Association, which later became The Evangelical Church, during his brief twelve-year ministry career.

Albright's family emigrated from the German Palatinate to Pennsylvania, where he was born. He was baptized and confirmed a Lutheran. How much he was influenced by Pietism in his youth remains debatable. On the one hand, Raymond W. Albright, a great-great-grandson of Albright, claims that his forebear came from a pietistic German home.[28] On the other hand, James Bemesderfer suggests that there is a lack of direct evidence for this early influence. Still, even Bemesderfer acknowledges a strong presence of Pietist influences in Albright's later life and ministry.[29] Indeed, these influences appear to have played a significant role in Albright's conversion to Christianity in 1791 and his subsequent acceptance of a call to preach in 1796.

If Pietist influences led to Albright's conversion and to his response to the call to preach, they were also advanced by the sorrow that Albright experienced over the sudden deaths of several of his children. These crises led Albright to consult with three different Pietist-oriented persons: Anthony Houtz, a German Reformed pastor who occasionally preached near Albright's home and who buried Albright's children; Adam Riegel, a United Brethren lay preacher in whose nearby home Albright experienced God's pardoning grace; and Isaac Davies, another neighbor and the leader of a Methodist class that Albright joined for a time. From each person, Albright received spiritual counsel that enabled him to live a devout Christian life and to hear God's call to an evangelistic ministry among the German-speaking populace of Pennsylvania.[30]

Not surprisingly, the Pietist orientation of the founding fathers of the Church of the United Brethren in Christ and The Evangelical Association can be seen in the character and ethos of the denominations themselves. For example, Pietist influence can be seen in the strong emphasis that these two denominations placed on *Wiedergeburt* and *Erneuerung*; in their calls to holiness of heart and life; in their development of a sanctification ethic that encouraged church members to refrain from drinking alcoholic beverages, smoking tobacco, dancing, cursing, playing cards, and both working and enjoying recreation on Sunday; and in their encouragement of family worship and private devotions. Buttressing all of this was a Pietist contention that doctrine, though important, was not ultimate in Christian discipleship. In good Pietist fashion, these two denominations placed greater stress on being reborn and living the new life in Christ than on adhering to a creed. To be sure, in the mid-nineteenth century the Evangelical General Conference forbade alteration of its Articles of Faith, and the United Brethren General Conference voted that the Confession of Faith could be changed only "by request of two thirds of the whole society."[31] Thus the articles of faith in both denominations provided theological parameters for ministry. Yet it is also clear that these documents were not considered a dogmatic straitjacket, as suggested in the Quadrennial Address at the 1901 United Brethren General Conference, which asserted: "There is no heresy known in our church and never has been in our history, unless it was an unloving heart or an impure life."[32] In saying this, the United Brethren were following the example of their Pietist fathers, Spener and Francke. They were attempting to walk the middle ground between dogmatic inflexibility and dogmatic indifference by insisting that the content that mattered most was the content of believers' hearts.[33]

THE SIGNIFICANCE OF THE EVANGELICAL UNITED BRETHREN CHURCH'S PIETIST HERITAGE FOR UNITED METHODISM TODAY

To this point, we have surveyed the origins and aims of early Pietism, and we have shown the influence of continental Pietism on the founding fathers of the United Brethren in Christ and The Evangelical Association (the two predecessor bodies that formed The Evangelical United Brethren Church when they merged in 1946). Other chapters in this volume will deal more extensively with the history, doctrine, polity, and practices of these groups. In the remainder of this chapter, it will help to say a word about how United Methodists today might benefit from taking their Pietist heritage more seriously.

Although there are dozens of ways that United Methodists today stand to benefit from careful engagement with their Pietist heritage, five areas of Pietist influence come especially to mind. The first is the need for a strong christological emphasis in United Methodist preaching and teaching. The gospel is not basically arousal to human activity but a stout proclamation about what

God has done and is doing for human salvation through Jesus Christ. Careful engagement with Pietist sources would help United Methodists to see this most clearly. For example, Spener contended, "Because sin is our greatest misery, the righteousness we have in Christ or which he has become for us is our greatest treasure. It liberates us from the greatest evil—sin."[34]

Elsewhere, stressing a theme that Philip William Otterbein would preach in a later century, Spener wrote:

> We are certainly obligated to preach not only *Christum pro nobis*, but also *in nobis* and do it often [2 Corinthians 13:3-5].... we not only believe that we will be saved through Christ's merits, but that he must also dwell in us, so that out of his power the image of his life shines forth and is discernible in our lives. The power of his death must kill the old Adam in us and the power of his resurrection must effect new life; so that everything happens not outside of us but in us.[35]

Church Pietists like Spener and Francke were confessional in the best sense of the word. They regarded as central the proclamation of God's redemptive action in Jesus Christ.

A second way that United Methodists might benefit from an engagement with Pietist sources has to do with the revival of the important theological concept of new birth. With the publication of the 1989 *United Methodist Hymnal* and its baptismal covenant emphasis, new sacramental language confronted United Methodist congregations, who are now reminded that through baptism "we are given new birth through water and the Spirit." Both Spener and John Wesley believed in baptismal regeneration, and both believed that the new birth conferred at baptism could be lost by subsequent sin. Therefore, persons needed new birth through the Word to complement the new birth conferred through the water of baptism. This would not necessarily call for a dateable conversion experience but, as Spener put it, for the confidence that we would die in the state of rebirth, being found in the grace of God.[36]

The concept of the new birth is not strange to historic United Methodism. John Wesley began his sermon "The New Birth" by citing two fundamental Christian doctrines—the doctrine of justification (which relates to the great work that God does *for us*, in forgiving our sins) and the doctrine of the new birth (the great work that God does *in us*, in renewing our fallen nature).[37] Otterbein, Boehm, Albright, and their successors all preached the necessity of the new birth.

Abuses of new birth language in the past have caused it to be neglected in many United Methodist congregations. Moreover, Protestant liberalism, embodied by many seminaries in the late nineteenth and twentieth centuries, minimized the doctrines of sin and grace. Surrendering the call to conversion, it opted for "salvation by education." However, the combination of our Pietist heritage and our newer baptismal discourse provides a marvelous opportunity for United Methodist pastors to recover a healthy concept of new birth. Such a recovery would provide many people with crucial doctrinal clarification for their self-understanding as Christian believers.[38]

A third way that engagement with Pietist sources would benefit United Methodists today has to do with the quality of Christian discipleship in The United Methodist Church. When the nascent Evangelical Association began its own small publishing house in New Berlin, Pennsylvania, in 1817, the second book it published was August Hermann Francke's *Menschenfurcht* (*Fear of Man*). Francke contended early in his treatise that unbelief is the root of all our problems. He quoted Romans 14:23, which concludes with the warning that "whatever does not proceed from faith is sin." Francke denounced pastors who were afraid to criticize worldly mindedness and were unwilling to stand against cultural norms. Such pastors would never see the glory of God or have any kind of joyful assurance.[39] He maintained that what destroys the fear of man is the fear of God.[40] The treatise is replete with calls to faith, buttressed by many scriptural admonitions. For Francke, faith was "a high and precious gift of God."[41] It comes as we ponder Christ's bitter passion.[42] Yet Francke could also speak of "the cheerfulness of faith."[43] Finally, he wisely reminded his readers that the true boldness of faith is most visible when it is active in love.[44]

The church's mission is, in part, to help people live "in Christ," providing them with resources to face life's challenges. Bishop Rueben Job expresses this well when he says:

> Living in the presence of and in harmony with the living God who is made known in Jesus Christ and companions us in the Holy Spirit is to live life from the inside out. It is to find our moral

direction, our wisdom, our courage, our strength to live faithfully from the One who authored us, called us, sustains us, and sends us out into the world as witnesses who daily practice the way of living with Jesus.[45]

The Pietists taught their people to pray and to trust God—to trust God because they prayed and to pray because they trusted God. Such an emphasis is always in season.

A fourth way that United Methodists would benefit from an engagement with their Pietist heritage involves what Pietists used to call *Gemeinschaft* (fellowship). It has been said of Count Nikolaus von Zinzendorf, the eighteenth-century Moravian Pietist leader, that he so emphasized God's gift of unity to Christians that he added fellowship as a third sacrament in Protestantism.[46] Even before the early Methodists were finding spiritual nourishment in their class meetings, Spener's *collegia pietatis*, a century earlier, provided a meaningful gathering place for earnest Christians to share their faith and to be encouraged by those who joined with them in weekly discussion and prayer.

The Evangelical United Brethren, inspired by both Methodism and Pietism, recognized the value of class meetings, midweek prayer services, and adult Bible studies together with children's Sunday school and catechism classes. Moreover, they looked very favorably on the use of small groups in which adults could be nurtured in the Christian faith. For example, a survey of the journal of Bishop Christian Newcomer, the United Brethren leader who followed Otterbein and Boehm, reveals how often he either organized or met with classes on his equestrian journeys.[47] Similarly, John Lawrence, an early United Brethren historian, commented on the class meetings held at what became known as "Old Otterbein Church" in Baltimore, Maryland, saying,

> This church, regarding the building up of each other in the most holy faith as the primary object of their union, did not only make careful attendance upon these meetings the duty of both men and women, but they ordained that no preacher unfavorable to class meetings should ever serve them as pastor.[48]

Although class meetings were not much in fashion in The Evangelical United Brethren Church in the 1960s, there was still a sense of *Gemeinschaft*. Because the denomination was relatively small in comparison with much larger church bodies, and because it retained a rural and small-town atmosphere with a homogeneous membership marked in many areas with the German or "Pennsylvania Dutch" ethos, the EUB members enjoyed a rather close-knit fellowship. Beyond that, however, the Pietist mutual understanding and support that church members could draw upon were key in providing, in most cases, a vital sense of camaraderie in the Christian faith.

It is not easy to suggest just how the concept and practice of *Gemeinschaft* could influence The United Methodist Church today. We live in an electronic, computer-driven, global-oriented world. The influence of localized small-membership groups seems to pale in comparison. Many United Methodists live in vast population areas and attend large congregations where anonymity is as prized by some as a sense of belonging is by others. Nevertheless, deep within our Methodist and EUB Pietist heritage is a conviction that Christian living is not a singular thing but plural—and that people, in Christ, need one another. Sensitive pastors and laypeople are still finding new ways to gather people in small groups for continued caring and accountability. Indeed, the phenomenal success of the DISCIPLE Bible Study and the increasing number of covenant groups are encouraging signs.

A fifth Pietism-inspired gift from The Evangelical United Brethren Church to The United Methodist Church is ecumenism. Because Pietism cuts across denominational lines irrespective of church doctrine and polity, it is inherently ecumenical. As we have seen, an ecumenical spirit was dramatically demonstrated in 1767 at Long's barn when the German Reformed pastor, Philip William Otterbein, heard in the sermon of Martin Boehm, a Mennonite lay preacher, an understanding of the gospel similar to his own and embraced him with the words, "We are brethren."

The ecumenical spirit of The Evangelical United Brethren Church was evident in several ways. For example, awareness of their denomination's size and its limited financial power motivated the EUB members toward cooperative ventures. This denominational cooperation was particularly evident on the mission field. Thus J. Steven O'Malley notes that an emphasis on ecumenical and indigenous expressions of Christian mission was made policy by the United Brethren in 1925 and was congruent with the understanding of mission adopted by assemblies of the World Council of Churches in which the former Evangelical United Brethren participated. Indeed, the EUB Board of Missions was given unusual freedom to pursue an ecumenical approach to mission.[49]

Additional evidence of the ecumenical spirit of The Evangelical United Brethren Church can be seen in the involvement of its leaders in ecumenical organizations. For example, Bishop John Stamm served as president of the Federal Council of Churches (1948–50), and Bishop Reuben Mueller was president of the National Council of Churches (1963–66).

Of course, the greatest evidence of the ecumenical spirit of The Evangelical United Brethren Church can be seen in its members' willingness to merge with a much larger denomination. At the time of the merger, EUB members knew only too well that their distinct history and identity would likely be swallowed up in the process. They knew that their story might be forgotten. Yet they deemed this sacrifice worthwhile because they believed that a new and even larger church would demonstrate how much Christians could accomplish when they set aside their differences and even their identities for the sake of Christ's mission to the world. Indeed, it may be that, above all else, this act of sacrifice for the sake of furthering Christ's mission to the world demonstrated the deep Pietist roots of The Evangelical United Brethren Church. More important, it may be that, in taking this aspect of their Pietist heritage seriously, United Methodists today might be inspired to sacrifice all that they hold most dear for the sake of Christ and for the world.

CHAPTER 2

Martin Boehm, Philip William Otterbein, and the United Brethren in Christ

Scott Kisker

The first German settlers to America came from among persecuted Christian minorities, assisted by converts to Pietism within the established confessions.[1] In 1683 thirteen families landed in Philadelphia, led by Franz Daniel Pastorius. Pastorius, a lawyer in Frankfurt, had come into contact with the leader of Lutheran Pietism, Philipp Jakob Spener, and the radical Pietist Johann Jakob Schütz.[2] To assist persecuted Christians, Pastorius arranged for the purchase of fifteen thousand acres outside Philadelphia, which became known as Germantown. The families who journeyed with him came from a variety of religious backgrounds and included Mennonites and Moravians, both of whom would be influential in the formation of The United Brethren in Christ (UBC).

More persecuted minorities followed. The Schwarzenau Brethren, also known as German Baptists or Dunkers, began arriving from southern Germany and Switzerland in 1719 and also settled in Germantown. More arrived with their founder, Alexander Mack, in 1729. In 1732, Johann Conrad Beissel, who had separated from the main group of Dunkers over Sabbath observance, arrived in Lancaster County, Pennsylvania, and developed a semimonastic community called Ephrata.

Members (at least nominally) of the established German churches also came. In 1709, Queen Anne of England encouraged thousands of Protestants to emigrate from the Palatinate, an area that had been a stronghold of Reformed Pietism.[3] In 1746, Michael Schlatter arrived to organize the German Reformed Churches in America. He became pastor of the united churches of Germantown and Philadelphia, and traveled among the German Reformed settlers of Pennsylvania, Maryland, New Jersey, and New York, organizing a synod, which met in 1747. On a visit to Europe in 1751, he published his journal (in Dutch, German, and English), emphasizing the need for pastors among Reformed congregations. In March 1752, he returned to Pennsylvania with six young ministers and more than £20,000 for the establishment of charity schools among the Germans.[4]

America also had its impact on these religious traditions. Though largely an English phenomenon, the First Great Awakening was more significant and divisive within colonial German religious culture than is generally recognized.[5] The revival influenced and divided all religious groups, even those stemming from the radical Reformation or those already influenced by continental Pietism.

THE MENNONITES AND MARTIN BOEHM (1725–1812)

Martin Boehm's grandfather was raised in the Swiss Reformed Church and became a Mennonite during his three-year traveling apprenticeship. Rejected by his family and community and wanting to escape imprisonment, he moved to the Netherlands. His son, Jacob, was twenty-two years old when, around 1715, he joined the second group of Mennonites to immigrate to Lancaster County, Pennsylvania. There, Martin Boehm was born. As a native-born American, Martin was reared within a religious community that no longer experienced, as a daily reality, the persecution that had defined its identity in the Old World.

By all accounts, Martin was a model member of this community. At age thirty-one he was a leader in his Meeting. In a conversation between Martin and his son Henry recorded shortly before his death, the elder Boehm said he began ministering "about year 1756. And about 3 years after I received full pastoral orders in the Mennonist society by nomination and lot."[6] Boehm's "ministry" is clarified by the firsthand account recorded by historian Henry Spayth. Boehm told Spayth that prior to his selection by lot, he had for "some two years past...been giving testimony at the close of the sermons, and frequently concluded the meeting."[7]

In 1758, Boehm was nominated with several others from his Mennonite community to succeed their pastor.[8] On the appointed day Bibles with slips of paper were laid on the table and each nominee chose. Boehm "stepped out with trembling, saying inwardly, Lord not me. I am too poor."[9] He chose the Bible whose slip had the words from Proverbs 16:33 (KJV) written on it: "The lot is cast into the lap; but the whole disposing thereof is of the LORD." Boehm was selected.

Boehm did not take over from the pastor immediately. Thus he says, "According to our usage, it was not expected from me to preach immediately thereafter, because our elder preacher was still able to preach; but it was my duty to assist him in preaching and exhortation as God would give me ability."[10] Boehm recounted to his son Henry, "I strove to live and preach, agreeably to the light I had. At this time I was a servant and knew of no person who professed experimental religion except my Mother's sister—Nancy Keagy."[11]

There are differing accounts of Boehm's conversion, both supposedly from Boehm himself. Spayth said Boehm attributed his conversion to the crisis provoked by his selection as pastor: "Sunday came, the elder brother preached, and in attempting to follow him by a word of exhortation, I failed.... The next Sabbath I was requested to take part, and rose up, but could say little or nothing."[12] Here he was "to be a preacher, and yet [had] nothing to preach." All he could do was "stammer out a few words, and then be obliged to take my seat in shame and remorse!"[13]

Boehm's testimony then follows the evangelical pattern of conviction of sin and an experience of justifying love. He says,

> *My salvation* followed me wherever I went. I felt constrained to pray for myself; and while praying for myself my mind became alarmed. I felt and saw myself a poor sinner. I was LOST! My agony became great. I was plowing in the field, and knelt down at each end of the furrow to pray. The word *lost, lost (verlohren)*, went every round with me. Midway in the field I could go no farther, but sunk behind the plow, crying, "Lord save, I am lost!"—and again the thought or voice said, "I am come to seek and save that which is lost." In a moment a stream of joy was poured over me. I praised the Lord, and left the field and told my companion what joy I felt.[14]

The following Sunday, Boehm "rose to tell my experience since my call to the ministry. When speaking of my lost estate and agony of mind, some in the congregation began to weep. This gave me encouragement to speak of our fall and lost condition and of repentance."[15] Spayth recorded Boehm's saying that this new preaching "caused considerable commotion in our church, as well as among the people generally."[16] Nonetheless, it did not prevent him from being considered an acceptable bishop. In 1761, he was selected senior pastor, or bishop, when Bishop Hostetter, whom he had been assisting, died.[17]

Boehm's son Henry, a preacher in The Methodist Episcopal Church (MEC), also recorded a conversation with his father about the elder Boehm's conversion. In this account Boehm's religious transformation occurred after he was bishop and was connected to an encounter with the First Great Awakening. Henry asked,

> "Father how did you come to a clear discovery relative to the necessity of a real change of heart...?" By preaching the doctrine of the fall and feeling the [want] of my Christ. I—about the year 1761 hearing of a great work among the New Lights in New Va.—resolved to find the truth more fully. Accordingly I visited those parts and found many gracious souls who could give a rational and scriptural account of the experience and acceptance with God. Now I was much encouraged to seek the same blessing in a greater degree.[18]

According to Spayth, "Some converts of the eminent George Whitfield had reached New Virginia, and commenced preaching a present salvation." Whitefield's message had evidently jumped the

English-German language barrier, likely among Dunkers. "With others, some members of the Mennonite families became seriously affected, through the preaching of these 'new-lights.'"[19]

Whether Boehm's experience of heart religion was entirely within a Mennonite framework or was the result of his contact with the First Great Awakening is impossible to determine. What is clear is that Boehm's conflict with his Mennonite tradition and his self-identification with an evangelicalism that crossed Reformation-era theological boundaries began with his return from Virginia. Mennonite historiography concurs that "the apostasy of Martin Boehm" occurred "during a visit to Virginia in 1761 [when] he came into contact with a revival movement and was greatly influenced by it."[20]

After 1761, Boehm's religious identity shifted in ways that alienated him from the community in which he had been raised and united him with people of different religious and ethnic backgrounds. He began to minister beyond his weekly duties at the meetinghouse: "Large congregations collected not only on the Sabbath, but also on weekdays, which was very displeasing to some of my brethren in the ministry."[21] Boehm also extended his ministry beyond Mennonites. Thus he says, "My heart was now enlarged so that I could not confine my labors to Jew only but also to Greek as far as my situation and ability would admit."[22] The controversy this caused did not discourage him: "Now some of the meeting houses were shut against me. But many doors opened in different directions."[23]

One of these doors involved the Virginia "New Light" preachers and the so-called Great Meetings. A. W. Drury writes:

> One of the important results of his trip to Virginia was the coming, at intervals, of the "Virginia preachers," as these lay evangelists of Virginia were called, into Lancaster County, Pennsylvania.... In Virginia they were called "New Lights." ... The preachers were sometimes spoken of as "English preachers," though some of them doubtless preached in the German. In Lancaster County they cooperated with Mr. Boehm in holding great meetings (*Grosse Versammlungen*). Great meetings did not belong to the economy of any single body of Christians. The name had been applied to meetings held in 1724, in which the

Dunkers were the most prominent, and in 1742, in which the Moravians were the most prominent.[24]

At one of these meetings Boehm encountered a German Reformed pastor named Philip William Otterbein, to whom we must now turn.

THE GERMAN REFORMED AND PHILIP WILLIAM OTTERBEIN (1726–1813)

Philip William Otterbein's religious background was quite unlike Martin Boehm's. Otterbein was raised in the established Reformed church in Germany. His father was a clergyman and rector of the Latin School where he grew up in Dillenburg, Nassau. Otterbein was well connected socially.[25] Whereas Boehm was relatively uneducated, Otterbein received a university education and, in 1749, followed his father and brothers into the ordained ministry.[26]

Two years later, Michael Schlatter came to Germany recruiting volunteers for America. Otterbein and five others responded. He was examined by the Reformed Synod in the Netherlands and landed in New York in 1752.[27] Otterbein was put in charge of the Reformed congregation in Lancaster—the largest parish outside Philadelphia.[28] Along with leading a frontier parish in a new country, he worked toward the establishment of a school.[29] He also built a new sanctuary.[30]

Otterbein may have come to an assurance of pardon while at Lancaster.[31] A.W. Drury, based on information from Spayth, suggests a date around 1754.[32] According to Drury, Francis Asbury, MEC bishop and Otterbein's close friend, asked Otterbein, "By what means were you brought to the gospel of God and our Savior?" Otterbein answered, "By degrees was I brought to the knowledge of the truth, while I was at Lancaster."[33] Drury then offers the following account:

> After Mr. Otterbein had preached an earnest sermon on repentance and faith, a man smitten with conviction came to him for advice....He knew not what answer to give to the awakened man. His only reply was, "My friend, advice is scarce with me to-

day." He then sought his closet, and ceased not his struggle until he obtained the peace and joy of a conscious salvation.[34]

Asbury recorded a somewhat different chronology in his *Journal*. After Otterbein's death in 1813, he wrote, "Forty years have I known the retiring modesty of this man of God.... He had been sixty years a minister, fifty years a converted one."[35] Asbury's recollection would date Otterbein's conversion around 1759, after he had left Lancaster.

In 1757, Otterbein threatened to leave Lancaster. In response the congregation agreed to strengthen discipline and clarify church membership:

> As it has been in many ways disorderly in our church, and we therefore do not know, especially among those who live outside of the city, who claims membership, we, Preacher and leadership, have therefore considered and found it necessary that everyone who calls himself a member of our church and for whom such is about a Christian life, shall therefore apply and sign his name to following Christian order.[36]

Although Otterbein's ministry in Lancaster produced fruit,[37] even with the agreement, he remained only one more year.[38]

From Lancaster, Otterbein moved to Tulpehocken, where he remained two years.[39] The character of this congregation was, according to J. Steven O'Malley, divided because of the proximity of the Ephrata cloister whose discipline and experimental religion Otterbein seems to have favored.[40] He preached during the week as well as on Sundays and introduced pietistic evening prayer meetings. Spayth writes:

> His custom was to read a portion of scripture, make some practical remarks on the same, and exhort all present to give place to serious reflections. He would then sing a sacred hymn, and invite all to kneel and accompany him in prayer. At first, and for some time, but few, if any would kneel, and he was permitted to pray alone.... After prayer he would endeavor to gain access to their hearts by addressing them individually with words of kindness and love.[41]

By 1760, Otterbein was certainly a New Light clergyman. A sermon he preached in Germantown that year, on Hebrews 2:14-15, was published in 1763.[42] It emphasized themes of conviction, new birth, assurance, and especially sanctification. "It is a teaching from hell itself," Otterbein preached, "which makes Christ into a mere cover for sin.... Christ has not even nearly concluded his work of salvation on the cross.... In the degree to which a man is subject to the power of Satan and sin, to that degree also he is subject to wrath, curse, and damnation."[43] For Otterbein, it was "an obvious error to imagine one cannot in this earthly life be freed from sin." Indeed, it is only "to the extent that Christ rids us of our sin,... [that we] are redeemed through Him. And wherever sin ceases in us, damnation also ceases, Romans 8:1. Thus to be born again, *Christ in us*, is nothing to sneer at."[44] Later in the sermon he links holiness in this life to a believer's eschatological state: "The more holy here, the more glorious there."[45]

Otterbein ministered in Frederick, Maryland, from 1760 to 1765.[46] While there, he connected with several people who were significant in the formation of the United Brethren. He began preaching at the farm of George Adam Geeting on Antietam Creek, very near another Sabbatarian Community founded by members of Ephrata.[47] Not far from there Methodist Robert Strawbridge had begun preaching around 1764 and had established a Methodist class meeting on Pipe Creek.[48] On Pipe Creek was also a Reformed congregation where Benedict Schwope was a lay elder.[49] However, Otterbein's connection to New Light Mennonites, and Boehm in particular, did not start until after he began ministry in York, Pennsylvania, in 1765.[50]

The Great Meeting at Long's Barn (Pentecost, May 10, 1767)

Boehm, now leader of the revival among Mennonites in the Lancaster area, had participated in Great Meetings for several years along with preachers from Virginia and elsewhere. The Great Meeting where he and Otterbein met "was called by Martin Boehm, and was to meet on Pentecost, 1767 at Isaac Long's barn, about six miles northeast of Lancaster."[51] The event drew people from various religious traditions who had been caught up in or were curious about the experiential religion of the First Great Awakening. Along with Mennonites and Dunkers, Lutherans and members of the German Reformed Church were present, including Otterbein, pastor at York.[52] Spayth summarized what happened, saying, "Boehm preached the first sermon, at the close of which, and before he had time to take his seat, Otterbein rose up, and folding Boehm in his arms, said with a loud voice, 'We are brethren.' "[53]

At the sight of such humility from a clergyman of the Reformed church toward a Mennonite bishop, "some praised God aloud, but most of the congregation gave place to their feelings—weeping for joy."[54] Such a sign of reconciliation was remarkable. "The Mennonites...still cherished the recollection of the cruel wrongs and persecutions which their fathers had suffered from the Reformed church in Europe."[55] However, such a scene was consistent with the experience of the Holy Spirit that those present had come to seek. As Drury puts it, "The occasion was, more than merely in name, a true Whitsuntide—a present Pentecost."[56]

At that Great Meeting, Otterbein, Boehm, and one of the "Virginia preachers" (who was likely a Dunker) decided to cooperate in evangelistic efforts while minimizing their differences over church order. They especially allowed freedom in the mode of baptism.[57] Boehm later recalled:

> I became acquainted with my much beloved friend and brother Willhelm Otterbein also with several other ministers who were cast out by their brethren with myself. We now had frequently social and large meetings, which generally lasted three days. These meetings were held extensively through Pennsylvania, west of Maryland, and New Virginia. Hundreds were made the subjects of grace in their penitence and pardon.[58]

The ministers "met in the capacity of a social devout band, from house to house, to make prayer and supplication for the continued influence of God's Spirit."[59] Their work resulted in a small revival in 1770 "conducted principally by Mssr. Otterbein, Boehm, Bochran, and Engles, representing the different bodies."[60]

In 1770, Otterbein left for Germany and returned in 1771.[61] That year a faction who had been influenced by revival preachers seceded from the German Reformed Church in Baltimore. They called Schwope, a lay elder at Pipe Creek who had visited Baltimore as an itinerant preacher, to be their first pastor. The new congregation bought property and organized what was called the German Evangelical Reformed Church. In 1774, the same year that he was ordained by the coetus (the governing presbytery of the German Reformed Churches), Schwope resigned as pastor and advised the congregation to call Otterbein. The coetus, desiring reconciliation between the two congregations, urged Otterbein to decline. Schwope was persistent. He enlisted Asbury to write and encourage Otterbein to accept the position, which he did.[62]

CROSS-LINGUISTIC COOPERATION

On Tuesday, May 3, 1774, the day before Otterbein began his pastorate in Baltimore,[63] Asbury recorded in his *Journal*, "Had a friendly intercourse with Mr. Otterbein and Mr. Swope, the German ministers, respecting the plan of Church discipline on which they intended to proceed. They agreed to imitate our methods as nearly as possible."[64] These methods, especially the class meeting, were spreading among some German Reformed congregations.

On May 29, 1774, Otterbein and Schwope organized "The Association of Reformed Congregations of Maryland, including Canawacke, Pennsylvania." The Association included evangelically minded Reformed pastors and congregations who wanted to adopt the discipline of class meetings: "The aim and purpose that those come together may minister to one another, pray and sing, and watch over one another."[65] The Association's first meeting at Pipe Creek listed class meetings (including leadership and meeting times) for congregations in Baltimore, Pipe Creek, Sam's Creek, Frederick, and Antietam. This association continued to meet biannually up to the Revolution.[66]

When rules were drawn up for the Baltimore church in 1785, they included the institution of the class meeting to define membership as follows:

> Each sex shall therefore meet apart once a week.... The rules for these special meetings are these: no one can be received into this society, who is not resolved to flee the wrath to come, and by faith and repentance, to seek his salvation in Christ, and be resolved

willingly to obey the disciplinary rules which are now observed by this church.... All such persons who may not attend our class-meetings, nor partake of the holy sacrament with us, but attend our public worship, shall be visited by the preacher in health and in sickness, and on all suitable occasions, admonish them, baptize their children, attend to their funerals, impart instruction to their youths, and should they have any children, the Church shall interest herself for their religious education.[67]

The rules also prohibited the teaching of standard Reformed doctrine: "No preacher can stay among us, who teacheth the doctrine of predestination, or the impossibility of falling from grace, and who holdeth them as doctrinal points."[68]

Boehm had also adopted the class meeting. His son Henry recounted, "As early as 1775, the year I was born, a class was formed at my father's house. Mother was one of the first who joined, and therefore belonged to the first race of Methodists in America."[69] It was Boehm's association with Methodists that had, according to him, led to his removal as bishop:

> I was excommunicated from the Mennonist society for keeping fellowship with people of other denominations and tongue viz. the Methodists whom I had received into my house, who soon formed a class which has continued, and still continues my companion in life.... I felt my heart enlarged to all religious persons of every denomination.[70]

Boehm invited preachers (including English-speaking Methodists) to preach on his property. The character of these evangelistic events can be seen from the journal of a Methodist lay preacher, Benjamin Abbott, who had been converted in 1772. Henry Boehm wrote, "My father had a very exalted opinion of Mr. Abbott, and felt it an honor to entertain him as his guest and listen to his powerful sermons."[71] Abbott described a meeting at Boehm's, saying,

> Next morning I set out with about twenty others for my appointment, where we found a large congregation. When I came to my application, the power of the Lord came in such a manner, that the people fell all about the house, and their cries might be heard afar off. This alarmed the wicked, who sprang for the doors in

such haste, that they fell one over another in heaps. The cry of mourners was so great, I thought to give out a hymn to drown the noise, and desired one of our English friends to raise it. But as soon as he began to sing, the power of the Lord struck him, and he pitched under the table, and there lay like a dead man. I gave it out again and asked another to raise it. As soon as he attempted, he fell also.... Mr. Boehm, the owner of the house, and a preacher among the Germans, cried out, "I never saw God in this way before." I replied, this is a pentecost, father. "Yes, be sure," said he, clapping his hands, "a pentecost, be sure!"[72]

Many Methodists used Boehm's house as a preaching stop in those early days. Henry Boehm wrote, "I heard Strawbridge preach at my father's house in 1781, and am the only man now living that has a personal recollection of him."[73] On July 31, 1783, Francis Asbury "preached at Martin Boehm's to many people."[74]

The leadership of the German- and English-speaking revivals also shared evangelistic concerns and held each other in great respect.[75] Otterbein took part in Asbury's ordination as deacon and elder and in his consecration as general superintendent at the 1784 conference where The Methodist Episcopal Church (MEC) was organized. As early as May 1786, Otterbein considered organizing the German revival preachers into a church similar to what the Methodists had done in 1784. That month, in Stevens City, Virginia, Asbury "called on Mr. Otterbein: we had some free conversation on the necessity of forming a church among the Dutch, holding conferences, and the order of its government, &c."[76]

Three years later Otterbein and Boehm called a conference "of all the preachers, in order to take into consideration, how, and in what manner they might be most useful."[77] The conference met in Otterbein's parsonage in Baltimore in 1789. Among those present were Otterbein, Boehm, Geeting, Christian Newcomer (a Mennonite from Lancaster County), Henry Weidner (a class leader and elder in Otterbein's church in Baltimore), Adam Lehman (a class leader at Sam's Creek), and John Ernst (a preacher who lived near Boehm in Lancaster County). Members reported absent were Schwope, Martin Crider (a Mennonite from near Lebanon), Christopher Grosch (a Moravian from Lancaster County), and Abraham Troxel (an Amish Mennonite who had been silenced because of his evangelical preaching). There are no extant minutes of this conference or of another that was held in 1791.[78] Despite these conferences, the organization of the German preachers continued from 1791 to 1800 mostly as it had before.

Cooperation between the English and German wings of the revival was now the norm. The plan of Boehm's Chapel, erected in 1791, "was furnished in 1790 by Richard Whatcoat, afterward [MEC] bishop. He was an elder at the time, and came there to administer the ordinances."[79] In June 1797, Asbury noted,

> In the afternoon I gave a short exhortation at Mr. Otterbein's church, on Howard's Hill.... I am trying to organize the African Church. I made interest for the use of Mr. Otterbein's church for Sabbath, in the morning and evening for the white people. I have attempted to promote society meetings at Old Town and the west end of the city, either at the Dunker's meeting house or Mr. Otterbein's church.[80]

Language and practice were now overlapping. Indeed, there is substantial evidence for this on both sides. For example, on the German side of the revival, Christian Newcomer recorded setting "out for the Quarterly, or Great meeting as it is generally called, at the Antietam...Sunday, June 1, 1800—This morning we had our Love Feast."[81] Similarly, on the English side, Asbury commented, "Bishop Whatcoat preached at Martin Boehm's church, on Psalm lxxii, 16-20.... Our *Dutch Methodists* are as kind and more lively than many of the American ones."[82]

"THE *UNSECTARIAN* PREACHERS"

The first regular annual conference of the German preachers was held at Peter Kemp's house near Frederick, on September 25, 1800. Otterbein, Boehm, Geeting, Newcomer, Lehman, John Hershey, Abraham Troxel, Christian Krum, Henry Krum, George Pfrimmer, Henry Boehm, Dietrich Aurand, and Jacob Geisinger were present. Drury describes what took place, saying, "Each person spoke first of his own experience, and then declared anew his intention with all zeal, through the help of God, to preach untrammeled by sect to the honor of God and [the good] of men." At this meeting they began the process to authorize preachers to perform the sacraments and resolved "that yearly a day shall be appointed when the *unsectarian* preachers shall assemble and counsel how they may conduct their office more and more according to the will of God, and according to the mind of God, that the church of God may be built up, and sinners converted, so that God in Christ may be honored." They elected Boehm and Otterbein as bishops and adopted the name "United Brethren in Christ [UBC]."[83]

Lack of sectarianism was a key component even as they continued to formalize their organization. The 1801 conference minutes describe Otterbein's discourse "that salvation depends on Christ alone and his mercy, and that whoever here becomes free from sin *and a party spirit* has God to thank."[84] Then "the preachers were examined" and were "asked who are willing to take charge of a circuit and preach at the appointed places."[85] The following year provision was made for the continuation of the organization after the death of Otterbein or Boehm.[86]

Asbury commented on August 2, 1803, that "there are now upwards of twenty German preachers somehow connected with Mr. Phillip Otterbein and Martin Boehm; but they want authority, and the Church wants discipline."[87] Certainly the "unsectarian preachers" were less hierarchical than the MEC under Asbury. At their October 5, 1803, annual conference, in contrast to MEC discipline, "It was left to the preachers in Maryland themselves to arrange." Resolution 7 stated, "Resolved that David Snyder and Abraham Mayer...shall make their own arrangement, how they shall serve their preaching places as may be best for the kingdom of God. May the Lord help them. Amen."[88]

At the UBC conference of May 29, 1805, this flexibility was proving unsatisfactory and possibly divisive. That year it was resolved that "the preachers who preach where they desire, according to their inclination, shall have no compensation. When, however, they receive money, they shall bring the same to the conference, to be given to the regular preachers."[89] Martin Boehm later reflected.

> Being conscious of the propriety and usefulness of a well ordered discipline, and not feeling any disposition of forming a separate body, and knowing of no discipline so well calculated to forward the work of God among those who are under the influence [of] grace in its several degrees as that among the Methodists, I generally advised serious persons to embrace the privilege of uniting

themselves with the Methodists. However several ministers met in conference annually, but still we felt our difficulties for want of a well-ordered discipline.[90]

At the 1806 conference neither Boehm nor Otterbein, the main advocates of tighter discipline, was present. That year the main business of the annual conference seems to have been setting the dates for the Great Meetings, much as the preachers had done before 1800.[91] This lack of tight organization was galling to Asbury. On June 18, 1808, he recorded, "Our German brethren of Otterbein's have shouldered us out, but have failed to establish themselves."[92]

GERMAN-ENGLISH UNION?

In March 1809 the Baltimore MEC conference addressed a letter to the UBC conference to address issues that made attempts "to establish a closer and more permanent union" difficult. The recommendations from the Methodist conference included "that each minister or preacher who is acknowledged by the United Brethren should receive...a regular license, which may introduce them to our pulpits and privileges and prevent impositions." The letter also recommended that the UBC "establish a strict discipline..., which might be a 'defense of your glory,'" and offered as a template "our Discipline [which] is printed in your language."[93] The issue of discipline, especially the institution of the class meeting, had long been an area of contention. As early as June 11, 1781, Asbury had written in his *Journal*, "I came to a Dutch settlement: the people love preaching, but do not understand class meeting."[94]

In response to the MEC letter, the UBC acknowledged that "the fundamental Christian doctrines as held by the two societies are the same; and all the differences between the two...consist in some external church regulations." Conference also agreed to supply UBC preachers with licenses "to prevent disorders as far as possible." However, they "deferred to our next conference" the majority of the issues of discipline among the members.[95]

Letters continued to be exchanged between annual conferences. Boehm was hopeful, saying on April 12, 1811, "Moreover I rejoice that there is a prospect of a union being form[ed] in sentiment and in practice, between the Methodist and the German brethren."[96] The following month the UBC conference met. "We have now formed our members in classes, as much as possible," they wrote to the MEC conference.

> However, there are a number yet among us who have not yet joined with us in this privilege, so long delayed by us. We earnestly hope that you will instruct your traveling preachers to bear with such as much as the order of your church will admit. We would further inform you that we have drawn up some regulations, or discipline, among us, and shall endeavor more and more, to put them into effect among ourselves and our members.[97]

Changing Leadership and Shifting Geography

By the time of this hopeful correspondence, Asbury, Boehm, and Otterbein, whose common ministry, mutual respect, and friendship had likely been the driving force behind union and the adoption of the class meeting, had limited time. On Friday, April 3, 1812, Asbury "received the first intelligence of the death of my dear old friend Martin Boehm."[98] On the Sabbath, April 5, 1812, he "preached at Boehm's chapel the funeral sermon of Martin Boehm."[99]

The following month, on May 13, 1812, the UBC conference addressed the MEC conference: "We are truly thankful for the delicacy and tenderness...as touching those members of our society that may not as yet be divested of certain peculiarities.... We have in many places succeeded in forming class-meetings and extending discipline, and, as far as prudence shall dictate, we will pursue."[100]

The caveat of prudence did not satisfy the Methodists. The MEC conference in May 1813 gave its official reply:

> Our doctrines are fixed and established; our discipline is binding upon [us] by the authority of our General conference, and we have long experienced and proved the great advantage of such regulations; consequently to these in our church communion and fellowship we feel ourselves bound by the most sacred obligations to have an especial regard. And might we not, brethren, rec-

ommend them to your consideration, that you may "prove all things, and hold fast that which is good?"[101]

On May 6, 1813, the UBC conference in Lancaster responded to that letter:

> We have it in lovely contemplation soon to have printed and circulated among our members a system of rules.... But as we cannot at present inform you in this letter concerning the general form of the Discipline we contemplate publishing, the bearers of this letter to your conference, our beloved brethren Christian Newcomer and Valentine Baulus, will be fully qualified, and shall have power, to give you any information that may be necessary.[102]

Asbury commented in October 1812 in his *Journal*, "O! what a work has there been done among the Germans, and would more abundantly have been, had they the discipline of the Methodists!"[103]

As the UBC expanded westward, the need was felt for more clergy and more legitimacy. At the 1813 Miami Annual Conference,

> "It was deplored that too little order was observed both in the reception and in the ordination of preachers. The Conference took under consideration whether it is proper to ordain preachers without the laying on of the hands of Elders." [Newcomer] was agreed to write to father Otterbein and ask him "to ordain, by the laying on of hands, one or more preachers, who afterward may perform the same for others."[104]

Otterbein granted the request and ordained Newcomer and two others in October 1813 to "the office of elder and preacher of the gospel." The ordinations were held in the vestry of Otterbein's church with "Br. Wm. Ryland, an Elder of the Methodist Episcopal Church, who had been invited for the purpose, to assist him in the ordination."[105]

In November 1813, Newcomer met with "the people denominated the Albright Brethren." The purpose of the meeting was "to try whether a union could not be effected." It could not. Newcomer blamed the fact that UBC "local preachers have a vote in the Conference as well as the traveling preachers."[106] That same month, Otterbein died.[107]

With Otterbein's death, the UBC conference received its last correspondence from the MEC regarding union. The letter evidences clear frustration with the lack of progress on discipline and union, concluding, "We think it unnecessary to continue the ceremony of annual letters, etc."[108] Asbury lived only two more years.

In August 1814, the Miami Annual Conference of the UBC, with Newcomer as bishop, issued a protest against "the present order of the Church,"[109] a Discipline written by the eastern conference (likely cowritten by Newcomer himself),[110] and called for a General Conference to meet in June 1815. This 1815 General Conference established the equality of the eastern and western annual conferences and issued a Confession of Faith and "definitions and rules." It also dealt with issues of ordination and membership, but it did not adopt the class meeting.

Conclusion

The theological backgrounds of those who formed the United Brethren in Christ included Mennonites, German Reformed, Moravians, and Dunkers. These theological streams were further influenced by the First Great Awakening, continental Pietism, the mystical Pietism of Ephrata, and Methodism. What brought these clergy and laypeople together was a perceived movement of the Spirit. It distanced them from their previous communities of faith and bound them together with those who shared their evangelical experience and evangelistic vision.[111]

The UBC began as an ecumenical, nonsectarian evangelistic association, mostly among the German-speaking population. As such, the UBC cooperated with and influenced other groups working to revive Christianity in America, particularly the MEC. Though separated by language, the groups were united by their sense of mission and through their leaders' ties of friendship. After the deaths of Boehm, Otterbein, and Asbury, emphases began to shift. For the second generation of leaders, the focus on building a church began to overshadow the focus on building the Church. Thus the UBC became a denomination alongside, yet distinct from, other revivalist denominations, including the MEC and "Albright's People."[112]

CHAPTER 3

JACOB ALBRIGHT AND THE EVANGELICAL ASSOCIATION

Kenneth E. Rowe

This chapter reviews the formative, and in many ways painful, first sixteen years (1800–1816) of the renewal movement that flowed from Jacob Albright's preaching among the Pennsylvania Germans, a missional initiative that Mother Methodism and Father Asbury, in their wisdom or folly, rejected. The chapter will briefly detail the movement's transformation from a "renewal group" within Lutheran and Reformed, Amish and Mennonite churches, through an attempt to become a German conference of The Methodist Episcopal Church, and finally to ecclesial independence in 1816. With great hope and patience Evangelicals waited sixteen long years for Mother Methodism to embrace them before finally and fully cutting their family ties. Although Evangelicals preferred the word *Association* (*Gemeinschaft*) to *Church* (*Kirche*), in time their Methodist-style lay-led classes, house churches, lay preachers, and camp meetings led to ordained preachers, superintendents and bishops, and books of discipline, doctrine, catechism, liturgy, and hymns, which is to say, historic marks of the one holy catholic and apostolic church, an intention affirmed in Albright's 1803 ordination certificate.

Along the way The Evangelical Association's original Wesleyan doctrine and ethos were heavily tinged by German Pietism in America, as several modern scholars affirm, most notably Professor J. Steven O'Malley.[1] My modest codicil to the O'Malley thesis is that German Pietism was first mediated to the

Evangelicals through Methodists in the period when they thought of themselves more or less as "Dutch" Methodists. The German Pietist tinging that Professor O'Malley so persuasively attests had already been initiated by their Methodist mentors in the founding period, as I shall attempt to show in an examination of the founding documents of The Evangelical Association.

CLASS MEETINGS FORMED

During the crisis of faith that followed the sudden deaths of several children in an epidemic of dysentery, Jacob Albright experienced an evangelical conversion in 1791, abandoned his Lutheran spiritual home, and sought and found spiritual nurture in a Methodist class led by his neighbor. Five years later (1796), at age thirty-seven, he felt called to preach to Pennsylvania's unchurched Germans.

True to his beliefs about a community of faith (*Gemeinschaft*), Albright proceeded rapidly to make his band of followers a formal one. Four years after beginning his itinerant preaching ministry (in 1800) he took the first step in organizing his German-speaking converts into a structure that would establish the results of his ministry, forming classes in the Methodist fashion in three widely scattered areas of eastern Pennsylvania—the Leisser class near the Coalbrookdale Iron Works near Barto (in Berks County near Reading), closest to home; the Walter class in Quakertown (in Bucks County, south of Allentown); and the Phillips class near Bangor (in Northampton County, adjacent to the Delaware River bordering New Jersey), with a total membership of about twenty. Additional societies were quickly organized near Allentown in Lehigh County, Pottsville in Schuylkill County, and Mifflin and Juniata in Juniata County along the upper Susquehanna River.[2]

In the fall, after the crops were harvested, Albright gathered his flock in 1802 for the first of many Great Meetings (*grosse Versammlungen*) at Coalbrookdale, near Reading, Pennsylvania. Converts expressed their joy in a variety of ways. Outbreaks of shouting, stamping in rhythm, or fainting often accompanied his passionate and persuasive preaching. To Albright, the emotional outbursts of the frontier camp meetings implied the presence and power of the Holy Spirit and of true religion. To the "church" people—Lutheran and Reformed—this display of emotion was offensive, and non-evangelicals regularly mocked his followers as "Bush Meeting Dutch" and more derisively as "holy rollers" (*Springbungen*, literally holy jumpers) or "knee-sliders" (*Knierutscher*) and foot stampers. Many feared Albright's itinerants as false prophets, deceivers, and bewitchers. Like Wesley before him, Albright tried to maintain a moderate course between relaxing in a false assurance and excessive exuberance, although what Albright called moderate emotionalism seemed excessive to the church Germans.

LAY PREACHERS RECRUITED, CIRCUITS LAID OUT

Young men who heard Albright preach began to join the evangelist's movement, became class leaders, and took up preaching. Two of the earliest became Albright's trusted assistants. John Walter (1781–1818), son of the leader of the Quakertown class, moved into the Albright home as a tile-making apprentice, giving Albright greater freedom to go on preaching journeys. A year later, in 1802, he joined Albright in another apprenticeship—preaching.[3] George Miller (1774–1816), a Lutheran from Pottstown, first heard Albright preach in 1798 and was impressed. Two years later, Albright stopped at his home to ask for lodging. Their conversations stimulated his interest in matters of faith, and in 1805 he took up preaching.[4] To their inspired preaching, some hearers responded, new classes formed, more circuits were added, and the Albright movement soon doubled in membership.

In the beginning, most preaching places were in private homes and barns. Some private homes were also the places where private lay-led class meetings were held twice a week, usually on Wednesdays and Sundays. Circuits were formed by linking anywhere from a dozen to twenty-five preaching places together in such a way that the circuit-riding preacher could get to each preaching place at least four times a year. By 1810, the circuits had expanded and were large enough to create three circuits. However, there was yet no official leadership, no book of discipline, no articles of faith, no liturgy, not even a denominational name, although they were popularly referred to as "Dutch Methodists" or "Albright's People" (*Albrechtsleute*).

ALBRIGHT ORDAINED

The first step to remedy these deficiencies was taken in November 1803. Albright called his two assistant preachers and his lay leaders together for a two-day organizing conference at the home of Samuel Leisser near Reading. Representatives of the forty-plus-member society[5] declared themselves to be a new church organization, affirmed the Bible as the sole guide of faith and practice, and elected and ordained Albright, probably with the laying on of hands and prayer—classic signs of ordination, though Paul Eller judged it to have been "ordination by resolution rather than ordination by rite."[6] Albright's ordination certificate, which survives, clearly indicates he was ordained "in the name of the entire society [*Gemeinde*], as a 'truly' or 'genuine' [*wahrhäftigen*] 'Evangelical' or 'Protestant' [*Evangelisch*] minister in word and deed, and a believer in the Holy Catholic Church and the Communion of Saints"—a clear reference to the ancient Apostles' Creed. The conference also commissioned two lay preachers as his ministerial associates. Here, perhaps for the first time on their own, Albright's little flock celebrated the Lord's Supper. This assembly is regarded as the formal beginning of The Evangelical Association, though that name was not adopted until the first General Conference in 1816.[7]

ANNUAL CONFERENCES BEGIN, ALBRIGHT ELECTED BISHOP

Four years after his ordination (November 1807), Albright presided at the first regular or annual conference. Four preachers—John Walter, George Miller, John Dreisbach, and Jacob Fry—and 28 of Albright's approximately 220 followers met at Samuel Becker's farm near Kleinfeltersville, Pennsylvania. (Note the departure from Methodist practice at this point—all the preachers and as many class leaders [that is, lay members] as possible were invited.)

In the record left by George Miller, "On brother Albright's advice, the Episcopal form of government was adopted," the assembly took the name Newly Formed Methodist Conference (*Neuformirten Methodisten Conferenz*), and they elected Albright bishop, acknowledging the leadership that he had already exercised among them. Albright licensed several lay preachers and ordained one of them, George Miller, an elder, making him a full-time itinerant elder and his chief assistant. Albright appointed the preachers to their circuits, providing a regular sacramental ministry to the growing number of scattered congregations. The conference also asked Albright to prepare and publish a German translation of the Methodist *Book of Discipline* and hoped Bishop Asbury and the Methodists would welcome the new conference as partners in ministry.

The German-speaking bishop and preachers, however, were not accepted by Asbury and the Methodists, partly because the ordinations were irregular—so much for their own mission-driven irregular ordinations!—partly because the preachers used the German language that Asbury and the Methodists believed would not long continue in this country, and also because Albright's absences while preaching had caused the membership in his Lancaster County Methodist class to lapse.

ALBRIGHT'S UNEXPECTED DEATH

Albright was determined to travel widely, but the new bishop's health failed. The next year, 1808, Albright traveled and preached with increasing difficulty. He convened the conference for the last time near Harrisburg on Easter Day. In speaking to his gathered flock for the last time, he said, "If it is God's will that you shall be a permanent association, God will also provide the elements necessary to success. God will raise up men from among you who will take up the burden I no longer can bear, and consummate the work. It is of God and in His hands and God will provide."[8]

Albright was worn out by his labors and by a tubercular condition, and his companions knew he could not make it to his home in Lancaster County, fifty miles away. So after thirty miles, the bishop rested at the home of George Becker in Kleinfeltersville. He died the next day, May 18, 1808, at a youthful age of forty-nine and was buried in the Becker family cemetery on the edge of the village two days later.[9] Methodist Bishop Asbury took little notice of Albright's death and preached no funeral sermon for Albright as he had done for United Brethren (UB) founder Martin Boehm and would do later (1813) for another UB founder, Philip Otterbein.

George Miller Assumes Leadership, Convenes the First Conference without Albright

Albright's death did not derail the community's determination to continue in union with the Methodists. George Miller (1774–1816) assumed leadership of the distraught religious community, and he convened the first annual conference without Albright in 1808 in the home of Henry Eby near Lebanon, Pennsylvania. The conference took a new name—the people called Albrights (*Die sogennanten Albrechtsleute*). Miller licensed a few lay preachers, for the first time ordained two preachers—John Dreisbach and John Walter—as elders (probably with the laying on of hands and prayer), and appointed all of them to their circuits. But Miller's leadership lasted only a brief time because at Christmas 1808 he suffered a heart attack that brought his itinerant ministry to an end.

Most important of all, the conference commissioned the preparation and publication of five documents that turned out to be crucial to the continuation of the new denomination. George Miller, recently retired, prepared three of them.

(1) A German translation of the Methodist *Book of Discipline*. The book, titled *Doctrine, General Rules and Discipline of the People-called Albrights* was presented to the 1809 General Conference and published a few months later.[10] It was modeled after an Asbury/Philadelphia Conference–sponsored German translation of the 1804 Methodist *Discipline* completed in 1807 but not published in Lancaster until early 1808 under the title *Lehre und Zuchtordnung der Bischoflich-Methodistenkirche*.[11] The translation was prepared by Dr. Ignaz Romer, a Swiss-born Roman Catholic–trained physician recently turned Methodist, from Middletown,

Pennsylvania, under the close supervision of Bishop Asbury's trusted adviser on German work, Henry Boehm.[12]

When comparing the 1804 MEC *Discipline* with the 1809 Evangelical *Discipline*, scholars have noted that Miller's *Discipline* generally followed the MEC *Discipline*, but modified it at several crucial points. First, Miller omitted all liturgical texts, suggesting that early Evangelicals may have preferred to pray with their eyes shut or that they hoped to continue as a German Conference within The Methodist Episcopal Church and needed none of their own. However, the Association's second and more complete *Discipline* (1817) did include a full set of revised Methodist liturgical texts, as I shall note below.

Second, Miller included the Twenty-five Articles of Religion of the Methodists without alteration, but filled two gaps in those doctrinal standards by adding a twenty-sixth Article, "Of the Last Judgment and God's Righteous Sentence of Rewards and Punishments"—borrowed from the Lutheran Augsburg Confession!

Third, and most significant of all, Miller appended to the Articles an extended essay on Christian perfection (*Von der Christlichen Vollkommenheit*), communicating the Wesleyan doctrine of sanctification in the genre of German Pietism, another topic strangely absent from English-speaking Methodism's doctrinal standards.[13] But where did Miller get the essay? Did he write it himself, or did he adapt or borrow it from someone else? The entire essay appeared in the 1808 Romer/Boehm German MEC *Discipline*. Thus, rather than drafting it himself or borrowing it from Pietist sources, Miller borrowed the first official Evangelical statement on Christian perfection from German-speaking Methodists. By whose authority were the eleven paragraphs "added" to the German translation of the official MEC 1804 English text? The title page suggests Romer and Boehm had full Asbury/Philadelphia Conference approval for the book.[14]

The latter part of the statement (paragraphs 14–16) in Miller's 1809 Evangelical *Discipline* is clearly a German translation of the section on perfection in John Wesley's "Large Minutes" of 1768, which Methodists traditionally printed in their *Disciplines* up to that time.[15] I have been unable to trace the precise origins of the first eleven paragraphs of the Romer-Boehm/later Miller text.

They are in the Wesleyan spirit, but are they from Wesley? Hezekiah Bowman, an Evangelical pastor writing in 1882, confidently suggested that the first "few paragraphs were afterwards supplied from Mr. Wesley's writings."[16] Bowman, I think, was trying to make the point that the Evangelicals were more Wesleyan than the Methodists on the matter. Who else could have drafted it? Bishop Asbury would have been too busy. Besides, he had his chance at improving or improvising Wesley on perfection in an annotated edition of the *Discipline* that he and Bishop Coke published in 1798, but did not choose to do so. When it came to the section on perfection, the bishops simply referred the reader to "Mr. Wesley's excellent treatise on that subject."[17] Henry Boehm says in his autobiography that he "aided" Dr. Romer in the translation and proofread the entire manuscript in addition to hiring the printer and footing the bill, but he takes no credit for the extra paragraphs on perfection. That leaves Romer. In his nine-page preface, Romer assures his German readers that the work before them is "eine getreue übersetzung der Methodistischen Kirchenzuchtsform, wie solche 1804" and does not mention any "additions."[18] The mystery remains.

From all of the above I conclude that if the original Wesleyan doctrine of the mature (mid-nineteenth-century) Evangelical Association was heavily tinged by German Pietism, as several modern scholars allege, most notably Professor J. Steven O'Malley,[19] the tinging had already been begun by the Association's Methodist mentors—in this case Henry Boehm and/or Ignaz Romer. The Evangelicals simply took their cue from their Methodist mentors as well as their Pietist-tinged neighbors in other faith communities.

(2) A biography of Albright. Miller prepared it to keep alive the ministerial memory of the charismatic leader. Based on Albright's journals and diaries, *A Short Account of the Empowering Grace of God by the Enlightened Protestant Preacher Jacob Albright* (*Kurze Beschreibung der würkenden Gnade Gottes, bey dem erleuchteten evangelischen Prediger Jakob Albrecht*) was published in Reading, Pennsylvania, in 1811.[20] Albright's personal narrative of his spiritual transformation—"Blessed joy coursed through my innermost self.... No longer was the practice of good a burdensome business to me. I was now inclined to hate sin and every evil. It was my joy to serve God and I had a sense of blessedness when I could converse with my God in prayer"—which Miller gives in the first person, continues to be the major primary source regarding Albright's life, thanks to Professor James Nelson's splendid recent English translation.[21]

(3) A handbook of faith and practice for ministers, parents, and children. *Simple and Plain Doctrines setting forth True and Practical Christianity* (*Kurze und deutliche Lehren zum Wahren und Thätigen Christenthum*), prepared by Miller and published in 1814, was an exposition on how to live out "true Christianity" based on the church's doctrinal standards.[22] The four chapters devoted to religion are largely an expansion of Miller's borrowed essay on Christian perfection in the church's *Discipline*: (1) "Man, by Nature, Sleeps Securely in Sin and Is Spiritually Dead," (2) "The Manner in which God Awakens Man from the Sleep of Sin and Spiritual Death, and Brings Him Back to Life," (3) "The New and Spiritual Life in Christ," and (4) "Growth in Grace and Perseverance in the Divine Life." Chapters 5–12 detail instructions for "Ministers of the Gospel," husbands and wives, parents and guardians, and children. The concluding chapter 13 gives "General Directions in Works of Love and Mercy for All Believers." The book thus functioned much as Wesley's less detailed General Rules for the Methodists—live simply by avoiding evil, doing good, and using all the means of grace.

(4) A catechism for children. John Dreisbach prepared *A Short Scriptural Catechism* (*Die kleine biblische Catechismus*), which was approved by the conference and published by the end of the year 1809.[23] The catechism was not Dreisbach's own work, but a translation of a small catechism prepared by John Dickins and first published for use in The Methodist Episcopal Church in 1793. The "principal design" of the Dickins/Dreisbach catechism was to introduce young children to the Bible. Its thirty-four lessons were heavy on duty to God, pastors, parents, and neighbors and harsh on derelicts—the final seven lessons warn about God's judgment for delinquents! The Lord's Prayer, the Apostles' Creed, and the Ten Commandments concluded the little catechism.[24]

(5) A hymnal. *A Little Collection of Old and New Spiritual Songs for the Upbuilding and Use of All God-loving Souls* (*Eine kleine Sammlung* *alter und neuer Geistreicher Lieder: zur Erbauung und Gebrauch aller Gottliebenden Seelen*) was edited by John Walter in 1810. From the very first, the meetings of the Albright People included singing, mostly the seventeenth-century Pietist chorales (hymns) of their Lutheran and Reformed heritage. Soon, however, a new century brought new forms of worship and outreach, the camp meeting, and a new form of sacred song, the camp meeting or "bush meeting" spiritual, ideally suited to the Methodist and Evangelical spirit. The simple rhythmic choruses sung around the campfires at English camp meetings were translated, adapted, and extended by the Pennsylvania German Methodists.[25] The Evangelicals preferred their indigenous spirituals to the hymnody of the Methodist revival. Walter's hymnal for use in prayer meetings and camp meetings, published in Reading, Pennsylvania, was the first of its kind for Germans in America. Among its fifty-seven texts are English hymns he translated into German, plus his own compositions. Among Walter's hymns is one of the most popular Pennsylvania Dutch spirituals composed in America, still known among German-speaking groups: "Come, Brethren, Come, We'll Journey On to the New Jerusalem."

These books of discipline, doctrine, catechesis, and hymns along with the biography of the revered Albright did much to provide a greater sense of cohesion and purpose to the distraught religious community. Miller reported that "all took courage to continue their union with God and among themselves, and many others were induced to unite with us and work out their soul's salvation."[26]

THE DREAM OF BECOMING A GERMAN CONFERENCE OF THE METHODIST EPISCOPAL CHURCH FADES

The new conference, fifty preachers and five hundred-pluss members strong, was ready to join the Methodists, but relations between the German Methodists and the English Methodists were never close. From the beginning, Albright was eager to have his followers become part of Methodism. But Asbury did not share Albright's dream. There is no evidence that the two leaders ever met. Asbury made many trips from Philadelphia westward across the mountains to western Pennsylvania, visiting Pennsylvania Dutch country along the way, at least twelve times during Albright's short ministry. There are no entries in Asbury's extensive published *Journal* referencing Albright and the Evangelicals. This stands in contrast to his many references to United Brethren names and events. He traveled from Philadelphia to Pittsburgh in the summer of 1803 and again in the summer of 1805.[27] In the latter trip he noted in his *Journal*: "We came off with courage, passing through Lancaster still unpropitious to Methodism."[28] In 1807, he visited Allentown, Kutztown, and Reading, only a few miles from the Albright farm, but never mentioned Albright's German Methodists.[29] At Albright's death, he sent no letter of condolence, offered no appreciation of his ministry, and preached no funeral sermon as he did at the deaths of the first two United Brethren bishops, Otterbein and Boehm, and yet Albright was a better Methodist than either of them! Not until after Asbury's death did The Methodist Episcopal Church begin an aggressive evangelization among the nation's swelling German immigrant population in the middle 1830s.

The rift between Evangelical *de facto* "bishop" John Dreisbach and Methodist Bishop Asbury over the use of the German language ended the dream of becoming a German Conference of The Methodist Episcopal Church.[30] On his journey down the Susquehanna River in early August 1810, Dreisbach "unexpectedly" met Bishop Asbury and traveled with him for two days. After conversing freely with Dreisbach on various topics relating to preaching and evangelism, the bishop, in order to enlist him for The Methodist Episcopal Church, made him an offer, which I give in Dreisbach's own words, written forty-five years later when he was editor of the Evangelical Church's weekly newspaper, the *Evangelical Messenger*, based on an original account that Dreisbach wrote in his journal at the time:

> The bishop made me a very favorable offer toward receiving me into the ranks of the Methodist clergy, which we, however, declined, because we, as a church, considered ourselves raised and destined of the Lord to labor in the Gospel for the good of the German people in our land, who so very much needed a revival

of true religion; and therefore, we could not consistently consent to leave in an individual capacity, and thus give up this important object, for fear we might become guilty of not fulfilling our duty. But we made the following proposition to the venerable Bishop: grant us to labor among the Germans; to have German circuits, districts, and conferences; the supervision of the latter to be by one of your Bishops; this being granted, we venture to state that we shall come over as a community to a man. However, the answer we received from the Bishop on this proposal was that it would be *inexpedient*. Then we must continue in our course, pursuing the object for which we believe ourselves raised and called by the Lord, was our answer to the Bishop. And when we departed, he... bid us God speed: and we saw him no more.

In retrospect the aged Dreisbach added,

But though it appeared inexpedient to the Bishop at that time to start a German work in the Methodist Church, yet some sixteen years ago this church did deem it expedient to commence one, and, as it appears, with good success.[31]

Bishop Asbury made no mention of the encounter (though he was in the area at this time) or the proposal in his *Journal*. Nor is it found in the *Reminiscences of Rev. Henry Boehm*. Asbury's last words on the Evangelicals were written four years later (1814) in a letter to Presiding Elder Jacob Gruber. Asbury wrote scathingly: "What are the Albrights but deceitful apers and opposers of Methodists."[32] Asbury clearly and stubbornly disliked preachers skilled only in German. He preferred bilingual preachers who would be able to interchange pulpits and turned down the idea of bringing the Germans and their German-only-speaking preachers converted by Albright and his successors into The Methodist Church.

After years of feeling strong bonds with the Methodists, Asbury's rebuff must have come as quite a shock. Dreisbach and Asbury were proud and determined men, and from then on, they went their separate ways. Only after this rift over missional strategy did Dreisbach, sole leader of the Albrights, take steps to fully organize an independent *German* Methodist church.

The Gradual Transition of the Albright People from Movement, Caucus to an Independent Methodist Church in and for the Conversion of German Americans

The transition of the Albright people from movement within The Methodist Episcopal Church to independent German Methodist church was completed at two conferences in 1816. The community had grown to number about fourteen hundred members, led by two district superintendents and about twenty itinerant preachers and forty local preachers.

In June, after the crops were planted, Dreisbach convened the regular annual conference in a barn in Dry Valley, Union County. Preachers were examined; new probationers, deacons, and elders were elected and ordained as usual. The conference also looked forward to becoming a permanent and independent church. Printed licenses were ordered for the first time, a seal was commissioned for official documents, and a committee was appointed to set up a publishing house. The conference also agreed henceforth to hold a delegated general conference every four years, with the first to be held in the fall that year after the crops were harvested. Twenty clergy delegates were elected.

In October 1816, Dreisbach convened an organizing General Conference near Lewisburg along the upper Susquehanna River, completing the gradual transition of the Albright People from movement to German *Methodist* church.[33] The conference took the name *Evangelische Gemeinschaft* (Evangelical Association), the first American church body to adopt the term *Evangelical* as its name. Evangelicals were fond of noting that their founding fathers did not want a church named after a man; they preferred, instead, the term used at Albright's ordination: he was declared to be "a truly [genuine, *wahrhäftigen*] Evangelical preacher in word and deed." The term *Church* would have to wait until 1922, but clearly they were forming one then and there. Delegates favored German-only ministry, and they approved expansion into Ohio and upstate New York. They rearranged and improved the *Book of Discipline* (published the following year, 1817), including this time full liturgical texts for baptism, Communion, marriage, burial, and ordination, modeled after the rites that Methodists inherited from John Wesley, though in revised form.

The first Evangelical Association *Book of Discipline* (1809) retained all five Methodist Articles of Religion on the sacraments: Article XVI. "Of the Sacraments," XVII. "Of Baptism," XVIII. "Of the Lord's Supper," XIX. "Of Both Kinds," and XX. "Of the One Oblation of Christ, Finished upon the Cross." The Evangelicals' dependence on Wesleyan/Methodist ways can also be seen in their revision of the 1792 Methodist Communion rite (*Form des Gedachtnissmahls*):

Following the sermon and offering, the elder would proceed as follows:

- *Exhortation:* The Service of the Table begins with a preparatory discourse and exhortation inviting self-examination on the words of institution and the warning against partaking of the supper unworthily of 1 Corinthians 11:23-29.
- *Confession:* The presider offers a prayer of confession "in the name of all those who are willing to receive the Holy Communion," all humbly kneeling. The prayer is an amalgam of the Methodist General Confession, Prayer for Pardon, Collect for Purity, Sursum corda, Sanctus, and Prayer of Humble Access, retaining the crucial sacramental words:

Grant us, therefore, Father of mercies, so to eat the body ["flesh" in the MEC rite] of thy dear Son Jesus Christ, and to drink his blood, that our souls and bodies may be made clean by virtue of his death ["by his body" in the MEC rite], and washed through his most precious blood, and that he may evermore dwell in us, and we in him.

- *Consecration, Dedication, or Thanksgiving Prayer:* This includes the following crucial words from the Methodist prayer:

Grant that we, receiving these thy creatures of bread and wine, according to thy Son our Saviour Jesus Christ's holy institution, in remembrance of his death and passion, may be partakers of his most blessed Body and Blood.

- *Distribution:* The Methodist words of delivery are slightly adjusted, but hardly weakened:

  Eat the bread, which we break, in remembrance that Christ had his body broken, who died upon Golgotha, the bitter death on the cross, that we might live forever; feed on Him in thy heart by faith with thanksgiving. Drink thereof in remembrance that Christ shed his blood for you, to the washing away of all thy sins, and to the sanctification of thy soul; partake of it by faith with thanksgiving.

- *Post-Communion Prayer:* Here the strong Wesleyan notion of the sacrifice of our persons is retained with slight verbal updating—for example, *"not weighing* our merits" becomes "not *considering* our merits."[34]

General Conference delegates further signaled their determination to henceforth be a church by authorizing the publication of a new collection of *more churchly* hymns and chorales from the Lutheran/Reformed tradition, *Das Geistliche Saitenspiel (Spiritual Lyre)* in 1817, as well as a revised prayer meeting/camp meeting hymnal retitled *Geistliche Viole (Spiritual Violin)*, published in 1818.[35] The two books, often bound together, were published by the church's newly established publishing house in New Berlin, Pennsylvania.

Delegates also agreed to explore union with the United Brethren. At a so-called social conference the following year (1817) between United Brethren and Evangelical leaders, actual proposals for merger were made, but incompatibility over polity and style ended the negotiation. Long after Asbury was dead and buried, the Methodist General Conference of 1840 voted to send three fraternal delegates to the Evangelical General Conference of 1843 for the purpose of establishing "closer friendship" between them and "to labor for the temporal and spiritual welfare of the neglected German people of this country."[36] The first step on the long road to reunion with the Methodists had been taken, but reunion would take another 128 years!

Jacob Albright: An Exemplary *Catholic* Methodist

Catholicity to Wesley meant, among other things, Christian diversity. Albright understood this better than Asbury, who in effect turned his back on developing a significant ministry among America's German-speaking community, as he did among African Americans. Not until twenty years after Asbury's death (1836) did The Methodist Episcopal Church realize its mistake and launch a mission with German-speaking preachers and German-language disciplines, hymnals, newspapers, and so on. By then it was too late to invite the Evangelicals back. The epicenter of this Methodist movement was in the state of Ohio, at first based in the city of Cincinnati.

Albright understood that catholicity is a complement of Christian unity. Better expressed, it is the church's power to remain itself in a great variety of differences, not only *tolerating* variety, but *seeking* it, even *enjoying* it!—something Bishop Asbury in his day, and we latter-day United Methodists, often fail to grasp. Catholicity means the ability for creative openness to the new, and as such is the essential power by which the church does its work. It is the ability to confront change—the new, the strange—in the spirit of worship, and to discover how Christ is Lord of it also, and how its newness and strangeness and variousness rightly belong to the riches of God's realm. Catholicity in this sense is a category of mission. It expresses the church's share in the spreading diversification of God's love. Catholicity means a church prepared to face the future and its surprises with confidence.

Evangelicals have been called "Methodists with a German accent" with considerable justification, as their organization and public preaching attest. In many ways Albright, in his brief twelve-year ministry, mimicked other leaders in the Methodist tradition. He shared their devotion to confessing Jesus as the way, the truth, and the life and professing its reality by a disciplined commitment to holy living and to missionary outreach. Evangelical Association class meetings, circuit riders, quarterly conferences, and annual and general conferences are pure Methodist patterns. But their primary message has a German Pietist as well as a Wesleyan cast, as Professor O'Malley has persuasively argued. Relations between them and the Methodists were close but, as we have seen, not always cordial. After Albright's death and Asbury's rebuff, Evangelicals did not think of themselves simply as German Methodists. Except for the very early years (to about 1816), both movements thought of themselves as quite separate denominations.

By reaching out in the face of shattering tragedy and accepting spiritual help from friends and from a supportive Methodist class, Jacob Albright became a teacher and example to many others not reached by Asbury's English-speaking preachers. By persistently following God's call to minister among German Americans in the face of self-doubt and ecclesiastical rejection, even at the cost of broken health and early death, Albright left behind a community of faith that was rejected by Mother Methodism two centuries ago but today is an important legacy of The United Methodist Church.

PART TWO
Doctrine and Theology

CHAPTER 4

THE THEOLOGICAL HERITAGE OF PIETISM

J. Steven O'Malley

Historians who have traced Pietist influences on The Evangelical United Brethren Church (EUB) have generally taken two approaches to their subject matter. On the one hand is a more generic approach that surveys the dominant persons and motifs associated with Pietism and then detects the ways in which those persons and motifs influenced EUB.[1] On the other hand is an approach that traces specific schools of Pietist thought that influenced key EUB figures, particularly Otterbein. These interpreters have paid close attention to the Herborn school of Reformed Pietism.[2]

Both approaches have validity as attempts to locate the denomination in a particular historical milieu. Their disadvantage, though, may reside in their tendency to view the EUB in a somewhat reified and hence detached way as occupying a narrow niche within a larger framework of development. As such, the EUB measure up as "also rans" who had their day and their say and whose memory deserves to be saluted at appropriate historical junctures.

Another and perhaps more fruitful approach would be to identify important, though sometimes obscured, motifs from the diverse and complex field of Pietist studies that appear to be critical for early Evangelical and United Brethren self-understanding and sense of mission. In what follows, I will identify one such motif that did much to set the ethos for the EUB, namely, the prophetic emergence of community as the end-time manifestation of a renewed Pentecost. As we will see ahead, later generations of proto- and veritable EUB would appeal to this motif at critical moments in their corporate life and mission. For now, however, we need to discern this motif in the work of pastors and musicians of the early eighteenth century known to historians as the German Reformed Pietists, as well as in a more exotic branch of visionaries now called the radical Pietists. The members of both groups were living in Germany, and their representatives were arriving in colonial Pennsylvania, during the closing decades of the seventeenth century and into the early part of the eighteenth century. We begin with the Reformed Pietists.

The Reformed Pietists

The theme of the prophetic emergence of community as the end-time manifestation of a renewed Pentecost appeared in late-seventeenth-century Rhineland and Holland among both the Reformed and the radical Pietists. Foundational to both groups was the work of Johannes Cocceius (1603–69). A German Reformed theologian teaching in Holland, Cocceius is perhaps best known for introducing the theme of salvation history (*Heilsgeschichte*) as the key to interpreting the Bible and Christian doctrine. However, he also exerted seminal influence within the official channels of "church" Pietism, especially within the Reformed territories of Germany, through his emphasis on a renewed Pentecost. Closely related to this motif was Cocceius's preference for reading Scripture through the lens of a symbolic-prophetic interpretation of the text, a way of reading for which he found a precedent in Irenaeus's use of the Adam/Christ typology in his anti-Gnostic Christology.

Cocceius's biblical/historical paradigm enabled Pietist writers of several confessional traditions to relate doctrine to life. More specifically, it helped define those persons as forward-looking, prophetic voices that presaged a more hopeful future for the world Christian movement. Indeed, the Pietists' adoption of Cocceius's hermeneutics enabled them to envision the revitalization of persons and faith communities and even the larger societies in which they were housed (for example, emerging nation-states like Prussia and the United States).

The Cocceian hermeneutic was the factor most responsible for turning mainstream church Pietism toward a program for the reformation of church and society in this period. Thus we can trace Cocceius's influence in such key figures as Spener, the Halle school, and the greatest biblical scholars of the day, most notably Campegius Vitringa at Franeker and Albrecht Bengel and his successors in Württemberg. These influences are in addition to Cocceius's influence on his home base, the key center of which included Bremen, Cocceius's birthplace and the site for the greatest leaders of Pietism within the German Reformed world, Theodore Untereyck and Friedrich Adolph Lampe.

Among the most important works influenced by Cocceius was Lampe's *The Secret of the Covenant of Grace* (*Geheimnis des Gnadenbundes*). Little known today, this work turned Cocceian biblical theology into a practical schema in which every seeker of salvation could trace the inward operation of the Spirit's ordering of salvation and outworking in the *praxis pietatis* in a stepwise fashion. Indeed, Lampe was building upon Cocceius's organization of history into grand dispensations, showing how the progressive unfolding of salvation history on a global scale may be fashioned into a micro-order of salvation (*Heilsordnung*) designed for each individual seeker of full salvation in Christ. In Lampe's hands, the goal of history on both the macro and the micro levels was the divine erection of Christ's reigning Kingdom within the human race.

Another important center for Cocceian thought among the Reformed in Germany was the Academy at Herborn (established 1584). The Herborn Academy was among the earliest centers for revitalizing the churches in an era of Aristotelian orthodoxy among Protestants in Europe. Hence it became known as a place to find a life-centered rendition of the message of the Heidelberg Catechism (1563), which was the main confessional symbol of the German Reformed churches. In the hands of these Calvinistic Pietists, the answer to the catechism's leading question, "What is your only comfort in life and in death?" was found in knowing the "greatness of my misery" in sin, the "greatness of my redemption in Jesus Christ," and the "greatness of my thankfulness," all expressed in daily living.[3] The answer reflected a practical Ramist theology that resulted in an emphasis on world missions.[4] Thus it was Herborn that produced John Comenius, the great missionary leader of the Bohemian Brethren in the seventeenth century (the *Unitas Fratrem* or Moravians). Recent scholars have argued that Comenius is the probable source of Spener's use of the conventicle at Frankfurt (the small group of earnest disciples, known as the *collegia pietatis*, which became the defining mark of Pietists). Herborn was also the home of the teachers of Cocceius, from whose influence his federal theology emerged.[5]

Most important, for our purposes, is the fact that Philip William Otterbein (1726–1813) went forth from Herborn to become the leading Pietist missionary to the German Reformed in colonial North America. Otterbein's education brought to the fore the prophetic, missional dimension inherent within the catechism, as expressed in the theological compendia of Lampe and Vitringa.[6] It was from this background that Otterbein learned to enunciate his hope for a coming millennium and for "a more glorious state of the church than ever has been."[7] He would find evidence for the emergence of this glorious new state in the "great meetings" for revitalization that he held in the Pennsylvania bush country on the eve of the Revolutionary War.

THE RADICAL PIETISTS

Now that we have seen how Reformed Pietism influenced the chief founder of the United Brethren, the time has come to examine the influence of the radical Pietists on the EUB. Of these two expressions of Pietism, the radicals are the more elusive to define. Who were they, and how did they come to influence the founders of the EUB?[8]

Before we attempt to describe the radical Pietists, we should note that some scholars prefer that Pietism be defined within the narrower parameters of a renewal movement within German Lutheranism, while others maintain those limits ought to be extended to include comparable impulses within Reformed and even Anabaptist traditions.[9] However, until recent decades, this more socially and theologically marginal body of writers, known as the radicals, has been largely ignored.

The radical Pietists operated through networks of their own, usually in opposition to the authorities within the state churches (*Landeskirchen*), although sometimes manifesting themselves within those entities. Through a confluence of social, economic, and political factors, radical Pietist writers gained popularity in the waning decades of the seventeenth century, particularly with their doomsday version of an approaching day of judgment. They expected this event to occur at the close of the century, which they were keen to note had been fraught with unprecedented levels of religious-motivated warfare.[10]

The earliest German center for the emerging radical Pietists was at Offenbach, where Conrad Broske was the local court preacher and senior pastor. Broske became a proponent of the radicals' message, arising from his contacts with the English Philadelphians. Here was printed Johann Heinrich Reitz's *History of the Reborn* (1698), which Schneider has called the first of a new genre of Pietist biographical anthologies that would be influential in the history of German intellectual and cultural thought.[11] The magnum opus of that genre, by the most luminous figure of radical Pietism, Gottfried Arnold (1666–1714), was also published at Offenbach. In this historical study, *The Unpartisan History of the Church and Heresy* (1699), Arnold traced the thread of apostolicity through history via the witness of a "mystical" theology perennially oppressed by Catholic and Protestant "scholastic theologies."[12] This distinction reflected Arnold's reading of the homilies of the Pseudo-Macarius, which he translated into German, as well as his study of the early church in *The First Love* (*Die Erste Liebe*, 1696). For Arnold, the outcome of history was to be the recovery of a true church of the Spirit. Thus he writes, "The Spirit's inward witness in the reborn constitutes the basis for the spiritual community of those not defined by the divisive biases of human confessions."[13] Macarius was also responsible for Arnold's attention to the doctrine of Christian perfection as "the final and foremost goal of the Christian life," a theme later popularized in Anglo circles by John Wesley and the Methodists.[14]

These authors were by varying degrees inspired by the original Philadelphian vision, whose principal spokesperson was Jane Leade (1624–1704). Leade's dispensational reading of the book of Revelation led her to affirm that the coming community of the redeemed would be a community of brotherly love modeled after the church of Philadelphia. If the present age was represented by the church at Sardis, then the coming age would be marked by a gathering of all God's children joined in a community of brotherly love out of the "Babylon" of conflicting sects (the established state churches). This millennial kingdom of Philadelphia would be the "bridal community of the Lamb" (Revelation 9:7-8) and salvation history would consummate in the final "restoration of all things" (Acts 3:21). The roots of this reading can also be seen in the German theosophy of Jacob Boehme,[15] as a popularized version of that system of thought was transferred to the Continent in the late seventeenth century.[16]

As Möller has observed, the German Philadelphians conflated this thinking with a spiritualized version of the historical dispensations set forth in Cocceius's schema for salvation history.[17] These Philadelphians became the spokespersons for a growing community of advocates who experienced exclusion from the state churches of the empire and the favored status that went with that culture. They came to prefer a counterculture defined by conventicles and networks that grew among disaffected craftsmen, women of nobility who married below their social class, and displaced nobility. Taken together, these networks comprised a new order of urban intelligentsia in an empire still largely controlled by decadent nobility.

At the Reformed Academy of Herborn we also discover the nurturing ground for an important leader of the radical Pietists, Heinrich Horch (1652–1729). Horch assimilated the covenant theology of Cocceius to the Philadelphian outlook. A faculty member there, he was dismissed for his separatist tendencies and for his production of the Marburg Bible, a translation of Scripture that made use of Cocceius's symbolic-prophetic hermeneutic to delineate a mystical-prophetic portrayal of the coming overthrow of "Babel" (Christendom as represented by the state churches). Using the Song of Songs and the Apocalypse of John as benchmarks for a "mystical and prophetic" reading of the entirety of Scripture, Horch sought to retrieve the "hidden seed from the shell of the dead letter" of Scripture.[18] In this context, the coming Age of the Spirit was envisioned not as a transmutation of the existing body of Christendom, but as a displacement of the old order altogether.

In its place, the coming reconciliation and reunion of humanity would occur in a common worship of the Lamb, signifying the emergence of the true Philadelphian community identified in Revelation 2–3.

Under Horch's guidance, the oppressed German Philadelphian societies were to be the agents of a global errand to the "faithful in all regions, who will receive you with joy for the sake of the gospel."[19] As we have seen, the year 1700 had been expected to be the time of judgment and retribution for a humanity dehumanized by the unprecedented destruction and brutality of the religious wars of the seventeenth century. Writing shortly after 1700, Horch began to shift from preparing people for an apocalyptic end of history to readying the faithful for a new dawning age. It would be a time in which the Kingdom was to emerge through the Spirit's equipping of the people of God across lines of nation and race. The case for the New Jerusalem, which was to fulfill the promise of Pentecost, was built on Horch's reading of the Heidelberg Catechism as declaring that God was gathering the church from all generations and all nations.[20] "Formerly," declared Horch, "the heathen were regarded as a wild thicket; now the elect among them will blossom as precious plants for the glory of the Lord."[21] Herein lay the birth of revivalism as a movement that would soon reach beyond the parameters of state church Christendom.

In the early eighteenth century, the main vehicle for Philadelphian aspirations was set up at Berleburg, the resident city of a count of Wittgenstein who became partial to the radical Pietists. That vehicle was the Berleburg Bible, a new German translation featuring an eight-volume commentary edited by Johann Friedrich Haug (1680–1753). The exegetical approach included mystical interpretations that had been rejected in the Reformation in favor of the literal sense of the text.[22] For his part, Haug appropriated themes of the earlier Philadelphians and mediated them to a world that had unexpectedly lived beyond the apocalyptic end of history that earlier Philadelphians had anticipated for the year 1700. In Haug's work, this vision lives on, but now it is refocused by contending that God speaks directly to the heart of the reader "through the finger of His Spirit," even as God spoke to the witnesses to Jesus' baptism.[23] Thus Haug's work represents the confluence of Coccean federalist themes with the mystical concerns for purity of heart and union with God through the Spirit's witness.

A more incendiary movement of radical revitalization arrived in the wake of the Philadelphians. These were the "New Prophets" or the Society of the Inspired, a group who traced their inception to the Camissard rebellion against the French Bourbon kings in the mid-seventeenth century. Now, their apocalyptic prophecies and uncontrollably ecstatic worship were disciplined by a new generation of leaders who linked this pneumatic witness to the aspirations of the German radical Pietists. The result was a fresh and energized hope for the coming of a new Pentecost as the vehicle for the realization of earlier Philadelphian aspirations.

Led by a Tübingen-trained pastor, Eberhard Ludwig Gruber, and by a Halle-trained missionary, Johann Friedrich Rock, these New Prophets set out to revitalize Christendom as then constituted, starting in Germany, in anticipation of the coming age of a renewed Pentecost.

Their message joined a coming Age of the Spirit with emphases on perfection and holiness of life. The latter emphases became marks of one's personal baptism in the Spirit. However, as their strategies became thwarted by unsympathetic state church authorities, the New Prophets (or Inspirationists) retrenched and set up their base in the Wetterau district near Wittgenstein.

Here one of their converts, a physician named J. S. Carl, began an ambitious project of publishing a spiritual almanac titled the *News of the Spirit* (*Geistliche Fama*), which chronicled outbreaks of revival occurring throughout the world of the early eighteenth century (1730–44). Carl's spiritual almanac linked the manifestations of Pentecost in a variety of cultures, including Asia, Africa, and the Western Hemisphere up to the time of the early stages of the Great Awakening in America (1734).

THE NEW PENTECOST AMONG EARLY UNITED BRETHREN AND EVANGELICALS

We are now ready to observe the theological influence of the Philadelphians and Inspirationists on the thought and work of German American revivalists in the late eighteenth and early nineteenth centuries.²⁴ There is substantial evidence for this influence. For example, the library of Philip William Otterbein, cofounder with Martin Boehm (d. 1812) of the Church of the United Brethren in Christ (1800), contained an edition of the leading radical Pietist Bible commentary, the Berleburg Bible. In addition, Otterbein provided direct mentorship for the quasi-radical Christian Stahlschmidt, a disciple of the renowned poet and protorevivalist, Gerhard Tersteegen, who has been described as both a mystical Reformed Pietist and a radical Pietist.²⁵

The Berleburg Bible and works by Gottfried Arnold and Tersteegen are also found in the library of Johannes Seybert (1791–1860), the first bishop of The Evangelical Association, and themes from these works guided his mystical piety. Moreover, these themes are woven through his extensive journal, reflecting his travels over 250,000 miles from Pennsylvania to Ontario and the Mississippi basin.²⁶ Similarly, the early journal of The Evangelical Association, *Der Christliche Botschafter*, the longest-running German American religious periodical (1816, 1839–1946), is replete with references to radical Pietist authors, and its style of reporting news of the revitalizing ministry around the globe closely resembles that of the radical Pietist J. C. Carl's *Geistliche Fama*.²⁷

It is also possible to specify several ways in which the stream of German radical Pietism provided United Brethren and Evangelicals with incentive for mission and for the pervasive transformation of human culture by the spirit of Christ. The early protocol of the United Brethren reflects Arnold's leading motif when it refers to the Brethren community as the "unsectarian [*unparteiische*] preachers." Otterbein addressed them, saying, "Whoever here becomes free from sin and a party spirit has God to thank," indicating that brotherly love was the foundation for the revival they were charged to superintend and extend.²⁸ This impulse among the early Evangelicals can also be seen in their preference for the term *Gemeinschaft* (Association) over *Kirche* (Church), the former term suggesting an inclusive fellowship in the Spirit.²⁹

As noted above, the Berleburg Bible is the most likely channel of this Philadelphian theme in Otterbein and the early United Brethren.³⁰ At Baltimore, Otterbein laid the basis for the United Brethren Confession of Faith (a lost draft was produced in 1789). The influence of the Berleburg Bible can also be seen in the

"Constitution and Ordinances" that Otterbein produced for his congregation.[31] Furthermore, traces of the Philadelphian hermeneutic are clearly visible in Otterbein's one published sermon, "Salvation Bringing Incarnation and Glorious Victory of Jesus Christ over the Devil and Death" (1760). For example, Otterbein appears to be deploying the Philadelphian hermeneutic when he declares that Christ's work both destroys "him who has the power of death" and delivers "those in lifelong bondage," and then goes on to suggest that persons who spurn this message with hard-hearted, pharisaic lives are like the Nicolaitans, whose lampstand will be removed from its place. Similarly, says Otterbein, those who heed the message are the pure in heart who, like the Philadelphians, will be summoned to enter the New Jerusalem.[32]

Readers of this sermon, which was first published in Core's anthology of Otterbein literature in 1968, have missed these implicit Philadelphian themes because the identifying names, Nicolaitans and Philadelphians, do not appear.[33] What we find are implicit references to them seen in such assertions that "blind is the person who does not at once realize it when God has removed the lampstand of his gospel from its place." Then, at another place, Otterbein asserts that the Spirit is to lead us to victory in the work of redemption, which is "Christ in us," "a ceasing of sin," the "fruits of holiness," and "a process of life which goes on steadfastly toward perfection." The purpose of this redemption is the formation of a new humanity who can "enter the New Jerusalem." Here he alludes to Revelation 21:2, which presupposes the earlier discussion of the New Jerusalem in Revelation 3:12 (RSV): "He who conquers, I will make him a pillar in the temple of my God; never shall he go out of it, and I will write on him the name of my God, and the name of the city of my God, the new Jerusalem which comes down from God out of heaven, and my own new name."

Early gatherings of the reborn among the United Brethren were intimate house assemblies where the meetings went by the name of the local host after the fashion of the Philadelphian societies reported by Hector de Marsay. For example, instead of being popularly known as United Brethren, local societies were instead referred to as *Lichtes Leute* (those meeting at the home of Felix Licht), or *Neidigs Leute* (after those meeting in fellowship at the Joh. Neidig home).[34]

The early societies and gatherings of the Albright People, at least through 1810, reflected another theme of radical Pietism. Early Albright meetings were consistently called "Pentecost meetings."[35] Similarly, the event that launched the United Brethren, the "great meeting" (*grosse Versammlung*) at the Isaac Long barn in Lancaster County, Pennsylvania, where Otterbein and Boehm declared, "We are brethren," not coincidentally occurred on Pentecost Sunday, 1767.

As with the German radical Pietists, the linkage to Pentecost became the definitive frame of reference by which they viewed the significance of their work in light of the prophetic fulfillment of salvation history. An unpartisan community of those reborn in Christ, which overcomes barriers of class, confession, race, and ethnic/national identity, and which was seen as the prophetic harbinger of the ultimate revitalization of the world Christian movement in the coming Age of the Spirit, was the controlling self-understanding for early United Brethren and Evangelical ecclesiology and for their view of history's imminent goal. This theme of Pentecost originated with Cocceius's symbolic prophetic biblical interpretation and the linking in his federal theology of the theme of covenant with the eschatological motif of the coming reign of God's kingdom on earth. The New Prophets (Inspirationists) identified that imminent event as a fulfillment of the universal promise of the outpouring of God's spirit on all flesh made known in the apostolic event of Pentecost.

There are also similarities between the Spirit-led worship patterns of early Evangelicals and United Brethren, and the conventicles of the Inspirationists in Germany. For example, Inspirationist worship featured fervent, extemporary prayer and singing, prophetic interpretation of biblical texts, and love feasts accompanied by footwashing.[36] Moreover, like their continental forebears, early Evangelicals and United Brethren engaged in street preaching under the influence of the Spirit's anointing and prophetic confrontations with civil and religious leaders over their neglect of godly living. In fact, early Evangelical missionaries in Germany concentrated their efforts in Württemberg, the region that had earlier been the primary base for the New Prophets. Gruber, the leader of the New Prophets, had sensed the need to impose standards of discipline. Thus he formulated twenty-four Rules of Godliness to distinguish true from false prophets. In addition, members of the New Prophets were grouped into "classes" led by a director and two elders, to lead worship, exercise prophetic-based discipline among members, and manage a fund for poor persons.[37] Here, then, is a pattern that would influence Moravian and Methodist practice in the years ahead. Each of these features was replicated among the early Evangelicals and to a lesser extent among United Brethren, including the use of children's catechisms and hymnals.[38]

We can also see the theme of Pentecost in other areas of early Evangelical and United Brethren doctrine and theology. For example, the Evangelicals' *Book of Doctrine and Discipline* (1809) described sanctification as experienced in their early "Pentecostal" meetings as a "baptism of fire," which produced a "powerful outpouring of the Holy Spirit."[39] Indeed, sanctification was to be lived out with eschatological fervor. And while we find entries in Seybert's journal that describe seasons of baptism in which diverse modes were used (immersion, sprinkling, and pouring in the same service), the emphasis clearly falls on the "baptism in the Spirit" in ways that mirror the testimonies of the Inspirationists in Germany of the previous century.[40]

For better or worse, the liveliness of these Pentecostal communities would not last. The decline of ecstatic interpretation led to the institutionalizing of the Inspirationists, who survive today as the Amana Colony in Iowa. A similar decline in spiritual vitality among Evangelicals led to an increasing institutionalization of the office of the bishop in the generation following Seybert and the systematizing of the doctrine of entire sanctification in Bishop John J. Esher's massive systematic theology.[41]

THE NEW PENTECOST IN MISSION AND CHURCH DIVISION

Despite the institutionalizing of the early Evangelical and United Brethren communities, the vision of a renewed Pentecost continued to inform their strategies for world mission at crucial phases in their history. For example, in 1897, the promising United Brethren mission to Sierra Leone was decimated by a brutal "hut tax" revolt of tribal people, but its real cause can be traced to policies of the

British colonial government. Hundreds were killed, and seven resident United Brethren missionaries were beheaded. In its wake, Bishop John S. Mills called for the brotherhood in America to remember the Pentecost vision of Otterbein joining with Boehm to produce a united brotherhood in Christ among former ecclesial enemies. Mills extended that vision to include the reconciliation of the warring tribes of that West African colony. Its capital, Freetown, with its diversity of tribal cultures and spoken tongues, was prophetically declared by Mills to be the "New Jerusalem," the rallying point for a "new Pentecost" that would sweep across all of Africa. Thus, in Mills's hands, a German American millennial vision became the basis for envisioning a new Christian Africa where indigenous people of many tongues would speak the one language of the baptism of the Spirit. The outcome was the present Sierra Leone Conference of United Methodism, which opened more than one hundred schools in that land and now represents more than one hundred thousand members.

Echoes of the renewed Pentecost vision can also be seen in the historic unions between the Evangelicals and the United Brethren and between the resulting Evangelical United Brethren Church and The Methodist Church. Thus the theme was invoked at Johnstown, Pennsylvania, when United Brethren and Evangelicals joined to create a new fellowship, The Evangelical United Brethren Church, in 1946. Similarly, there were allusions to Pentecost in Dallas in 1968 when Bishop Reuben Mueller joined hands with Methodist Bishop Lloyd Wicke to bring into existence The United Methodist Church.

However, there were also occasions when the radical Pietist legacy was remembered in counterproductive ways. Thus the theme of a renewed Pentecost became the focus of disputed interpretation in the course of church controversies. This tendency can be seen in both predecessor bodies of the EUB. It surfaces, for example, in the time of United Brethren and Evangelical church divisions in the nineteenth century, when each side in those divisive controversies saw itself as the protector of the legacy of the founders. Thus it can be seen in Bishop Milton Wright's appeal to the sanctity of the original constitution and Confession of Faith of the United Brethren in Christ. The early protocol asserted that they were to be a people without "division and a party spirit" (Protocol of 1812). For Wright, this statement was a mandate that there be no tolerance for secret societies within the membership, a position that had prevailed without challenge in the early decades of the denomination. He made known his position on this issue during the years leading up to the fateful General Conference of 1889, which produced the schism between the so-called radical and liberal United Brethren. The former was the minority party and the latter the majority.

At stake in this division were the larger political debates of the nineteenth century. Thus in the years following that division, members of the minority party were divested of their hold on church property, despite their conviction that changes in the constitution could occur only if these reflected the "consent of two thirds of the entire membership." By contrast, the liberal party, represented by J. J. Glossbrenner, John S. Mills, and others, was willing to accept into membership those belonging to Masonic orders so long as they did not violate their Christian obligations as members of the brotherhood. They were more interested in limiting the two-thirds rule to those actually voting. On each side, there was a tendency to see only those features of the United Brethren tradition that would support their respective positions. For the majority, members of Masonic orders could be embraced as United Brethren if they were guided by genuine Christian intentions and character and were willing not to hold allegiance to the lodge where that might stand in conflict with obligations to their brotherhood "in Christ."

Likewise, when the members of The Evangelical Association took the path to church division in 1891–94, each side produced historians and theologians intent on showing that their way was more faithful to Jacob Albright's vision of bringing to birth the godly life among the spiritually deadened ranks of German Americans. They were caught up in a web of divisive issues that were even more complex than the divisive issues surrounding secret societies had been for the United Brethren. Underlying the discussion was the question of how one should rightly remember the vision of the early Albright People, who were intent on manifesting the apostolic meaning of Pentecost, understood as full salvation from sin through the Spirit's baptism.[42]

In the case of The Evangelical Association, the majority party was committed to a defense of German-language worship and the original German version of their doctrines of Christian perfection and entire sanctification (these doctrines had been produced in German by George Miller in 1809). Furthermore, they saw the Anglicizing tendencies of the minority group to be a threat to the ways of their forefathers and foremothers. They were also energized by the fact that the first English-speaking preacher admitted into the Association had to be deposed for denying their doctrines of Christian perfection and entire sanctification.

The majority group was located geographically within the fast-growing western sectors of the denomination (the upper Midwest), where their numbers were being augmented by the arrival of new generations of German immigrants in the latter decades of the nineteenth century. From these new immigrants came stalwart apologists for the "old Evangelical way" who were brought into the fold through the German camp meetings held throughout the connection. Their leader, Bishop John J. Esher, produced the definitive (German) systematic theology for The Evangelical Association. It had its longest use in the Germany conference, which Esher organized in Stuttgart in 1865. This overseas conference—the first of four European conferences formed in the late nineteenth century throughout German-speaking Europe—became the embodiment of the majority group's mission to fulfill Albright's commitment to preach exclusively to his German-speaking neighbors. Now the mission was being extended to take the message of full salvation in Christ to the people of the German fatherland.

By contrast, the minority group in Pennsylvania was championing a new constitution and Articles of Faith that introduced more democratic elements into the polity of the denomination, including limitations on the office of the bishop and provision for lay representation in church conferences at all levels. They were second- and third-generation descendants of the original Evangelicals, now Anglicized and more acclimated to nineteenth-century American culture. They were ready to give up the old language of their Germanic parents (including the German bush meeting hymns and attending idioms of worship), so long as the message of Albright could be refashioned for a new day. This meant that when they constructed their new version of the Articles of Faith, they replaced the old articles with a set of doctrines written by Methodist theologian Milton Terry of Union Biblical Institute in Evanston, Illinois. Of crucial importance in this document was its well-developed statement on world missions, which affirmed the need to take the message of the gospel to all peoples.

The schism between these two groups led the minority group to organize the United Evangelical Church in 1894. The division remained until partial reunion was effected in 1921. Following the reunion, the doctrinal articles written by Terry were retained. They did not include the time-honored exposition of entire sanctification once cherished by the majority body (The Evangelical Association).

THE THEOLOGICAL HERITAGE OF PIETISM AND THE RENEWAL OF METHODISM TODAY

The radical-Reformed Pietist Gerhard Tersteegen (1697–1769), whom Reginald Ward once called "the most fascinating character in the whole history of religious revival," and who was the most frequently reprinted Pietist writer in the periodical of the Evangelicals (the *Christliche Botschafter*), was a product of Inspirationist preaching in his native Muhlheim an der Ruhr.[43] His hymns were mainstays of Evangelical and United Brethren worship.[44] He also became the major voice of a revival that swept through Holland and the lower Rhineland of Germany between 1730 and 1769.

Avoiding the ecstatic frenzy of the Inspirationists, Tersteegen borrowed their language (but without their appeal to ecstatic signs and wonders) to articulate a winsome message that reached masses of unchurched urban religious seekers in that cosmopolitan region. In the revival address "The Outpouring of the Holy Spirit," delivered before a crowd of listeners in Amsterdam in 1753, he linked the work of sanctification within believers of all sectarian persuasions to a grand "baptism of the Holy Spirit," which he projected would ultimately bring together all streams of the church into one unified Christian witness.[45] His words may best be read as a fulfillment of the Philadelphian hope, expressed in the language of a renewed Pentecost. It is also a picture of world revitalization for the twenty-first century—a picture of the heavenly city becoming manifest in local communities and cultures around the world. It images taking the gospel to every locale and culture so that Christ may be all in all. The aspiration also takes the form of a prophetic prayer:

> O, let us study to be unanimous! Let us incessantly and unweariedly strive after it! If we cannot outwardly unite with [others of faith], let us at least do it in spirit. I am certain that, according to Zeph 3:10, the Lord will bring souls together more and more from all places and corners of the earth, from all the different religious bodies, and lead and guide them all to the one thing needful! The vital need for all is the baptism with the Spirit and the heavenly unction to the conversion and the renewal into the image of God which entirely depends upon it, to the great mystery which has been hid from the beginning of the world and from all ages but which is now revealed to the saints of God, which is Christ in us.... Amen.[46]

Here we come to the heart and soul of the theological vision of the EUB and its predecessor bodies, The Evangelical Association and the United Brethren. Indeed, it is a vision that is embedded deep in the history of German Reformed and radical Pietist theology. It is a vision that stresses unity in purpose and mission and that yearns prayerfully for the outpouring of the Holy Spirit throughout the world. Surely this is a vision that can inspire United Methodists today.

CHAPTER 5

DOCTRINE AND THEOLOGY IN THE CHURCH OF THE UNITED BRETHREN IN CHRIST

Tyron Inbody

The Church of the United Brethren in Christ began as a pietistic, revivalistic movement among the German population of Pennsylvania and Maryland in the late eighteenth century and became an original American church at the beginning of the nineteenth century.[1] The church existed as a separate denomination until 1946, when its 421,689 members merged with The Evangelical Church to form The Evangelical United Brethren Church. Within twenty-two years (1968), its 750,000 members were united with The Methodist Church to form The United Methodist Church (UMC).

This chapter will begin with a set of six generalizations about the character of United Brethren doctrine and theology, followed by four characteristic doctrines of that church (human nature, soteriology, ecclesiology, and sacraments). The chapter will conclude with reflections on the impact of UB doctrine within United Methodism today.

The Character of United Brethren Doctrine and Theology

Emphasis on Conversion

The roots of United Brethren doctrine and theology lie in German Reformed Pietism and American revivalism. The movement was first and foremost an extension of the Second Great Awakening to Germans in the middle colonies, especially Pennsylvania and Maryland. At the core of its beliefs and practices lay an evangelical experience of conversion and consciousness of salvation. Christian faith was not so much an intellectual affirmation or baptism as it was a way of life initiated by an experience of a new birth. Of supreme importance in the Christian life were the emotions, the religion of the heart. Orthopathy (right feelings) was as important as orthodoxy and orthopraxis. Assurance as an experience of peace with God was emphasized. Religion was individualistic: individuals were offered and found salvation in a conversion experience, and individuals were summoned to the Christian way of life as described by pietistic perfectionism, the overcoming of sin. There was none of William James's "once born" religion here, but the absolute necessity of repentance and an instantaneous born-again experience, followed by a stress on the transformation of the whole person, including the emotions and behavior, as evidenced by conservative teachings about alcohol, tobacco, capital and labor, Sabbath, public schools, amusements, secret societies, civil government, and divorce, which were a primary focus of the movement.[2] The means of conversion was evangelistic effort through revivalism. To the extent the United Brethren had a theology, it was a "revival theology."[3] There was one purpose for the denomination to exist: the salvation of souls.[4] Indeed, "in the early history of the church, the function of evangelism was almost the sole function of the church."[5]

The Inseparability of Doctrine and Piety

Both the United Brethren and the Evangelical churches had Wesleyan Methodist ties with a strong Arminian emphasis on human freedom. But the United Brethren also had even stronger ties to the Reformed and Mennonite churches through Otterbein and Boehm. In contrast to British evangelicalism, whose revivalism occurred within Anglicanism, United Brethren piety and doctrine were shaped by the Reformed Pietism of the Continent.[6] One characteristic of United Brethren doctrine, therefore, was the way experiential religion was shaped by the teachings of the evangelical symbol of the German Reformation, specifically, the three-part structure of the Heidelberg Catechism, which served not so much as a textbook for doctrine but as a practical guide to the Christian life through the recognition of one's sin and guilt, the recognition of one's redemption and freedom, and the recognition of one's gratitude and obedience.[7] The influence of this form of Pietism on doctrine is evident in its first Confession of Faith of 1789, in which the first two of the five articles are common foundational articles, but the third article on the Holy Spirit expresses the true Pietist emphasis on two elements of salvation: (1) deliverance from the legal guilt of sin and moral cleansing or sanctification, and (2) the conversion experience related to the change wrought in regeneration, which is completed when reaching the point of assurance.[8] Through Otterbein and the Confessions in the early *Disciplines*, German Reformed Pietism became a part of United Brethren evangelicalism as Puritanism was mediated through the English divines and Dutch Pietism through Freylinghausen.[9] This German Reformed version of evangelicalism kept United Brethren doctrine closer to continental Reformed doctrine than to a radical Anabaptist theology (although the Mennonite influence on United Brethren doctrine was significant) or to a thoroughly subjectivist experiential theology (which would have led to a more liberal theology). Thus the denomination was a representative and defender of Pietism *and* conservative doctrine, which the members believed were inseparable, as any relinquishment of orthodoxy was not only heresy but, even more significantly, cut the nerve of the church's mission of making converts.

A Nontheological Denomination

The United Brethren denomination had a reputation and a self-image as a nontheological, even antitheological, denomination.[10]

Little distinction was made between preaching and theology. This perception, however, is both true and false. First, it is true in the sense that the United Brethren had a pietistic understanding of faith. The leaders of the church had no interest in theological innovation, in speculative theology, or even in theology for its own sake. This kind of theology was empty, distracting, and above all threatening to the church's mission of evangelization. There was nothing unique, even distinctive, about the doctrine and theology of the United Brethren. Rather, the denomination preached a very conservative form of Arminian theology. It accepted above all the distinctly Protestant doctrine of *sola scriptura*. Its beliefs were simply what the Bible taught, undiluted and undisputable. Any belief could simply be proof-texted; theological reflection belonged to the haughty, pretentious accommodaters to infidelity. United Brethren modesty required one to eschew any arrogant speculation that went beyond what the Bible plainly taught. During the first half of the nineteenth century, then, the denomination simply ignored the theological developments within liberal Protestantism.

Second, however, after 1850, United Brethren defenders against infidelity began to resemble the theological scholasticism of other denominations, appealing to reason (as well as, and often instead of, the Bible), attempting to beat infidelity at its own game through a rationalistic defense of the Bible.[11] When the "infidel threat" appeared during this period, sentiment shifted toward defense of the creeds as a guard against error and debilitation of the mission of the church. Philosophy, the old enemy, now became a valuable ally, especially Scottish common sense realism with its self-evident truths and rationalistic Kantian intuitionism. Leaders began to discuss the need for a theology textbook to combat heresy in the church and eventually produced a new Confession of Faith in 1889. Many of its leaders, through its magazine, its journal, and its seminary, became interested in apologetics. Eventually they began to open themselves to some discussion of liberal theology as this white, lower-middle-class, northern, conservative German denomination sought to become less a sect in its identity and self-perception and more a successful, middle-class American church.

Nevertheless, the church never provided a significant systematic theologian, theological text, or major or even notable player, either outside or inside the denomination, as a contributor to theological discussions of the second half of the nineteenth century or even as a representative voice of the church. The United Brethren never produced a Gamertsfelter. United Brethren doctrine and theology were consistently antiliberal in understanding and defense of classical Christianity because they remained devoted to a pietistic version of conservative Protestant theology as the undergirding of the singular mission of the United Brethren. Liberal forms of Pietism (a la Schleiermacher) never appeared within the United Brethren horizon. In short, throughout the nineteenth century, and especially during the latter part, United Brethren thinking held together two concerns in an uneasy alliance, namely, the cultivation of simple piety and a serious attention to the defense of conservative Christian doctrine. As Drury argued, "Christianity both promotes doctrine and is promoted by it."[12] Heresy and spiritual death always go together.[13] The United Brethren, then, were interested in defending orthodox doctrine on pragmatic grounds: the truth and importance of a doctrine lay in its power to undergird the pious life and the mission of the church (practical theology).[14] Orthodox doctrine is an indispensable basis for a theology of subjective faith; subjective faith is not the basis for doctrine, as in liberal theology.

The Role of a Confession of Faith

The United Brethren adopted the first Confession of Faith in 1789. Five Reformed pastors (and two Mennonites) wrote it. Their guide was the Heidelberg Catechism, which, except for Otterbein's distinct Arminianism, held to the doctrines of the preexisting historic creeds, emphasizing universal atonement, moral competence, and new life through evangelical conversion.[15] The first General Conference of 1815, after much internal debate, revised and enlarged it, though no exposition was ever attempted and it was never used for instruction. In 1889 the United Brethren split over the acceptance by the majority of a new constitution and the thirteen articles of a new Confession of Faith. Some phrases were reminiscent of the Helvetic and Heidelberg Catechisms, a Calvinism infused with Pietism, confirming the Church of the United Brethren in Christ belonged to the sixteenth-century Protestant Reformation.[16] In the new Confession of Faith the United Brethren now had a "creed of its own," the first statement of distinctive

United Brethren doctrine. In 1891 the *Quarterly Review* provided a series of essays based on the new Confession of Faith to give the church "a desirable and much needed literature."[17] Instead of the Thirty-nine Articles of Religion from Anglicanism or the Twenty-five Articles of Religion from Methodism, the threefold division of the Heidelberg Catechism formed the core of the thirteen articles that constituted the Confession of Faith.[18] If there was such a thing as United Brethren theology outside this Confession of Faith, however, its theology was only apparent and available in various articles in the *Religious Telescope*, the *Quarterly Review*, and Weaver's *Christian Doctrine*.

Quest for Identity

The United Brethren were not interested in playing on the theological field until the latter part of the nineteenth century for several reasons. First, the denomination was about revivalism and conversion, not theological reflection; second, members wanted to avoid the formalism and sterility of the established denominations and the indifference of the mass of immigrants from the European churches; third, they had a bad taste in their mouths from past experience and their current knowledge of the rationalistic theology in Germany and its deadly results. Consequently, they became interested in theology only when confronted by infidelity in the late nineteenth century. Interest in theology arose more because of a quest for self-identity as a small and seemingly unnecessary denomination than as a claim about anything novel or even distinctive about United Brethren doctrine.[19]

Part of the quest for United Brethren identity lay in the question of their relationship with Methodism. Although much has been made in recent years about the cordial and cooperative relations between the United Brethren and The Methodist Episcopal Church in the early nineteenth century, United Brethren historians argue that "the UB is in no historic sense an offshoot from the Methodist Church, its origins being entirely separate and distinct, its typical characteristics have naturally classed it with the Methodist family of churches."[20] A reading of Drury's biography of Otterbein makes it abundantly clear that even at the close of the nineteenth century, the United Brethren had a distinct and proud sense that they were not Methodists.[21] They were in this country involved in a revival movement before any Methodist preachers were; they had spurned efforts to get them to merge with the Methodists; when Otterbein began to preach an evangelical experience and to hold prayer meetings in the 1750s, unlike Methodists they provided little organization of the revival movement;[22] there were no organized or appointed Methodist preachers in America in their early years[23] (they were shaped by German Pietism independent of any Wesleyan class meetings); the United Brethren movement and loose organization resisted the authoritarianism of Methodist bishops.

By 1890 the United Brethren had become interested in the question, why be a member of the denomination?[24] Given their minority status and sectarian identity, they eventually needed to explain and justify their reason for being. They had Teutonic roots; they were Saxons in a pervasively Anglo-Saxon environment; they were overwhelmingly the poorest and least cultured among those Saxons (those Germans).[25] The mother church was German Reformed, not Anglican, and the fatherland was Germany, not England. They were humble and proudly cultivated the virtue of their humility. They argued, however, that the denomination "contains all the elements of a much needed American church," namely, its government is "unique, flexible, and republican"; its spirit is progressive; it holds to the two essential doctrines of repentance and assurance; it has a record and attitude of moral reform and a spirit of aggressive evangelism and of Christian brotherhood—all part of the progressive spirit of the late nineteenth century.[26] It had (or tried to create and defend) a sense of being a uniquely American church with ecumenical significance.

A Maturing Ecumenical Denomination

The organizationally weak United Brethren denomination was, from its beginning, an ecumenical denomination. In part, of course, this was a practical necessity in an environment in which it was a minority; this small ethnic church was never tempted to denominational triumphalism! Instead of retreating to a sectarian mentality, however, throughout its entire history, it reached out in many ways in an ecumenical spirit. From Otterbein through its many formal and informal discussions with like-minded movements and denominations, including the Methodists, through the late-nineteenth- and early-twentieth-century ecumenical movements, the denomination participated in various transdenominational movements, including a persisting series of merger discussions and open participation in various ecumenical movements. The denomination was also characterized by the optimistic mood of the late nineteenth century, which is very apparent not only in its participation in the missionary movement but also in the optimism about history apparent in its literature, which set it over against the pessimism of some of the new dispensational movements of the later nineteenth century. The *Quarterly Review* reflected the optimistic triumphalism of the coming Christian century at the end of the century.[27] Church leaders also began to engage the new progressive theology, so in 1898 the *Quarterly Review* could publish the article "The Economics of Jesus," which argued that the nation is Christian when its public institutions are created by the people, not when the stock market determines everything.[28] Although 92 percent of the United Brethren churches were still rural churches in 1906,[29] the denomination began to develop a sense of engagement with the social order as it began to deal with issues such as the home, family, marriage, morality, citizenship, war, labor, and economics.[30] Its Social Creed of 1909, inspired by the social creeds of the Federal Council of Churches, moved it beyond its earlier days of almost exclusive accent on personal morality.

CHARACTERISTIC UNITED BRETHREN DOCTRINES

There are, at the same time, some notable theological themes in the literature produced by the bishops and leaders of the denomination in books, a church magazine, and a journal. Four of these are noteworthy as characteristic of (though not unique to) United Brethren doctrine.

Total Depravity

The doctrine of total depravity was "the only great doctrinal subject that has seriously divided the ministry of the church."[31] The

United Brethren retained, from the Heidelberg Catechism and from Otterbein's extant sermon,[32] a strong Reformed doctrine of total depravity. Nevertheless, this doctrine always stood in tension (including Otterbein) with an equally strong Arminian emphasis on freedom, which led to a quasi-Reformation understanding of synergism. Throughout much of its history, there was controversy in the United Brethren over this doctrine. The debate centered on a strong emphasis on moral agency, which repudiated a strong Reformation doctrine of the bondage of the will and affirmed a semi-Pelagian view of human nature. The ambiguity of the United Brethren teaching on the doctrine was evident in the very first volume of the *Religious Telescope,* in which an editorial rejected the doctrine of original sin as total depravity in infants and finally rejected a strong doctrine of original sin as an offense to common sense.[33] To be sure, the Confession of Faith of 1817 affirmed the fall of Adam, and by 1841 the United Brethren had added language of depravity. But some objected at once, with some promoting the language of partial depravity and some the language of total depravity.

The matter led to heated debate at the eleventh (1853) and twelfth (1857) General Conferences, occasioned by a debate over the proper ordination question on this issue. It was settled by affirming that the question was "before" or "after" grace. The debate was intense and, because of fear of division, came to a climax when a committee offered an explanatory amendment to read "abstract of the grace of God."[34] Disagreement continued as late as Weaver's *Christian Doctrine,* in which Thompson argues for the defacement but not obliteration of the image of God, while Mobley focuses on total depravity as what Scripture teaches.[35] At the end of the century the *Quarterly Review* interpreted the statement in the 1889 Confession of Faith to teach that depravity is fundamental, that we are born into a state of sin as the result of the fall, that "totally depraved" means sin touches every part of our being but that we are not condemned because of Adam's sin, and that our "inherited depravity" gives us a bias toward sin and makes it certain that, but for grace, we would choose sin and grow worse and worse continually.[36] The point is that regardless of the emphasis on moral agency and the implications of that emphasis for sin and salvation, the United Brethren retained a strong doctrine of total depravity—so much so that, by 1962, when merger with the Methodists was imminent, any hint of a strong affirmation of total depravity was written out of the Confession of Faith in order to sound more Wesleyan instead of Reformed in the article on human nature.[37]

Salvation and the Changed Life

The tension between the United Brethren teaching on depravity and the emphasis on moral agency played itself out in the teaching about salvation. Otterbein had taught that the work of Christ alone without us is not sufficient for salvation.[38] Salvation is God's work outside us and inside us; there is also a necessary work from our side. There is a common stress in United Brethren doctrine, therefore, from Otterbein onward on a form of synergism. A distinction is made between justification (the beginning of the Christian life) and acquittal (the consummation of the Christian life), so conversion and regeneration are necessary for salvation.[39] Justification is treating the sinner as justified and making the sinner just in actual experience. Both are not only contemporaneous "but absolutely the same."[40] To be justified is to be restored in relation and character to the favor of God. Justification, therefore, is a higher and different act than pardon alone. Pardon forgives a fault by removing guilt; justification removes guilt of all its liabilities and pronounces us blameless. It signifies a state of worthiness before God, even though pardon and justification are God's acts.[41] So the United Brethren taught a conditional understanding of justification. O'Malley calls this, relative to standard Reformation teaching, a doctrine of "qualified justification." Justification is not imparted unless we fit ourselves for justification by growing up rightly and continuing to grow that we might be ready for judgment.[42]

At the center of the United Brethren teaching about sin and conditional justification, then, is the expectation that salvation would lead to a changed life. The United Brethren taught "holiness, without which no man shall see the Lord."[43] God requires all God's children to be holy. The United Brethren doctrine of conversion and discipline are inseparably bound up with each other in the practice of holiness. Here again God's grace and human cooperation are stressed. There is no sanctification (God's work) without consecration (our work).⁴⁴ Although both the Evangelicals and the United Brethren taught holiness, the degree of emphasis was a point of difference between them. The severest battle in the nineteenth century among Evangelicals was over the doctrine of entire sanctification, and they nearly split over the doctrine of perfection.⁴⁵ There is no teaching on Christian perfection in the essay on sanctification in Weaver's *Christian Doctrine*,⁴⁶ and the *Quarterly Review* essay notes that there was no place in the Confession of Faith for this article until the present quadrennium of "what our church has written and taught" on this doctrine, interpreting the church's teaching to be both complete in regeneration and continuous, both instantaneous and gradual. Both a work of God and our own efforts are essential for it to be complete.⁴⁷

Polity

One of the persisting, even growing, influences of United Brethren doctrine and theology and sources of tension in the contemporary United Methodist Church is the underlying egalitarian impulse and looser structure of United Brethren polity.⁴⁸ United Brethren literature was consistent and persistent in its stress on democracy in its ecclesiology. In the very first volume of the *Religious Telescope* one finds a long editorial on ecclesiology and polity, "Declaration of Rights: Explanatory of the Reasons and Principles of Church Government," which reads like a philosophical defense of democracy, stressing all are created equal, church government of the people, suspicion of the clergy, and the rights of the laity.⁴⁹ Ultimate power lay in the hands of the people.⁵⁰ Furthermore, the United Brethren movement was predominantly a lay movement. The leaders were plain people, mostly farmers, who underwent a religious experience that propelled them to proclaim their gospel.⁵¹ The ecclesiastical background of the founders was also significant for its polity. Otterbein and his fellow churchmen were German Reformed with a Reformed polity, while Boehm and his Mennonite associates brought an Anabaptist ecclesiology and polity. With the pronounced increase of Mennonites in the movement after 1800, which eclipsed the German Reformed element, efforts at strong and centralized organization were resisted. Thus there was a very loosely knit quality to the United Brethren movement, as it undervalued outward forms of church government.[52]

Of the three main forms of church polity (episcopal, presbyterian, and congregational), United Brethren leaders, refusing to adopt a pure form of any of these three polities, often argued that "probably no other church includes these features in a more just equipose than does the UB church."[53] Theirs was a "composite polity."[54] Nevertheless, the fundamental principle in their ecclesiology was that "the supreme earthly authority in our church is visited, not in the ministry, but the whole society."[55] The United Brethren "cannot properly be called an episcopal church" but were "not far away from churches that exalt their Congregationalism." The United Brethren, then, prized a fuller participation of congregational participation in church affairs than the Methodists and even Evangelicals, which were more connectional and itinerant according to the The Methodist Episcopal Church *Discipline*.[56]

Indeed, the United Brethren maintained a predominantly presbyterial form of polity as "the prevailing character of the government of the church, though they repudiated the aristocratic class features of that system."[57] They claimed "centralization is the natural law of Episcopal Methodism," as there is "no power but General Conference."[58] In contrast, decentralization was the tendency of the United Brethren polity and practice.[59] Through their chosen representatives the people administered the church, so it was democratic without being chaotic, authoritative without being tyrannical. It was a representative form of democracy through a graded series of conferences—quarterly (a station or circuit), annual (ordained and licensed and lay delegates from each circuit), and general (equal number of lay and clergy).

They derived from this principle "a class of churches having an ascending series of church courts under a common jurisdiction."[60] So United Brethren polity can be described as a "modified Presbyterianism" with elected representatives who administered a church government that was democratic without being subject to chaos.[61] From the Reformed tradition Otterbein took the threefold pattern of two lay offices and a single ordained order. Local preachers and itinerant preachers shared equally in the conference, while the primary governing authority was in the local church. Authority for Word and Sacrament lay with the conference, and ordination was done in the local church. The two irrepressible issues that provoked long debate, beginning in 1837, were lay representation in conferences and prorated representation of conferences in General Conference. Although the church was episcopal to the extent that it had bishops, it was clear that the bishops were not a separate order; they were agents of supervision; they held an administrative, not a priestly, office; they had a specified term of office and acted for and by the authority of the General Conference. There was only one ministry in the church, an office of ministry, which was not an order.[62]

Sacraments

A persisting controversy within the Church of the United Brethren in Christ was the issue of the sacraments, especially baptism. This revivalistic denomination so emphasized the new birth that the importance and meaning of the sacraments were diminished.[63] Though the use of the sacraments was recommended, they taught that salvation was available without them. Indeed, in the original Confession of Faith the observation of the sacraments was only recommended, in part in order to clearly reject baptismal regeneration. Beginning around 1840, the practices of infant baptism and rebaptism were heatedly debated in the church. Over the years the United Brethren had sustained a Mennonite influence on infant baptism.[64] However, in the 1853 General Conference when infant baptism was contended, the conference formally forbade disrespect for infant baptism and those who practiced it.[65] But they emphasized that baptism was not a saving ordinance in the sense of containing or imparting the means of grace for salvation. They continued to reject baptismal regeneration, and many insisted the church did not teach infant baptism. Even though they called it baptism, it was nothing but consecration, they argued.[66] Although the Church of the United Brethren in Christ never rejected infant baptism, it was often interpreted as infant dedication. The 1897 Catechism taught that "baptism of children shall be left to the judgment of believing parents."[67] However, a prescribed order for infant dedication first appeared only in the very last United Brethren *Discipline* in 1945 as a supplement to another piece of legislation on children's membership record. McCabe, however, insists that the language of the two rites was so close to each other that this was "a distinction without a difference."[68] The continuing debate in United Methodism today is intensified by the rejection, or at least ambiguous teaching and practice, of the United Brethren on infant baptism.

Continuing Legacy of the Church of the United Brethren in Christ in The United Methodist Church

The union of the United Brethren with the Evangelicals in 1946 and with The Methodist Church in 1968 tied The United Methodist Church directly to continental Protestantism in general and to Reformed and Mennonite piety, doctrine, ecclesiology, and polity in specific. United Brethren genes brought Reformed and Mennonite piety and theology directly into the Methodist tradition. They are now part of the Methodist inheritance.

Continental Pietism

To be sure, Anglican theology is rooted in Reformed continental Protestant theology more than in the Lutheran continental Protestant confessions. However, through the Church of the United Brethren in Christ, the Reformed tradition and confessions, especially the Heidelberg Catechism, are direct, explicit, and persisting influences in United Methodism, traceable to the two founding fathers of the denomination, specifically in the Pietism of the Church of the United Brethren in Christ through Otterbein, and through Boehm, to the Mennonite tradition on the Continent, and so to the Anabaptist tradition. Methodism is now a more inclusive form of Protestantism than it has ever been. Continental Protestantism is now a genetic inheritance of Methodism in America, adding the richness of Reformed and Mennonite forms of faith that was not as apparent in Anglican Puritanism and Wesleyan revivalism.

German Reformed Pietism is now formally a part of the Methodist heritage in America, alongside Anglo American, Anglican, and Puritan forms of Christianity (and the Moravian

Lutheran form of Pietism that influenced Wesley). The Evangelical United Brethren General Conference in 1964 reduced the Reformed heritage of Otterbein and moved toward a more Wesleyan theology in regard to total depravity (the Reformed heritage in the article that said we are "inclined to evil and only evil" omitted the phrase "only evil" from the 1964 EUB Confession). And the United Brethren statement on sanctification could be interpreted either in a Wesleyan-Evangelical or a Lutheran-Calvinistic fashion, although it was formulated in the EUB Confession of Faith in a Wesleyan-Evangelical fashion and also more in line with the Evangelicals' more extensive emphasis on sanctification.[69]

Reformed Ecclesiology and Polity

The Church of the United Brethren in Christ and The Methodist Episcopal Church had two *very different ecclesiologies*. For Asbury the church was the conference, the annual quarterly conference, and the General Conference, where preachers were sent to, not called to, a local congregation, so the local church was an expression of the conference, whereas Otterbein began with the local congregation and built up from there.[70] In short, the Church of the United Brethren in Christ had a modified Reformed presbyterial polity, while The Methodist Episcopal Church was a modified Anglican episcopal polity. These recessive United Brethren genes continue to shape the contemporary United Methodist Church. Although both were mixed and not pure forms of any of the three basic polities, the dominant democratic impulse and free church polity of the United Brethren remain a powerful strain within The United Methodist Church episcopal polity, played out in contemporary UMC polity struggles between lay and clergy in General and Annual Conferences and in theological debates over the nature and role of ordination as well as over the authority of bishops.[71]

The downside of this new inheritance in The United Methodist Church has been the persisting and unresolved tension between the essentially Reformed and Anabaptist ecclesiology and polity of the United Brethren and the Anglican-Episcopal ecclesiology and polity of The Methodist Episcopal Church. The United Brethren tradition contains views of authority associated with its Reformed and Mennonite beginnings (the United Brethren made little use of the Methodist *Discipline*, while the Evangelicals adopted a translation of the Methodistic discipline for their own use),[72] so that all who denote themselves today as United Methodists share a diversity and ambiguity of heritage regarding their polity and understanding of ministry.[73] Though the United Brethren adopted a modified episcopal polity, with bishops, the literature frequently identifies episcopacy as aristocratic, concentrated, and authoritarian power. Thus the United Brethren insisted that bishops were superintendents, an office (not an order) with four years' tenure and subject to the will of the people; the ordination of women, the rights of individual church members, and the centrality of the laity: all of these are reiterated in the literature. The United Brethren were suspicious of and resistant to organization and authority, whereas Asbury had made organization, order, and authority central to Methodist polity.

These tensions are not apparent in any conflicting statements between the Confession of Faith and the Articles of Religion, but persist more subtly in the ethos or in the bloodstream of persons shaped by German Reformed Pietism and polity in contrast to Anglican Puritanism and episcopal polity. The United Brethren tradition also had a more clear sense of being a distinctly new American denomination instead of a transplanted and newly shaped and independent Old World English denomination adapted to a new setting. The tensions between German Reformed Pietism and polity and English Anglican Puritan episcopacy continued to influence and play out even as United Brethren, Evangelical United Brethren, and Methodist Episcopal Church members were deeply shaped by the American evangelical revivalism they shared in common. The United Brethren rejection of Methodist "authoritarianism" from the beginning, the temperament of modesty inherited from Otterbein and his followers, the feeling of being a distinct minority within The United Methodist Church (The Evangelical United Brethren Church was one-tenth the size of The Methodist Church in the 1968 union), and the difference in the ethos between the denominations, traceable in part to the difference between the Anglo and continental forms of Pietism, have contributed to the sense of disillusionment, alienation, and at times even exclusion that some former United

Brethren and Evangelical United Brethren members feel in The United Methodist Church even to this day.[74]

Some in The United Methodist Church today see a persisting and disturbing influence of the United Brethren tradition in United Methodism, which is a challenge to its historic connectionalism. In 1996 the General Conference moved from the Anglican tradition of Asbury to something more akin to Otterbein's Reformed tradition (Albright inhabited a more middle ground between Asbury and Otterbein).[75] Indeed, in some ways the United Brethren tradition has seemed to triumph in The United Methodist Church in regard to its polity (authority of General Conference over bishops) and ordination (a pattern of single ordination to ministry) and especially the increasing significance of the local congregation in our understanding of the church.[76] Frank, for example, argues that the increasing use of the term *congregation* in the *Discipline* is now a polity term and not simply a reference to a gathering in a particular place. The *Discipline*'s use of *congregation* as an organizational term in the chapter on the local church continually (112 times) suggests that somehow United Methodism has, or is moving toward, congregations in the political sense as self-constituted associations. "While the Constitution still asserts the annual conference is the basic body of the church, many current practices suggest that the local church is the basic body."[77] This change is undoubtedly a reflection of the undercurrent of populism in American culture, but it is also a strain in the ecclesiology and polity of the United Brethren (as well as Evangelicals; The Methodist Episcopal Church, South; and other movements within Methodism). The tension can be traced all the way back to the difference in views of polity and ministry between Asbury and Otterbein, namely, connectionalism versus congregationalism. The growing emphasis in the *Discipline* on the local church and on our understanding of the orders of ministry reflects the continuing influence of the United Brethren tradition.[78] This is evident in the creation of an ordained order without sacramental authority (deacon in full connection) and a nonordained order with sacramental authority (local pastor). Harnish suggests this was a radical break with the long-standing tradition of Methodism and is traceable, in part, to the continuing influence of United Brethren ecclesiology and polity.[79]

CHAPTER 6

DOCTRINE AND THEOLOGY IN THE EVANGELICAL ASSOCIATION/CHURCH

William Naumann

Jacob Albright had prospered on the fertile land of a Pennsylvania farm until 1790 when the deaths of several of his children plunged him into religious crisis. Help emerged for this German Lutheran from several of his neighbors: evangelical Reformed minister Anthony Houtz preached the funeral sermons; in the home of United Brethren lay preacher Adam Riegel, Albright yielded his life to Christ and experienced glorious conversion; a nearby Methodist class provided Christian fellowship; and through the influence of pietistic neighbors, he savored a growing personal relationship with God. Soon Jacob Albright began to preach. And from that beginning emerged The Evangelical Association.

BASIC DOCTRINE—PIETISTIC AND WESLEYAN

The supreme importance of Christian experience was the central core of Albright's convictions and the dominant note of his sermons. Early Evangelicals were convinced that people did not become Christians in the cool detachment of the philosopher's armchair. Nor did it happen gradually, unconsciously, or imperceptibly. To confront Christ squarely was to be decisively converted, and this meant transformation of the whole person, not least of which were the emotions.

So important are the "religious affections" that the journals of early Evangelical ministers are filled with accounts of their religious feelings.[1] John Seybert, the Asbury of the Evangelicals, always recorded it as a mark of success when emotions were aroused and people wept or shouted.[2] Evangelicals agreed that "a child of God needs no further argument that Christ is God than that he feels him in his soul as the living power of God."[3] "Religion of the heart" was definitely superior to "religion of the head."[4]

The colorful "bush meeting spirituals," which they composed and sang, added to the emotional fervor of their meetings.[5] Both John Walter, Albright's first assistant, and John Dreisbach, first presiding elder, wrote songs that were among the most popular German hymns ever written in America.[6] But the embrace of the emotions had its dangers. "Heart religion" occasionally became noisy, boisterous—and offensive to some. Jacob Vogelbach, a promising young minister who formed the first missionary society in 1838 and frequently contributed to the church's German periodical, left the church because of his opposition to boisterous worship.[7]

Instantaneous conversion was expected to issue in assurance, a certainty that one had made peace with God. The exhortation to seek conversion was based on the belief in human depravity. In 1839 The Evangelical Association reprinted one of John Fletcher's works in order to publicize that doctrine.[8] Human sinfulness was basic to the whole effort of converting sinners in the quarterly meetings, revivals, and camp meetings in which they continually were engaged.[9] And these were publicized widely. Detailed reports and advice for promoting them were frequent features in the denominational journals.[10] A later historian asserted that without evangelization there would be no good reason for his church's existence.[11]

The overcoming of sin also was central. One circuit rider engaged in spirited argument with a "defeatist" he encountered in his travels:

> I told him, that if he had religion, perhaps he could live better, but he did not know what genuine religion is. I sought to make it plain

to him, but he would not believe it, saying that he commits sins every day and that no man on earth lives who does not sin daily.... Then I asked him why man cannot live without sinning since it is not God's will?... He answered, but no one can become so perfect in this world for he must sin every day. But my dear friend, said I, how do you expect to stand before the righteous judgment seat of Christ if you are still a sinner? He had no answer, and broke out weeping, saying, pray for me. Yes, I said, I will pray that God shall enlighten your darkened understanding.[12]

Despite their humble social standing and modest material resources, these early Evangelicals exhibited an air of success. They were convinced that a Christian could live above sin. God demanded holiness, and common sense decreed that what God commanded, humans could fulfill.[13]

Private meditation and family worship were the means for cultivating pious feelings and maintaining a close relationship to God. John Arndt strongly advocated a devotional reading of the Bible each morning, and these people were his avid devotees.[14] As early as 1809, a conference requested George Miller to prepare devotional material for use among members.[15]

Scripture, common sense, and good works were the three criteria for evaluating Christian experience. The statement that Jacob Albright was "a thorough student of the Bible and consequently based much of his preaching directly on the Scriptures" was true of every preacher.[16] The first catechism contained no article or question on the Bible, but every question was answered by a biblical quotation with no other comment.[17] Like other Pietists, Evangelicals earnestly defended the Bible against all detractors.[18] Early preachers were careful to speak clearly and simply, taking some pride in being methodical and logical.[19] The appeal to common sense was supported by the evidence of God's handiwork in nature. The soil on which most of these thrifty Germans settled in Pennsylvania and Ohio was good, and they found nature and the good earth to be bountiful and generous.[20] Nature could be trusted to lead one to God.[21]

George Miller, venerated compiler of the Evangelical *Discipline*, illustrates the focus on good works with his *Practical Christianity*, a book that went through at least three editions. Miller's book was a call to live a devout life; no one need remain unchanged and at the mercy of propensities to evil. Rigid discipline of both laypersons and ministers was enforced. Eventually this established a reputation for integrity that contributed to growth and counteracted the losses resulting from strict discipline.

MINISTERIAL TRAINING

This new movement achieved enough success in its first few years that, in 1810, John Dreisbach declared his loyalty to it in his notable response to Bishop Francis Asbury's invitation to leave the movement and join The Methodist Church.[22] Dreisbach and his associates were clear about their calling to work mainly among the German population—and they were committed to it.[23]

Dreisbach, as the first presiding elder, was an important transitional leader between Albright and John Seybert. Although he was criticized for it, Dreisbach strongly advocated education for ministers.[24] Fear of education had been with Evangelicals from the beginning. The gospel they proclaimed was a simple message, and the stress on emotional experience and the lay character of the movement strengthened that tendency. Questions of orthodoxy and efforts at theological precision were less important than the winning of souls. Formal theological training for the ministry seemed unnecessary and often detrimental.[25]

George Miller's influential book, *Practical Christianity*, insists that the most important aspect of a minister's preparation is that he be spiritually alive. The wisdom he requires for his work must come from God. Miller concedes that "learning is necessary and good in its place, if properly applied," but the wisdom that is essential for the minister "cannot be obtained in... schools of learning, or found among the dead languages, however useful learning may be in its proper place."[26] His help must come through prayer.

John Walter, an associate of Albright and Miller, was "so completely uneducated that at first he had to spell the texts which he desired to read to his congregations."[27] This did not hinder his effectiveness, for he was probably the most powerful of the early Evangelical preachers.[28]

Eventually the fear of an educated ministry began to subside. Jacob Albright tried to compensate for his academic deficiencies by avid reading habits.[29] And John Seybert and Joseph Long were leaders who, despite their misgivings about educated ministers, were ardent readers and careful students. Seybert gave away thousands of books to poor persons and sold even more on his trips westward. In 1841 he purchased 23,725 books, which he took west for distribution on his evangelistic journeys.[30] When ill health compelled Bishop Long to "locate" for eight years, he spent much of his time reading, particularly the standard theological works of the time.[31]

The "standard theological works" were, of course, the writings of the Pietists, especially John Arndt's *True Christianity*.[32] Another religious tradition was represented by Richard Baxter and Joseph Alleine, English Puritan leaders of the seventeenth century.[33] The first Evangelical *Discipline*, published in 1809, included several doctrinal essays taken from the writings of Wesley and Fletcher.[34]

In 1843 the Evangelicals set up a Course of Study that included Watson,[35] Fletcher, Mosheim, Collier, Wesley's sermons, Josephus, Rotteck's world history, a German grammar, the church *Discipline*, biblical natural history and geography, works on the existence and attributes of God, and the Bible.[36] Similar to the internship arrangement in the days of Jonathan Edwards, persons entering the ministry, who were being supervised by experienced pastors, used the Course of Study. Although the early prejudice against education for ministers had begun to fade by the 1840s, the fear of overemphasizing education was still present. The first report of the Evangelicals' committee on ministerial training concluded with this warning:

> Finally, we surely want to remind everyone again that without the unction of the Holy Spirit and divine equipment from heaven, all the study and science in the whole world does not make a man fit for the ministry; wherefore we counsel every man, before everything else, to pray God for the necessary grace, unction, and wisdom which are indispensable for his calling.[37]

Other denominations were establishing theological seminaries, but the fear of "preacher factories" prevented Evangelicals from doing so until later in the nineteenth century.

Official Doctrine

In 1839 The Evangelical Association made its statement of faith unalterable. This action of General Conference and the Evangelicals' policy of forbidding ministers to publish doctrinal books without permission show that they regarded Christian doctrine as a clear and indisputable set of statements about which little discussion was needed. The task of theology was simply to expound truth, defending one's articles of faith by reference to the authority of the Bible, experience, and common sense. This is why the Evangelicals were indifferent to creeds. At first the Bible seemed sufficient. When it became advisable to have a statement of faith, they simply borrowed from the Methodists. It is not a unique document welling up from the vitality of the church's experience. Rather, they adopted it to provide cohesion and unity. They conceived of their task as the repetition of eternal truths in traditional language. Actually, in their preaching and in conversation with their neighbors, they did what they failed to do in their more formal theological pronouncements, that is, point out the relevance of the gospel for contemporary life.

What early Evangelicals believed about theological language and the task of theological activity in the life of the church may be summarized thus: (1) Affirmations about God and human relations to God are eternally true propositions requiring no revision. (2) The essentials of the simple gospel require few words to express them. (3) Christians should not waste their time on such theoretical matters; they are better occupied in efforts to convert the lost. (4) One may have unshakable confidence about the absolute truth of the Christian faith and the possibility of making this perfectly clear to others.[38]

The certainty about basic convictions was a strength and a weakness. Their confidence invigorated them for evangelism. However, to their successors they left a set of working ideas demanding reevaluation. Among these were the negative attitude toward formal education; the willingness to borrow from outside sources for theological statements; the elevation of individual and subjective norms above the corporate witness of the church, past and present;[39] and the preference for the emotional appeal, the devotional life, and the comfortable feeling of assurance over disciplined theological study.

Growth of Theological Awareness

The period 1840 to 1890 witnessed enormous growth and change. Membership grew more than twelvefold, Sunday schools multiplied rapidly, and foreign missions were begun. Youth societies sprang up, colleges were organized, and a seminary was established. Interest in theology rose, particularly over the doctrine of Christian perfection. Two editors of the *Evangelical Messenger* lost their jobs over the issue, and Solomon Neitz, a popular presiding elder from Pennsylvania, twice was accused of heresy for questioning the Wesleyan doctrine of perfection. The issue agitated The Evangelical Association from 1857 until the editor of the *Messenger* was dismissed in 1870.[40]

Gradually education acquired greater prestige. In an important editorial the venerable John Dreisbach called for theological training in natural theology, revealed theology, moral theology, speculative theology, and scholastic theology.[41] Responsible persons were beginning to realize that better education was an absolute necessity if ministers were to be effective. Conversions were unlikely if preachers were not well trained.[42]

Another motivation was the flood of Germans coming to America who had been affected by the atheistic rationalism that pervaded some of the mid-nineteenth-century liberal movements.[43] Editor T. G. Clewell pointed out the challenge, indicating that uneducated ministers were no match for the clever arguments of "polished infidels." He saw the truth suffering because of "the incompetency of its advocates." Calling for the addition of "a thorough erudition to the piety of our ministry," he suggested that "missionary institutes" be provided for training.[44] After the interruption of the Civil War, he returned to this theme to plead once again for "biblical institutes."[45] Infidelity without and heresy within became potent arguments.

Beginning as early as 1857, district ministerial meetings were held to discuss theology. The first one, in Greensburg, Ohio, lasted four days.[46] These district meetings were supported by the

Episcopal Address to the General Conference of 1863.[47] Finally, in 1876 Union Biblical Institute opened at North-Western College with eight men enrolled.[48]

Philosophy, the old enemy, more and more was embraced as a valuable ally. In fact, Anton Huelster, who taught theological students at North-Western College, wrote that at its "highest step of perfection," it "passes over into theology."[49] However, the philosophy that was adopted was Scottish common sense realism. Sydney Ahlstrom pointed out that this philosophy had come "to exist in America...as a vast subterranean influence, a sort of water-table nourishing dogmatics in an age of increasing doubt."[50] Negatively, for Evangelicals it reduced the fear of higher education and German rationalism. Positively, it fitted the pattern of engaging in theological activity to affirm and defend the faith, for it "was an apologetical philosophy, par excellence."[51] With its vindication of the substantial, personal self and the appeal to concrete evidence, it suited the practical temper of these common people who could not have appreciated the epistemological subtleties of Kant.[52] Also, it furnished an appropriate weapon to defend orthodoxy without becoming deeply involved in philosophical speculation. Thus armed, they were immune from accusations of anti-intellectualism by the infidel. It provided a basis for biblicism and a shelter against the unpredictable currents of an uncontrolled empiricism.

The names of prominent promulgators of the Scottish philosophy appeared frequently in denominational literature.[53] Joseph Haven's *Mental Philosophy* and Richard Whateley's *Logic* were integral parts of the ministerial Course of Study for many years.[54] Another evidence of the prevalence of the Scottish philosophy is the heavy reliance on the idea of "self-evident truths," a trademark of the system.[55] Anton Huelster appeals to the principle to support a contextual approach to a biblical interpretation of the millennium[56] and also to support belief in the existence of God.[57] The conviction that truth is essentially unchangeable was in harmony with a substantialist understanding of the nature of reality and a clear-cut distinction between subject and object that saw the subject as having no modifying effect on the objects grasped by it.[58]

The significance of Scottish realism for theology is noteworthy. Ahlstrom notes that "by a firm separation of the Creator and His creation, the Scottish thinkers preserved the orthodox notion of

God's transcendence, and made revelation necessary."[59] This position buttressed Watson's emphasis on the human need for a revelation coming from outside ourselves, and Watson remained a theological mentor of Evangelicals throughout most of this period.

JOSEPH COOK

Joseph Cook's lectures at Boston's Tremont Temple between 1874 and 1895 became another significant means of coping with threatening developments like higher criticism and the New Theology. At first printed in newspapers, his lectures later appeared in book form, filling eleven volumes. They covered a variety of subjects, but his reputation was built on his ability to explain the ideas of contemporary European thinkers and to comfort the orthodox by showing that what scientists were saying "was either incorrect or was wholly compatible with revealed religion."[60]

Though he was a voice coming from outside the denomination, Cook was the most important single influence on the theological understanding and activity of Evangelicals during the late 1870s and the 1880s. His name appears everywhere, being almost universally praised, quoted, and copied. His significance is twofold. On the one hand, Cook reinforced the pattern of engaging in theological activity for defensive purposes; he was an apologist and a polemicist. On the other hand, because he was such an orthodox apologist, he provided a safe means of becoming acquainted with the larger theological world. Once acquainted with this larger world beyond their limited theological horizons, Evangelicals began to modify some of their theological and philosophical convictions. Intellectual curiosity led them to explore and experiment with new ideas, and it all seemed perfectly safe with Joseph Cook as their reliable guide.[61]

Reports and articles about Cook that were appearing in the church periodicals were written by ministers, college professors, bishops, and editors. Cook became far and away the most quoted authority. "As Joseph Cook says" became absolutely confirmatory evidence. He seemed to deal a deathblow to infidelity and heresy.

Furthermore, he helped the faithful meet the challenge of science,[62] providing comfort with regard to the new Darwinian theories.

Cook's viewpoint was a compound of Scottish philosophy modified by what he liked of Rudolph Lotze's personalism and sprinkled with scientific ideas supporting his disdainful rejection of materialism. His strong emphasis on self-evident truths, which are the result of rational intuitions, reveals his affinity with Scottish philosophy. In his attempt to come to terms with science, Cook understood correctly his contemporaries' anxiety about the new biological theories and what they might mean for religion. Evangelicals could not accept the liberalism of a theology like Ritschl's, which rejected original sin and attempted to outflank science with an immanental view of God.[63] Joseph Cook stepped in and supplied the resources for reconciling science and religion. He was involved in a reinterpretation of the Christian faith, and that was something Evangelicals had not done before. After Joseph Cook, the role of theology could no longer be the same.

HISTORICAL CRITICISM AND PROTESTANT LIBERALISM

As the end of the nineteenth century approached, Evangelicals were divided by the tragic fracture that split the denomination in two. Much of their attention necessarily was turned toward organizational matters. However, both groups were swept up in larger movements. Both were charter members of the Federal Council of Churches in 1908 and would affiliate with the International Council of Religious Education.[64] These connections brought them into contact with the larger theological movements of their time.

During the 1890s, the number of young liberals who came to influential positions in American theological education was notable.[65] In one of its more liberal moments the journal of the United Evangelicals advertised the summer session of the University of Chicago at which such men as Shailer Mathews, Herbert Willett, and President William Rainey Harper were scheduled to teach.[66] However, what seemed even more dangerous was the threat of higher criticism. Beyond Anton Huelster and S. J. Gamertsfelder, few understood its methods and wrestled with its implications for interpretation of the Bible. United Evangelicals were listening increasingly to James Gray of Moody Bible Institute, and he was advising a hard, uncompromising line in the warfare against higher criticism and the New Theology. To accept any of the procedures of the higher critics, he said, was tantamount to giving up the Bible: "You think you can give up the written Word and still hold on to the Word Incarnate, but in the long run that will be found impossible."[67] How to estimate the strength of fundamentalism and dispensationalism among United Evangelicals is difficult. They had based their new Articles of Faith on the work of Milton Terry, a biblical scholar at Garrett. Terry was no fundamentalist. While H. B. Hartzler was fulminating against higher criticism and liberalism in the pages of *The Evangelical*, his brother Jacob wrote the church's catechism (1901), which shows no evidence of dispensationalism.[68] United Evangelicals did not speak with a united voice.

If the official pronouncements of bishops and General Conferences are valid indicators of the mood of their respective denominations, the general attitude toward the newer methods of Bible study remained defensive until about the middle 1920s. The addresses of the bishops to the United Evangelical General Conferences of 1902, 1906, and 1910 contained especially strong warnings against higher criticism. The editors of the church's periodicals were even freer in calling names in their opposition to higher criticism in higher education.[69]

As the fundamentalist controversy moved toward its peak in the 1920s, the pressure mounted to line up enemies on one side and friends on the other. This polarization resulted in the clear-cut identification of supporters of the New Theology as enemies, including heretics, Unitarians, Universalists, Harnack, Eliot, Fosdick, the religious education movement, liberal institutions of higher education, and others.

Friends included familiar names: William Biederwolf, A. B. Simpson (founder of the Christian Missionary Alliance), Mel Trotter, C. I. Scofield, Robert Dick Wilson, A. C. Gaebelein, R. A. Torrey, Clarence Macartney, and Billy Sunday. The church periodicals kept readers informed about the dangers to Scripture coming from some scholars. In 1919, an editor wrote:

Prof. H. F. Rall, of Garrett Biblical Institute, was president of Iliff School of Theology before going to Garrett. He is a German and was educated in Germany. He unloaded his German U-boat theology upon Iliff and is now doing the same at Garrett. He is the supremely moving spirit in the Commission on the Course of Study for our young preachers, and is more than any one responsible for the un-Methodistic, anti-Biblical, faith-wrecking infidel character of this course.[70]

But the lure of liberalism was too strong for many to resist. S. J. Gamertsfelder led the way by introducing newer patterns of thought at Evangelical Theological Seminary. These made their way into the training of ministers, as shown through the book lists on the Courses of Study:

United Evangelical Church
1910   H. C. Sheldon, *System of Christian Doctrine*
        Shailer Mathews, *Social Studies*
        George Stevens, *The Theology of the New Testament*[71]

Evangelical Association
1911   George Stevens, *The Theology of the New Testament*
        Walter Rauschenbusch, *Christianity and the Social Crisis*
1919   Horace Bushnell, *Christian Nurture*

German theology was no longer universally rejected. Bishop Rudolph Dubs sent his son to Germany for four years of theological study after his graduation from Oberlin College.[72] Apparently Germany did not corrupt C. Newton Dubs, for he then dedicated himself to a lifetime of missionary service in China.

Gamertsfelder taught theology for twenty-eight years and published his text *Systematic Theology*, which contained the substance of his lectures.[73] He, too, was willing to learn from German theologians, especially after spending the summer of 1906 in Germany.[74] Throughout his works, one can detect interest in the themes of Evangelical liberalism: tentativeness, tolerance, immanentism, comparative religion, the glorification of humanity, Christocentrism, personality, and openness to science.[75] But he wrote and taught from within the mainstream of Evangelical tradition. Ted Campbell has characterized him as a "progressive evangelical."[76]

As the fundamentalist controversy intensified in the 1920s, Evangelicals were reluctant to put their stamp of approval on Gamertsfelder's *Systematic Theology*. Too many liberal ideas appeared in the 1913 edition. So he went to work, softening his criticism of the substitutionary atonement and removing other telltale signs of liberalism, and the revised product was approved and published by the denomination in 1921.

Ecumenism and the Social Gospel

Ecumenism and the social gospel also exerted their influence on the denomination. Theology and theological differences became less important, for they were divisive. Evangelicals had good reason for trying to maintain unity, for they had suffered a grievous split. Therefore, the United Evangelical bishops in 1898 advised that "no differences of opinion...must be allowed to disturb the unity of the spirit."[77] As a matter of fact, many were not comfortable in serious theological discussion. In the summer of 1903, Bishop Rudolph Dubs delivered the lecture "The Consciousness of God as Conditioned by Christianity" at a Bible conference. The response of the reporter dramatizes the perennial ambivalence of Evangelicals toward theology:

> This was a gigantic production from the giant mind of this masterful servant of God. The reporter in following this lecture was soon beyond his depths; and as he was not able to swim well in these waters, he was compelled to remain nearer shore. Hence, no report of this lecture. The committee is requested to either secure a more competent reporter, or have less profound themes discussed at the next conference.[78]

When the fundamentalist crusade was exerting its divisive influence in the 1920s, Ammon Hangen, editor of *The Evangelical*, urged his fellow churchmen not to forget the bitter lessons they had learned from their own past: "Perfect agreement is a sign of mental indolence and atrophy. As long as men think, they will differ. There are those who think that no *doxy* but theirs ought to be held by any man, but they mistake uniformity for unity and contend for that literalness which paralyzes and kills."[79] Hangen then counseled

United Evangelicals to avoid both extreme fundamentalism and extreme liberalism.

Both groups of Evangelicals needed to maintain unity in 1922, for they were preparing to reunite later that year. President G. B. Kimmel of Evangelical Theological Seminary rejoiced "that our church as a whole has...refused to be drawn into any of the theological controversies of our day. We have refused to be divided. We have kept faithfully to our task of preaching and teaching a warm, practical, positive gospel that saves from sin and transforms human lives."[80] Advising his readers to avoid both premillennialism and postmillennialism, W. H. Bucks, editor of the *Evangelical Messenger*, saw that the fervent espousal of either position could lead to serious divisions within the denomination.[81]

The traditional emphasis of Evangelicals on good works prepared them to appreciate the social gospel. John Stamm, professor of systematic theology at Evangelical Theological Seminary, put strong emphasis on the ethical in his master's thesis at the University of Chicago in 1926, the year he was elected bishop. Stamm took a long look at the statement of Jacob Albright about his motivation for beginning to preach: "God, my helper and protector, also strengthened my heart and mind by his grace, that I was not only able to preach pure doctrine to those whom He had entrusted to me, but also to establish them by my own example."[82] He then concluded that by "pure doctrine," Albright did not mean "philosophical or speculative" truths, but ethical verities. Albright meant holy living according to the Scriptures, for he and other founders "did not think of Christianity as primarily a system of doctrines and beliefs, but as an ethical and spiritual force." With accurate historical understanding Stamm wrote:

> This church did not originate as a protest against some theological doctrine, but as a protest against the low moral and spiritual standards of their times, especially as exemplified in the lives of many who professed to be Christians.... [Jacob Albright] believed that he was preaching "pure doctrine" when he emphasized the ethical and spiritual content of Christianity. He believed people were true to "pure doctrine" when they lived so truly Christian that the principles of Jesus and the Apostles were being exemplified in their thought and conduct. This initial emphasis is the key to the doctrinal consciousness of the Evangelical Church.

Her doctrinal interests have always been in the field of the ethical rather than the theological.[83]

This emphasis on the ethical permeated the two seminaries, which were training effective ministers, not professional theologians. Theology was understood as auxiliary to the religious life and not as the main course. As Newell Wert aptly expresses it, "Personal experience of Jesus Christ was basic to Christian living and took precedence over creeds and church structure. The Godly life was central."[84]

CHAPTER 7

THE CONFESSION OF FAITH: A THEOLOGICAL COMMENTARY

Jason E. Vickers

In 1968, The Evangelical United Brethren Church (EUB) merged with The Methodist Church to form The United Methodist Church (UMC). As a part of this merger, the EUB Confession of Faith (CF) was incorporated into the United Methodist *Book of Discipline* alongside the Twenty-five Articles of Religion (AR) as standards of doctrine for the newly formed church. It remains there today. Unfortunately, like the AR, the CF is seldom used and little known in many quarters within United Methodism. When it is used, it is often to support heresy charges against bishops or clergy. In other words, it is used primarily as a test of orthodoxy.

The fact that many United Methodists turn to the CF and AR only when they are (rightly or wrongly) upset by the teachings of their bishops or other clergy is symptomatic of a deeper problem, namely, a limited and, in my judgment, misguided view of the primary role of confessions of faith in the life of the people of God. The very language "standards of doctrine" tends to consign the CF and AR to a very limited role as tests of orthodoxy and therefore of doctrinal and theological heresy. As such, they are only too readily perceived in negative terms. After all, no one likes a test. Many of my United Methodist students view the CF and AR as things that they are supposed to believe (or at least say that they believe) if they want to make it past the Board of Ordained Ministry.

In saying this, I am not suggesting that there are not times in the life of the church when we need doctrinal standards or tests of orthodoxy. At times, confessional statements can function to help us sort out orthodox from heterodox teaching. My criticism is not that the CF and AR are sometimes called upon to function this way, but that many Methodists seem to view this as their primary function, if they view them as having a function at all.

The point here is that we need to be more attentive to the primary function of confessions of faith in the history of Christianity. Confessions of faith have been around since the earliest days of the church. In the earliest days, their primary use was not to settle theological disputes or serve as tests of orthodoxy. Rather, their primary use was in catechesis and worship.[1] In catechesis, confessions of faith were taught and even memorized. They gave to inquirers and initiates a basic outline of the Christian faith. They were relatively short summaries of the most basic Christian beliefs, indicating who God was and what God had done "for us and for salvation." In worship, confessions of faith helped to keep these things in the minds and hearts of the people of God and thereby to evoke wonder, thanksgiving, and praise. The greatest evidence that these were the primary functions of confessions of faith in the life of the early church can be seen in the use to which the Nicene Creed was put after the Arian crisis had passed. To be sure, the Nicene Creed functioned at the height of the Arian crisis primarily as a test for orthodoxy. Yet soon after the matter was resolved, the creed was put to use primarily in catechesis and worship. You can see this, for example, in the use that Chrysostom makes of the creed in his *Baptismal Instructions*.

In The Methodist Church from 1784 to 1968, the Twenty-five Articles of Religion have functioned primarily as tests of orthodoxy or standards of doctrine. They do not appear to have functioned widely in catechesis and worship. To be sure, we put the AR in the front of the *Book of Discipline*, and we even adopted a restrictive rule prohibiting their alteration. But this is a far cry from memorizing them, teaching them to our children, reciting them at our baptism and in public worship, and the like.

I can think of at least two reasons the AR have not been especially important for faith formation and teaching in American Methodism. First, in the early going, it may be that many Methodists perceived the AR as something foisted upon them by John Wesley, a vestige of English rule to be sloughed off together with the Sunday Service. There are more than a few reminders of our Anglican roots in the AR.

Second, the AR, even as modified by John Wesley, reflect at many junctures the ecclesiastical and theological crisis in which they were written, namely, the crisis of the English Reformation. Thus they are frequently polemical in tone. As often as not, they are concerned with denouncing doctrines, for example, purgatory and transubstantiation. Here we have to do with a confessional statement that was originally intended to function more as a test of orthodoxy than as a means of grace in faith formation and worship—and it shows! Notice that the AR were written in the third person rather than in the first person plural. The effect is that they sound more like something to be enforced by a king than something to be humbly and joyously confessed at one's baptism! Indeed, this may be a very important difference between the theological genre known as *articles* and the genre commonly referred to as *confessions*. Articles would appear primarily to call for intellectual assent. The very word *confessions* suggests a liturgical setting with the accompanying activities of worship, repentance for sin, thanksgiving, and the like.

In The Evangelical United Brethren Church, the CF was composed primarily for faith formation. It was used primarily in settings of catechesis and worship. Written in the confessional first person plural, it readily lent itself to public recitation by the gathered people of God.[2] Moreover, in good Evangelical United Brethren fashion, the CF is rarely, if ever, polemical. It does not go out of its way to identify false teachings or to prohibit belief in certain doctrines or practices. Rather, it sticks closely to what its architects deemed essential to Christian faith and Christian living. It is truly a summary of essentials. For this reason, the CF is one of the Evangelical United Brethren's greatest gifts to

United Methodism. Unfortunately, The United Methodist Church does not appear to have recognized the uniqueness of the CF over against the AR. We have not noticed the truly confessional nature of the CF—that it is a statement intended for use in catechesis, in initiation and formation, and in worship. We seem to have assumed that it simply belongs alongside the AR as a standard of doctrine or a test of orthodoxy rather than in the mouths and hearts of the people called United Methodists.

It is often said that Christianity in America is a mile wide and an inch deep. Indeed, there are now startling studies of American religious illiteracy. Fewer and fewer people can name the four Gospels, let alone provide a basic, well-ordered outline of the essential teachings of the Christian faith.[3] This is not simply a matter of a lack of knowledge, as though not knowing the essential teachings of the Christian faith is like not knowing all the elements of the periodic table. On the contrary, lack of knowledge of the essential teachings of the Christian faith is at the heart of all sorts of problems in both church and society. It is causally linked to what Ellen Charry calls "the atrocities of our age." Unaware of who God is and of what God has done for us and for our salvation, we are left to lead reckless, self-serving, ungrateful, and hedonistic lives.[4] We are left to live out of fear and hatred rather than out of confidence and love. We are wholly given over to distrust, and it shows. We do not know who we are.

The United Methodist Church is blessed with a ready remedy for this situation. In the CF, we have a robust, yet economical statement of who God is and what God has done for us and for our salvation. It is a statement that should be taught to initiates preparing for baptism and confessed publicly in worship. This is not to suggest that it should be taught and confessed in lieu of, say, the Nicene Creed, but that it should have a place alongside the creed as an expression of a distinctively United Methodist way of understanding the essentials of the Christian faith.

In what follows, I want to make the case that the CF is theologically more robust than the AR. To be sure, this is a theological judgment on my part, but it is one that I am prepared to discuss and to defend. Suffice it to say that part of this judgment has to do with its usefulness for Christian initiation and formation. As I read it, the ordering of the CF is tailor-made for initiation into the life of the church in a way that the AR are not.

Having said all of this, the remainder of this chapter will unfold in two stages. First, I will provide a chart (see below) by which the two documents can be usefully compared. Second, I will provide a theological commentary on the CF, noting those places where the CF adds significant theological content to AR and therefore to United Methodist standards of doctrine.

At this stage, I need to say a word or two about how to read the following chart. The reader will notice that the CF occurs twice, both to the left and to the right of the AR. This is intended as a heuristic device. In the first column, the CF appears in its original order. By comparing the CF in this column with the AR in the second column, the reader can readily observe crucial differences between the ordering of the CF and the ordering of the AR. Also of note in the first column are articles that appear in italics. These articles are entirely unique to the CF, that is, they are *not* contained in the AR.

The second column contains the AR in their original order. Articles that are underlined in column two appear in the AR but not in the CF.

Column three represents a revised ordering of the CF, enabling the reader to compare directly the articles that occur in both the CF and the AR. Doing so helps material differences stand out more than they would otherwise. Finally, the reader will observe that the titles of some articles in column three are in italics. Italics in column three indicate that an article in the CF has been divided into two or more sections in order to enable direct comparison with the relevant material in the AR.

EUB Confession of Faith—Original Order	Methodist Articles of Religion—Original Order	EUB Confession of Faith—Revised Order
Article I—God We believe in the one true, holy and living God, Eternal Spirit, who is Creator, Sovereign and Preserver of all things visible and invisible. He is infinite in power, wisdom, justice, goodness and love, and rules with gracious regard for the well-being and salvation of men, to the glory of his name. We believe the one God reveals himself as the Trinity: Father, Son and Holy Spirit, distinct but inseparable, eternally one in essence and power.	**Article I—Of Faith in the Holy Trinity** There is but one living and true God, everlasting, without body or parts, of infinite power, wisdom, and goodness; the maker and preserver of all things, both visible and invisible. And in unity of this Godhead there are three persons, of one substance, power, and eternity—the Father, the Son, and the Holy Ghost.	**Article I—God** We believe in the one true, holy and living God, Eternal Spirit, who is Creator, Sovereign and Preserver of all things visible and invisible. He is infinite in power, wisdom, justice, goodness and love, and rules with gracious regard for the well-being and salvation of men, to the glory of his name. We believe the one God reveals himself as the Trinity: Father, Son and Holy Spirit, distinct but inseparable, eternally one in essence and power.
Article II—Jesus Christ We believe in Jesus Christ, truly God and truly man, in whom the divine and human natures are perfectly and inseparably united. He is the eternal Word made flesh, the only begotten Son of the Father, born of the Virgin Mary by the power of the Holy Spirit. As ministering Servant he lived, suffered and died on the cross. He was buried, rose from the dead and ascended into heaven to be with the Father, from whence he shall return. He is eternal Savior and Mediator, who intercedes for us, and by him all men will be judged.	**Article II—Of the Word, or Son of God, Who Was Made Very Man** The Son, who is the Word of the Father, the very and eternal God, of one substance with the Father, took man's nature in the womb of the blessed Virgin; so that two whole and perfect natures, that is to say, the Godhead and Manhood, were joined together in one person, never to be divided; whereof is one Christ, very God and very Man, who truly suffered, was crucified, dead, and buried, to reconcile his Father to us, and to be a sacrifice, not only for original guilt, but also for actual sins of men.	*Article II—Jesus Christ, Part I* We believe in Jesus Christ, truly God and truly man, in whom the divine and human natures are perfectly and inseparably united. He is the eternal Word made flesh, the only begotten Son of the Father, born of the Virgin Mary by the power of the Holy Spirit. As ministering Servant he lived, suffered and died on the cross.
Article III—The Holy Spirit We believe in the Holy Spirit who proceeds from and is one in being with the Father and the Son. He convinces the world of sin, of righteousness and of judgment. He leads men through faithful response to the gospel into the fellowship of the Church. He comforts, sustains and empowers the faithful and guides them into all truth.	**Article III—Of the Resurrection of Christ** Christ did truly rise again from the dead, and took again his body, with all things appertaining to the perfection of man's nature, wherewith he ascended into heaven, and there sitteth until he return to judge all men at the last day.	*Article II—Jesus Christ, Part II* He was buried, rose from the dead and ascended into heaven to be with the Father, from whence he shall return. He is eternal Savior and Mediator, who intercedes for us, and by him all men will be judged.

EUB Confession of Faith—Original Order	Methodist Articles of Religion—Original Order	EUB Confession of Faith—Revised Order
Article IV—The Holy Bible We believe the Holy Bible, Old and New Testaments, reveals the Word of God so far as it is necessary for our salvation. It is to be received through the Holy Spirit as the true rule and guide for faith and practice. Whatever is not revealed in or established by the Holy Scriptures is not to be made an article of faith nor is it to be taught as essential to salvation.	**Article IV—Of the Holy Ghost** The Holy Ghost, proceeding from the Father and the Son, is of one substance, majesty, and glory with the Father and the Son, very and eternal God.	**Article III—The Holy Spirit** We believe in the Holy Spirit who proceeds from and is one in being with the Father and the Son. He convinces the world of sin, of righteousness and of judgment. He leads men through faithful response to the gospel into the fellowship of the Church. He comforts, sustains and empowers the faithful and guides them into all truth.
Article V—The Church We believe the Christian Church is the community of all true believers under the Lordship of Christ. We believe it is one, holy, apostolic and catholic. It is the redemptive fellowship in which the Word of God is preached by men divinely called, and the sacraments are duly administered according to Christ's own appointment. Under the discipline of the Holy Spirit the Church exists for the maintenance of worship, the edification of believers and the redemption of the world.	**Article V—Of the Sufficiency of the Holy Scriptures for Salvation** The Holy Scripture containeth all things necessary to salvation; so that whatsoever is not read therein, nor may be proved thereby, is not to be required of any man that it should be believed as an article of faith, or be thought requisite or necessary to salvation. In the name of the Holy Scripture we do understand those canonical books of the Old and New Testament of whose authority was never any doubt in the church. The names of the canonical books are: Genesis, Exodus, Leviticus, Numbers, Deuteronomy, Joshua, Judges, Ruth, The First book of Samuel, The Second Second Book of Samuel, The First Book of Kings, The Second Book of Kings, The First Book of Chronicles, The Second Book of Chronicles, The Book of Ezra, The Book of Nehemiah, The Book of Esther, The Book of Job, The Psalms, The Proverbs, Ecclesiastes or the Preacher, Cantica or Songs of Solomon, Four Prophets the Greater, Twelve Prophets the Less. All the books of the New Testament, as they are commonly received, we do receive and account canonical.	**Article IV—The Holy Bible** We believe the Holy Bible, Old and New Testaments, reveals the Word of God so far as it is necessary for our salvation. It is to be received through the Holy Spirit as the true rule and guide for faith and practice. Whatever is not revealed in or established by the Holy Scriptures is not to be made an article of faith nor is it to be taught as essential to salvation.

EUB Confession of Faith—Original Order	Methodist Articles of Religion—Original Order	EUB Confession of Faith—Revised Order
Article VI—The Sacraments We believe the Sacraments, ordained by Christ, are symbols and pledges of the Christian's profession and of God's love toward us. They are means of grace by which God works invisibly in us, quickening, strengthening and confirming our faith in him. Two Sacraments are ordained by Christ our Lord, namely Baptism and the Lord's Supper. We believe Baptism signifies entrance into the household of faith, and is a symbol of repentance and inner cleansing from sin, a representation of the new birth in Christ Jesus and a mark of Christian discipleship. We believe children are under the atonement of Christ and as heirs of the Kingdom of God are acceptable subjects for Christian Baptism. Children of believing parents through Baptism become the special responsibility of the Church. They should be nurtured and led to personal acceptance of Christ, and by profession of faith confirm their Baptism. We believe the Lord's Supper is a representation of our redemption, a memorial of the sufferings and death of Christ, and a token of love and union which Christians have with Christ and with one another. Those who rightly, worthily and in faith eat the broken bread and drink the blessed cup partake of the body and blood of Christ in a spiritual manner until he comes.	**Article VI—Of the Old Testament** The Old Testament is not contrary to the New; for both in the Old and New Testament everlasting life is offered to mankind by Christ, who is the only Mediator between God and man, being both God and Man. Wherefore they are not to be heard who feign that the old fathers did look only for transitory promises. Although the law given from God by Moses as touching ceremonies and rites doth not bind Christians, nor ought the civil precepts thereof of necessity be received in any commonwealth; yet notwithstanding, no Christian whatsoever is free from the obedience of the commandments which are called moral.	

EUB Confession of Faith—Original Order	Methodist Articles of Religion—Original Order	EUB Confession of Faith—Revised Order
Article VII—Sin and Free Will We believe man is fallen from righteousness and, apart from the grace of our Lord Jesus Christ, is destitute of holiness and inclined to evil. Except a man be born again, he cannot see the Kingdom of God. In his own strength, without divine grace, man cannot do good works pleasing and acceptable to God. We believe, however, man influenced and empowered by the Holy Spirit is responsible in freedom to exercise his will for good.	**Article VII—Of Original or Birth Sin** Original sin standeth not in the following of Adam (as the Pelagians do vainly talk), but it is the corruption of the nature of every man, that naturally is engendered of the offspring of Adam, whereby man is very far gone from original righteousness, and of his own nature inclined to evil, and that continually.	*Article VII—Sin and Free Will, Part I* We believe man is fallen from righteousness and, apart from the grace of our Lord Jesus Christ, is destitute of holiness and inclined to evil. Except a man be born again, he cannot see the Kingdom of God.
Article VIII—Reconciliation through Christ We believe God was in Christ reconciling the world to himself. The offering Christ freely made on the cross is the perfect and sufficient sacrifice for the sins of the whole world, redeeming man from all sin, so that no other satisfaction is required.	**Article VIII—Of Free Will** The condition of man after the fall of Adam is such that he cannot turn and prepare himself, by his own natural strength and works, to faith, and calling upon God; wherefore we have no power to do good works, pleasant and acceptable to God, without the grace of God by Christ preventing us, that we may have a good will, and working with us, when we have that good will.	*Article VII—Sin and Free Will, Part II* In his own strength, without divine grace, man cannot do good works pleasing and acceptable to God. We believe, however, man influenced and empowered by the Holy Spirit is responsible in freedom to exercise his will for good.

EUB Confession of Faith—Original Order	Methodist Articles of Religion—Original Order	EUB Confession of Faith—Revised Order
Article IX—Justification and Regeneration We believe we are never accounted righteous before God through our works or merit, but that penitent sinners are justified or accounted righteous before God only by faith in our Lord Jesus Christ. We believe regeneration is the renewal of man in righteousness through Jesus Christ, by the power of the Holy Spirit, whereby we are made partakers of the divine nature and experience newness of life. By this new birth the believer becomes reconciled to God and is enabled to serve him with the will and the affections. We believe, although we have experienced regeneration, it is possible to depart from grace and fall into sin; and we may even then, by the grace of God, be renewed in righteousness. **Article X—Good Works** We believe good works are the necessary fruits of faith and follow regeneration but they do not have the virtue to remove our sins or to avert divine judgment. We believe good works, pleasing and acceptable to God in Christ, spring from a true and living faith, for through and by them faith is made evident.	**Article IX—Of the Justification of Man** We are accounted righteous before God only for the merit of our Lord and Saviour Jesus Christ, by faith, and not for our own works or deservings. Wherefore, that we are justified by faith, only, is a most wholesome doctrine, and very full of comfort. **Article X—Of Good Works** Although good works, which are the fruits of faith, and follow after justification, cannot put away our sins, and endure the severity of God's judgment; yet are they pleasing and acceptable to God in Christ, and spring out of a true and lively faith, insomuch that by them a lively faith may be as evidently known as a tree is discerned by its fruit.	**Article IX—Justification and Regeneration** We believe we are never accounted righteous before God through our works or merit, but that penitent sinners are justified or accounted righteous before God only by faith in our Lord Jesus Christ. We believe regeneration is the renewal of man in righteousness through Jesus Christ, by the power of the Holy Spirit, whereby we are made partakers of the divine nature and experience newness of life. By this new birth the believer becomes reconciled to God and is enabled to serve him with the will and the affections. We believe, although we have experienced regeneration, it is possible to depart from grace and fall into sin; and we may even then, by the grace of God, be renewed in righteousness. **Article X—Good Works** We believe good works are the necessary fruits of faith and follow regeneration but they do not have the virtue to remove our sins or to avert divine judgment. We believe good works, pleasing and acceptable to God in Christ, spring from a true and living faith, for through and by them faith is made evident.

EUB Confession of Faith—Original Order	Methodist Articles of Religion—Original Order	EUB Confession of Faith—Revised Order
Article XI—Sanctification and Christian Perfection *We believe sanctification is the work of God's grace through the Word and the Spirit, by which those who have been born again are cleansed from sin in their thoughts, words and acts, and are enabled to live in accordance with God's will, and to strive for holiness without which no one will see the Lord. Entire sanctification is a state of perfect love, righteousness and true holiness which every regenerate believer may obtain by being delivered from the power of sin, by loving God with all the heart, soul, mind and strength, and by loving one's neighbor as one's self. Through faith in Jesus Christ this gracious gift may be received in this life both gradually and instantaneously, and should be sought earnestly by every child of God. We believe this experience does not deliver us from the infirmities, ignorance, and mistakes common to man, nor from the possibilities of further sin. The Christian must continue on guard against spiritual pride and seek to gain victory over every temptation to sin. He must respond wholly to the will of God so that sin will lose its power over him; and the world, the flesh, and the devil are put under his feet. Thus he rules over these enemies with watchfulness through the power of the Holy Spirit.*	**Article XI—Of Works of Supererogation** <u>Voluntary works—besides, over and above God's commandments—which they call works of supererogation, cannot be taught without arrogancy and impiety. For by them men do declare that they do not only render unto God as much as they are bound to do, but that they do more for his sake than of bounden duty is required; whereas Christ saith plainly: When you have done all that is commanded you, say, We are unprofitable servants.</u>	

EUB Confession of Faith—Original Order	Methodist Articles of Religion—Original Order	EUB Confession of Faith—Revised Order
Article XII—The Judgment and the Future State We believe all men stand under the righteous judgment of Jesus Christ, both now and in the last day. We believe in the resurrection of the dead; the righteous to life eternal and the wicked to endless condemnation.	**Article XII—Of Sin after Justification** <u>Not every sin willingly committed after justification is the sin against the Holy Ghost, and unpardonable. Wherefore, the grant of repentance is not to be denied to such as fall into sin after justification. After we have received the Holy Ghost, we may depart from grace given, and fall into sin, and, by the grace of God, rise again and amend our lives. And therefore they are to be condemned who say they can no more sin as long as they live here; or deny the place of forgiveness to such as truly repent.</u>	
Article XIII—Public Worship We believe divine worship is the duty and privilege of man who, in the presence of God, bows in adoration, humility and dedication. We believe divine worship is essential to the life of the Church, and that the assembling of the people of God for such worship is necessary to Christian fellowship and spiritual growth. We believe the order of public worship need not be the same in all places but may be modified by the church according to circumstances and the needs of men. It should be in a language and form understood by the people, consistent with the Holy Scriptures to the edification of all, and in accordance with the order and Discipline of the Church.	**Article XIII—Of the Church** The visible church of Christ is a congregation of faithful men in which the pure Word of God is preached, and the Sacraments duly administered according to Christ's ordinance, in all those things that of necessity are requisite to the same.	**Article V—The Church** We believe the Christian Church is the community of all true believers under the Lordship of Christ. We believe it is one, holy, apostolic and catholic. It is the redemptive fellowship in which the Word of God is preached by men divinely called, and the sacraments are duly administered according to Christ's own appointment. Under the discipline of the Holy Spirit the Church exists for the maintenance of worship, the edification of believers and the redemption of the world.

EUB Confession of Faith—Original Order	Methodist Articles of Religion—Original Order	EUB Confession of Faith—Revised Order
Article XIV—The Lord's Day *We believe the Lord's Day is divinely ordained for private and public worship, for rest from unnecessary work, and should be devoted to spiritual improvement, Christian fellowship and service. It is commemorative of our Lord's resurrection and is an emblem of our eternal rest. It is essential to the permanence and growth of the Christian Church, and important to the welfare of the civil community.*	**Article XIV—Of Purgatory** <u>The Romish doctrine concerning purgatory, pardon, worshiping, and adoration, as well of images as of relics, and also invocation of saints, is a fond thing, vainly invented, and grounded upon no warrant of Scripture, but repugnant to the Word of God.</u>	
Article XV—The Christian and Property We believe God is the owner of all things and that the individual holding of property is lawful and is a sacred trust under God. Private property is to be used for the manifestation of Christian love and liberality, and to support the Church's mission in the world. All forms of property, whether private, corporate or public, are to be held in solemn trust and used responsibly for human good under the sovereignty of God.	**Article XV—Of Speaking in the Congregation in Such a Tongue as the People Understand** <u>It is a thing plainly repugnant to the Word of God, and the custom of the primitive church, to have public prayer in the church, or to minister the Sacraments, in a tongue not understood by the people.</u>	

EUB Confession of Faith—Original Order	Methodist Articles of Religion—Original Order	EUB Confession of Faith—Revised Order
Article XVI—Civil Government We believe civil government derives its just powers from the sovereign God. As Christians we recognize the governments under whose protection we reside and believe such governments should be based on, and be responsible for, the recognition of human rights under God. We believe war and bloodshed are contrary to the gospel and spirit of Christ. We believe it is the duty of Christian citizens to give moral strength and purpose to their respective governments through sober, righteous and godly living.	**Article XVI—Of the Sacraments** Sacraments ordained of Christ are not only badges or tokens of Christian men's profession, but rather they are certain signs of grace, and God's good will toward us, by which he doth work invisibly in us, and doth not only quicken, but also strengthen and confirm, our faith in him. There are two Sacraments ordained of Christ our Lord in the Gospel; that is to say, Baptism and the Supper of the Lord. Those five commonly called sacraments, that is to say, confirmation, penance, orders, matrimony, and extreme unction, are not to be counted for Sacraments of the Gospel; being such as have partly grown out of the corrupt following of the apostles, and partly are states of life allowed in the Scriptures, but yet have not the like nature of Baptism and the Lord's Supper, because they have not any visible sign or ceremony ordained of God. The Sacraments were not ordained of Christ to be gazed upon, or to be carried about; but that we should duly use them. And in such only as worthily receive the same, they have a wholesome effect or operation; but they that receive them unworthily, purchase to themselves condemnation, as St. Paul saith.	*Article VI—The Sacraments, Part I* We believe the Sacraments, ordained by Christ, are symbols and pledges of the Christian's profession and of God's love toward us. They are means of grace by which God works invisibly in us, quickening, strengthening and confirming our faith in him. Two Sacraments are ordained by Christ our Lord, namely Baptism and the Lord's Supper.

EUB Confession of Faith—Original Order	Methodist Articles of Religion—Original Order	EUB Confession of Faith—Revised Order
	Article XVII—Of Baptism Baptism is not only a sign of profession and mark of difference whereby Christians are distinguished from others that are not baptized; but it is also a sign of regeneration or the new birth. The Baptism of young children is to be retained in the Church. **Article XVIII—Of the Lord's Supper** The Supper of the Lord is not only a sign of the love that Christians ought to have among themselves one to another, but rather is a sacrament of our redemption by Christ's death; insomuch that, to such as rightly, worthily, and with faith receive the same, the bread which we break is a partaking of the body of Christ; and likewise the cup of blessing is a partaking of the blood of Christ. Transubstantiation, or the change of the substance of bread and wine in the Supper of our Lord, cannot be proved by Holy Writ, but is repugnant to the plain words of Scripture, overthroweth the nature of a sacrament, and hath given occasion to many superstitions. The body of Christ is given, taken, and eaten in the Supper, only after a heavenly and spiritual manner. And the mean whereby the body of Christ is received and eaten in the Supper is faith. The Sacrament of the Lord's Supper was not by Christ's ordinance reserved, carried about, lifted up, or worshiped.	***Article VI—The Sacraments, Part II*** We believe Baptism signifies entrance into the household of faith, and is a symbol of repentance and inner cleansing from sin, a representation of the new birth in Christ Jesus and a mark of Christian discipleship. We believe children are under the atonement of Christ and as heirs of the Kingdom of God are acceptable subjects for Christian Baptism. Children of believing parents through Baptism become the special responsibility of the Church. They should be nurtured and led to personal acceptance of Christ, and by profession of faith confirm their Baptism. ***Article VI—The Sacraments, Part III*** We believe the Lord's Supper is a representation of our redemption, a memorial of the sufferings and death of Christ, and a token of love and union which Christians have with Christ and with one another. Those who rightly, worthily and in faith eat the broken bread and drink the blessed cup partake of the body and blood of Christ in a spiritual manner until he comes.

EUB Confession of Faith—Original Order	Methodist Articles of Religion—Original Order	EUB Confession of Faith—Revised Order
	Article XIX—Of Both Kinds The cup of the Lord is not to be denied to the lay people; for both the parts of the Lord's Supper, by Christ's ordinance and commandment, ought to be administered to all Christians alike.	
	Article XX—Of the One Oblation of Christ, Finished upon the Cross The offering of Christ, once made, is that perfect redemption, propitiation, and satisfaction for all the sins of the whole world, both original and actual; and there is none other satisfaction for sin but that alone. Wherefore the sacrifice of masses, in the which it is commonly said that the priest doth offer Christ for the quick and the dead, to have remission of pain or guilt, is a blasphemous fable and dangerous deceit.	**Article VIII—Reconciliation through Christ** We believe God was in Christ reconciling the world to himself. The offering Christ freely made on the cross is the perfect and sufficient sacrifice for the sins of the whole world, redeeming man from all sin, so that no other satisfaction is required.
	Article XXI—Of the Marriage of Ministers The ministers of Christ are not commanded by God's law either to vow the estate of single life, or to abstain from marriage; therefore it is lawful for them, as for all other Christians, to marry at their own discretion, as they shall judge the same to serve best to godliness.	

EUB Confession of Faith—Original Order	Methodist Articles of Religion—Original Order	EUB Confession of Faith—Revised Order
	Article XXII—Of the Rites and Ceremonies of Churches It is not necessary that rites and ceremonies should in all places be the same, or exactly alike; for they have been always different, and may be changed according to the diversity of countries, times, and men's manners, so that nothing be ordained against God's Word. Whosoever, through his private judgment, willingly and purposely doth openly break the rites and ceremonies of the church to which he belongs, which are not repugnant to the Word of God, and are ordained and approved by common authority, ought to be rebuked openly, that others may fear to do the like, as one that offendeth against the common order of the church, and woundeth the consciences of weak brethren. Every particular church may ordain, change, or abolish rites and ceremonies, so that all things may be done to edification.	
	Article XXIII—Of the Rulers of the United States of America The President, the Congress, the general assemblies, the governors, and the councils of state, as the delegates of the people, are the rulers of the United States of America, according to the division of power made to them by the Constitution of the United States and by the constitutions of their respective states. And the said states are a sovereign and independent nation, and ought not to be subject to any foreign jurisdiction.	**Article XVI—Civil Government** We believe civil government derives its just powers from the sovereign God. As Christians we recognize the governments under whose protection we reside and believe such governments should be based on, and be responsible for, the recognition of human rights under God. We believe war and bloodshed are contrary to the gospel and spirit of Christ. We believe it is the duty of Christian citizens to give moral strength and purpose to their respective governments through sober, righteous and godly living.

EUB Confession of Faith—Original Order	Methodist Articles of Religion—Original Order	EUB Confession of Faith—Revised Order
	Article XXIV—Of Christian Men's Goods The riches and goods of Christians are not common as touching the right, title, and possession of the same, as some do falsely boast. Notwithstanding, every man ought, of such things as he possesseth, liberally to give alms to the poor, according to his ability.	**Article XV—The Christian and Property** We believe God is the owner of all things and that the individual holding of property is lawful and is a sacred trust under God. Private property is to be used for the manifestation of Christian love and liberality, and to support the Church's mission in the world. All forms of property, whether private, corporate or public, are to be held in solemn trust and used responsibly for human good under the sovereignty of God.
	Article XXV—Of a Christian Man's Oath <u>As we confess that vain and rash swearing is forbidden Christian men by our Lord Jesus Christ and James his apostle, so we judge that the Christian religion doth not prohibit, but that a man may swear when the magistrate requireth, in a cause of faith and charity, so it be done according to the prophet's teaching, in justice, judgment, and truth.</u>	

THEOLOGICAL COMMENTARY

Now that we have the CF and the AR before us, the time has come to examine the theological contents of the CF. Along the way, I will note differences between the CF and the AR, most notably when the CF adds something theologically substantial to the AR. I will conclude by noting the most striking theological differences between the CF and the AR.

Article I—God

Several things stand out in the CF article on God. First, there is a list of divine attributes. The CF describes God as one, holy, and alive. It also declares that God is infinite in power, wisdom, justice, goodness, and love. Second, there is an emphasis here on the gracious character of God's dealings with human persons. Thus we confess our faith in a God who governs the world with a view toward the well-being and salvation of human persons. Third, the CF calls attention to the trinitarian nature of divine revelation. God reveals God's self as Father, Son, and Holy Spirit. Fourth and finally, the CF emphasizes divine power. Thus, early on there is mention of the infinite nature of divine power, and the article ends with a declaration that all three divine persons are eternal not only in essence but also in power.

Generally speaking, the CF's statement on God mirrors the statement in the AR. What is unique to the CF is not the divine attributes or the emphasis on power. Nor is it the emphasis on the Trinity. Rather, what is unique here is the emphasis on God's gracious dealings with human persons—on divine concern for the well-being of people! This emphasis on divine grace and concern for persons is noticeably absent from the AR's statement on God.

Article II—Jesus Christ

Following our confession of faith in a triune God who is graciously disposed toward human persons, the CF directs our attention to Jesus Christ. Essentially Chalcedonian in outlook, it stresses the divinity and humanity of Jesus Christ, as well as the perfect union of the two natures. This Chalcedonian note is followed immediately by Nicaean language. Thus the CF emphasizes that the Son is both eternal and begotten of the Father, and that he was born of the Virgin Mary by the power of the Holy Spirit. It then provides a thumbnail sketch of the life, death, resurrection, ascension, and second coming of Jesus, stressing that he is Savior and Mediator and that he intercedes *for us*. Finally, there is a reminder that all persons will be judged by Christ.

One crucial difference between the statement on Jesus Christ in the CF and the statement in the AR is worth noting. The CF includes a reference to the Holy Spirit that, maximally interpreted, can be taken to mean that the whole of Christ's life was undertaken in the power of the Holy Spirit. In the AR's statement on Jesus Christ, there is no mention of the Holy Spirit.

Article III—The Holy Spirit

The article on the Holy Spirit in the CF is significantly more robust than the statement on the Holy Spirit in the AR. Like the AR, the CF includes the filioque clause, indicating that the Spirit proceeds from the Father *and* the Son. However, the AR are content to stress the fullness of the Spirit's divinity and the manner of the Spirit's relationship to the Son and the Father. The CF, by contrast, goes on to discuss the work of the Spirit. Thus the CF reminds us that the Spirit convicts the world of sin, of righteousness, and of judgment. Moreover, it declares that the Spirit leads people through faithful response to the gospel *into the fellowship of the Church*. The Spirit also comforts, empowers, and guides the faithful into all truth.

This is a tremendous account of the workings of the Holy Spirit. It shows that the Christian life is from beginning to end a matter of the presence and work of the Spirit. Most important, it stresses that, to the extent that it is the work of the Spirit, the Christian life is a life of fellowship in the church. In the CF, the Spirit draws Christians together in the body of Christ. Thus there is a close linkage between pneumatology and ecclesiology that is absent in the AR!

Article IV—The Holy Bible

Like the AR, the CF next turns to Scripture. The CF stresses that the Scriptures contain what is necessary for our salvation. Thus the CF presents Scripture as a means of grace by which we come to know and love God. The most important thing to note, however, is the emphasis on the Holy Spirit. The Scriptures are to be received *through the Holy Spirit*. If I may be allowed an interpretive gloss here, I would suggest that the Scriptures are only of saving significance when they are so received.

Interestingly enough, the article on Scripture in the AR includes no reference to the Holy Spirit. By contrast, the Evangelical United Brethren appear incapable of writing a single statement in their CF without at least some reference to the Holy Spirit!

Article V—The Church

Until this point, as noted above, the CF and the AR mirror each other in their ordering. Both move from the Trinity to Christology to pneumatology and then to an article on Scripture (the AR actually have three articles on Scripture). Following the article on Scripture, the ordering of the CF departs significantly from the ordering of the AR. After the articles on Scripture, the AR proceed directly to matters related to the doctrine of the Christian life, including articles on original sin, free will, justification, good works, works of supererogation, and sin after justification. Only then do the AR take up the doctrine of the church. Thus six articles stand between the doctrine of God and the doctrine of Scripture on the one hand and the doctrine of the church on the other in the AR.

By contrast, the CF moves from the doctrine of God and the doctrine of Scripture directly to the doctrine of the church (Article V) and of the sacraments (Article VI). Only then does the CF take up the doctrine of the Christian life, including sin and free will, reconciliation through Christ, justification and regeneration, good works, and sanctification and Christian perfection. The resulting impression is that, in the CF, the Christian life is something that happens within the church and by means of the sacraments. In the CF the church and the sacraments literally precede the Christian life. In the AR the church and the sacraments come after the Christian life, leaving room for the impression that the church and the sacraments are incidental to salvation.[5]

The difference in the ordering of doctrinal material related to the church and to salvation in the CF and the AR raises at least one crucial theological question: Where do United Methodists stand with regard to the theological axiom *extra Ecclesium nulla salus* (outside the church, there is no salvation)? Neither organizational pattern would seem to require adherence to this theological axiom, especially if it is understood to mean that there is no hope of salvation apart from participation in the church and its sacraments. However, whereas the ordering of the AR can make the church appear *incidental* to salvation, the ordering of the CF suggests that the church is *instrumental* to salvation. To be sure, there is a rich theological discussion to be had here, but that only strengthens the case that we stand to benefit from careful reflection on the two doctrinal statements of The United Methodist Church.

In addition to differences in ordering, there are important content differences between the two statements on the church. The CF enhances United Methodism's doctrinal standard on the church in two important ways. On the one hand, the CF adds the Nicene marks of the church, according to which the church is one, holy, apostolic, and catholic. By contrast, the AR limit the marks of the church to the right preaching of the Word and the due administration of the sacrament (the classical Protestant marks, which are also included in the CF's statement on the church). On the other hand, the CF stresses the relationship of the Holy Spirit to the church, saying, "Under the discipline of the Holy Spirit the Church exists for the maintenance of worship, the edification of believers and the redemption of the world." Thus, while the CF's statement on the Spirit (Article III) points to the church, its statement on the church (Article V) points back to the Holy Spirit, making clear the intimate relationship between the two.

Article VI—The Sacraments

Generally speaking, the statement on the sacraments in the CF mirrors the statement in the AR. For example, both stress that the sacraments are outward signs of inward grace, both stress two sacraments (baptism and the Lord's Supper), both allow for and encourage infant baptism, and both offer a memorialist view of the Lord's Supper. What then does the CF add to the doctrinal standards of United Methodism? The addition is a subtle but important one. The AR indicate that baptism differentiates Christians from other folk. Yet the differentiation that baptism signifies has clearly to do with the baptized's status as regenerate. By contrast, the CF stresses that baptism signifies "entrance into the household of faith." In other words, baptism does not simply have to do with personal regeneration. It also has to with incorporation into the life of the church. Thus it is not just in the ordering of the CF that we can see an emphasis on the church—it is also in the content of the articles on the Holy Spirit and the sacraments. In these ways, the church features more prominently in the CF than it does in the AR.

Article VII—Sin and Free Will

In its article on sin and free will, the CF adds two crucial things to the doctrinal standards of United Methodism. First, there is the addition of the term *holiness*. Missing from the AR statement on sin, the emphasis on holiness anticipates the statement on sanctification and Christian perfection ahead. I will say more about this when we get to that statement. The second and more significant addition has to do, once again (!), with the emphasis on the Holy Spirit. In the AR, there is no mention of the Holy Spirit in connection with sin and free will. By contrast, the CF stresses that it is only as we are influenced and empowered by the Holy Spirit that we can be responsible freely to exercise our will for good!

Article VIII—Reconciliation through Christ

The interesting thing about this article is that it appears to enshrine a particular understanding of the atonement at the level of the doctrinal standards of United Methodism. The AR's statement on Jesus Christ uses the language of sacrifice in connection with Christ's death, and the language of sacrifice is present here too. Thus Christ is said to be the perfect and sufficient sacrifice for the sins of the whole world. What is new is the term *satisfaction*. By introducing this term, the CF appears to advocate for a satisfaction theory of the atonement. To be sure, the statement falls well short of a theory. Nonetheless, it surely orients our understanding in that direction. In the current climate, this may be unfashionable, if not downright reprehensible, to some, as it purportedly implies a wrathful deity. For now, I will leave this matter in midair, saying only that the rejection of the language of sacrifice and satisfaction reflects a poor understanding of the metaphorical nature of atonement language as well as a failure to think about the subjective and doxological dimensions of the issue.[6]

Article IX—Justification and Regeneration

In its statement on justification and regeneration, the CF adds significantly to the statement on justification in the AR. Not surprisingly, the crucial addition has to do with the person and work of the Holy Spirit. Whereas there is no mention of the Holy Spirit in the statement in the AR, the Holy Spirit is central to the statement in the CF. Regeneration is through Jesus Christ, but it happens by the power of the Holy Spirit. Most interesting here is the language "partakers of the divine nature"—for here we have to do with the language of theosis or divinization. In regeneration, the Holy Spirit makes us like God. We are reconciled to God, and we are enabled to love and to serve God with the will and the affections.

Article X—Good Works

The article on good works is virtually identical to the statement in the AR. Here we can see most clearly the influence of the AR on predecessor confessional statements of the Evangelical United Brethren. Suffice it to say, the Evangelical United Brethren clearly expected that good works would follow true faith.

Article XI—Sanctification and Christian Perfection

With the article on sanctification and perfection, we come to what is quite obviously the most significant addition to the Methodist standards of doctrine. It is interesting that, until the incorporation of the Evangelical United Brethren Confession of Faith, The Methodist Church lacked a doctrinal standard for what John Wesley once called the *Grand Depositum*—the very purpose for which God raised up the people called Methodists! And what a fascinating and instructive standard it is! Indeed, four important aspects of the statement deserve to be highlighted. First, the CF sets the bar high. Sanctification involves a cleansing of sin in thought, word, and deed. Second, the CF makes it clear that entire sanctification as perfect love for God and neighbor is something that "every regenerate believer" may obtain "in this life." Third, the CF emphasizes that entire sanctification is a gift that may be received both gradually and instantaneously. Fourth and finally, the victory over enemies obtained in entire sanctification occurs in and through the power of the Holy Spirit!

Article XII—The Judgment and the Future State

This is a fascinating addition to the Methodist standards of doctrine insofar as it would appear to commit us to the currently rather unfashionable doctrine of eternal damnation. To be sure, it does not positively exclude the possibility that all might be saved, but it clearly implies that at least some will be deemed wicked and judged accordingly. Although some Methodists today may reject this view, we must recognize that it is consistent with much ecumenical Christian teaching across the centuries. The real challenge here is to think anew and afresh about how even this doctrine might be salutary.

Article XIII—Public Worship

I want quickly to highlight three features of this article. First, the emphasis on proper dispositions for worship is one that would resonate with John Wesley and is sorely needed in many quarters of United Methodism today. Worship is to be done in adoration, humility, and dedication. Second, we once again see the centrality of the life of the church in the CF—worship in the church is here deemed essential to fellowship and spiritual growth. Third, there is a delicate balance struck between the need for order and discipline in worship and the need for flexibility and creativity. This last point reflects a hard-won wisdom in the Evangelical United Brethren tradition!

Article XIV—The Lord's Day

In Article XIV, the Evangelical United Brethren were ahead of the curve. In recent years, there has been a growing concern to recover a more robust notion of Sabbath rest. Numerous Christian theologians have been advocating for the rediscovery of the true meaning of Sabbath.[7] We are, they tell us, overworked, overstressed, overcommitted, and overly tired. We are addicted to being consumers, to getting ahead, and to being entertained. We have forgotten what it means to take our rest and our joy in God.

Surely this article has something to say to United Methodists today!

Article XV—The Christian and Property

For United Methodists living in North America, this article in the CF ought to be particularly challenging. After all, many Americans regard private property as a right rather than a responsibility. Yet if we would take the CF seriously, we would have to begin to think creatively about what it might mean to use private property for "the manifestation of Christian love and liberality" and in support of "the Church's mission in the world." Once again, the CF appears to go out of its way to make the individual Christian with all of her rights and concerns subordinate to the church into which she has been baptized and in which she has come to know and to love God and her neighbor as herself!

Article XVI—Civil Government

In recent years, many Methodists in the United States of America have found themselves at odds with one another over the justifiability of war. Unlike the AR, the CF goes out of its way to speak directly to this issue in its statement on civil government, saying, "We believe war and bloodshed are contrary to the gospel and spirit of Christ." Although this may not resolve the issue of whether war is ever justifiable, it ought to give United Methodists who take seriously their standards of doctrine pause over the matter. Surely it is neither a light nor an easy thing to engage in or support activity that one's church has deemed "contrary to the gospel and spirit of Christ"!

Conclusion

By now, the careful reader will have noticed one thing above all about the CF as compared to the AR. Whatever other theological contribution the CF might make to United Methodist standards of doctrine, it infuses them from beginning to end with a very robust pneumatology. Indeed, eight out of sixteen articles in the CF include references to the Holy Spirit. By contrast, only three out of the twenty-five AR do so. The weight given to the person and work of the Holy Spirit in the CF by comparison with the AR is truly stunning. Given this weighting of pneumatology, it is hardly surprising that the Evangelical United Brethren Confession of Faith also exhibits a rather robust ecclesiology. There is, after all, the most intimate connection in Christian theology and the Christian Scriptures between the work of the Holy Spirit and the life of the church. One can only wonder what difference it might make if United Methodists would put the CF to work in their worship and church membership classes—if they would teach it to their adults and their children and confess it together in a spirit of repentance and thanksgiving to God.

PART THREE
Polity and Practices

CHAPTER 8

EPISCOPACY AND ORDINATION

James E. Kirby

In attendance at the first General Conference of the organizing Evangelical United Brethren was a fraternal delegate from The Methodist Church, Bishop G. Bromley Oxnam. At the meeting he declared that "he had been authorized by the Board of Bishops of the Methodist Church to state that if at any time after we had come far enough in our own union that we would care to open negotiations with them, they would be pleased to receive such overtures."[1] The fact that Oxnam spoke for the Methodists is significant. Oxnam was and had been the secretary of the Council of Bishops ever since its formation in 1940. He held that position for a total of sixteen years and upon retirement said that he thought he was giving up "the most powerful position in the Church." As secretary of the council, Oxnam continued in his office from quadrennium to quadrennium while presidents of the council served a one-year term. Because of his personality and his office, Oxnam was responsible for setting the council agenda, which, on occasions, the president did not see until the council convened; he was largely responsible for appointing fraternal and denominational representatives to ecumenical and other gatherings, organizing committees, and the like.

I begin with what may seem trivial information because I am uncertain just how much substantial authority was behind Oxnam's offer. He was fully capable of going on his own, and I am frankly leery of the consensus behind his remarks. By 1958, the

Commission on Church Federation of the Evangelical United Brethren had been in conversation about union with several groups, including the Methodists. Out of these informal conversations, it was decided that the best opportunity was with the Methodists, and the talks became "formal" in nature. The subject of union with the Evangelical United Brethren came up during the 1960 meeting of the Council of Bishops. One of those present was William C. Martin, then presiding bishop of the Dallas–Fort Worth area, who noted the fact with a terse entry into his diary: "Question of union with the EUBs was discussed, but not much interest was expressed." Now, Martin had a lot on his plate at the time, and it would have taken a serious topic to get his attention. He was the second president of the National Council of Churches, and both the council and the Methodists had been in the eye of the storm of the anti-Communist crusade; racial issues were seriously troubling his church, his city, and the nation; and he had spent six months writing the Episcopal Address that he delivered at the 1960 General Conference in Denver. But there is no doubt in my mind that any serious talk about uniting with the Evangelical United Brethren was not high on Martin's agenda.

It is not the purpose of this chapter to reexamine the details of that union, but I am interested in the amount of capital that was brought to the table by the Evangelical United Brethren and how much bargaining power they had in the discussions leading up to 1968. When I moved to Drew in 1976, I was quickly told that I should not forget that we were The "United" Methodist Church and almost as quickly informed that some former Evangelical United Brethren members thought the results of the merger were little more than "United" in the name of the new body and a few hymns in the hymnal.

We are all aware that the developments of Methodism, the United Brethren in Christ, and The Evangelical Association were concurrent and in many ways parallel. The Methodist Episcopal Church was organized into an independent denomination in 1784; the followers of Otterbein and Boehm met for the first time in conference in 1800; Asbury and Otterbein were friends; Otterbein took part in Asbury's ordination and Boehm's son became a Methodist and a traveling companion of Asbury. Boehm and his family even allowed a Methodist chapel to be built on their property. In 1810 formal arrangements were made allowing Methodists and United Brethren to share buildings and class meetings, and even then there was talk of formal union. Jacob Albright joined a Methodist class meeting after the tragic deaths of his children in 1790 and decided to preach six years later. Albright's People consisted of three classes organized and modeled on the Methodist class meeting. In 1807, when they were uncertain whether they could continue, they renamed themselves the Newly Formed Methodist Conference, and "at the suggestion of Albright they adopted an episcopal form of church government" like that of the Methodists.[2] Reuben Yeakel in his *Life of Albright* says, "It is clear from the fact that in doctrine and usage the conference was Methodistical, that they had a Methodistical conception of the word bishop."[3] I wonder if Albright, had he lived to serve in the episcopal office to which he had been elected, would have modeled his episcopal direction after Asbury and provided the kind of direction that would have led to a strong itinerancy. The fact that The Evangelical Association did not elect another bishop until 1839 is testimony to the fact that most appear not to have favored such a form of church government. The obvious question is why these closely associated groups were not united before 1968. The common wisdom is that language kept them separate. Raymond Albright says that "the language barrier was the only reason Albright's People did not unite with the Methodists."[4] That explanation, though logical and with some merit, is far too simple to be completely satisfactory. We know, for example, that although German-speaking persons were not the first priority for Asbury's Methodists, there were German-speaking Methodist congregations with German-speaking leaders. It is also significant that the first *Discipline of The Evangelical Church* was based on the one used by these German-speaking Methodists. Asbury himself gave another answer to the question. He noted first that none of the German groups had "a master-spirit to rise up and organize and lead them." But that was not his most serious reservation about them. He said that all of the ministers "located" and "only added to their charge partial traveling labors." Both the Brethren and The Evangelical Association lacked a viable itinerancy. Their preachers were largely independent, and Asbury questioned whether "a reformation in any country, or under any circumstances, can be perpetuated without a well-directed itinerancy."[5]

Only a strong central organization directed by a powerful leader could produce a "well-directed itinerancy." And he was convinced that no revival could be successful on the frontier without such an itinerancy. One advantage enjoyed by the Methodists on that frontier was that they had an unlimited supply of pastors who were part of an infinitely expandable organization with strong central control. Every pastor in every part of American Methodism was appointed once a year by Francis Asbury. When the Methodist Protestants organized in 1830, their failure to keep pace with The Methodist Episcopal Church in growth was attributed to their democratic organization.

Asbury's vision of the Methodist organization did not go untested. In 1792 a leading member of the Virginia Conference, James O'Kelly, lodged a formal protest against Asbury's powers in the form of a motion made at the first General Conference to allow persons who were not satisfied with their appointments to appeal them to the annual conference. After a lengthy debate, during which Asbury removed himself from the chair, they considered two important questions: "1st Shall the bishop appoint the preachers to the circuits? 2nd Shall a preacher be allowed an appeal?"[6] The answer given to the first was "Yes," and the second was defeated by a large majority. It was a resounding personal affirmation for Asbury and a resounding commitment to the system of itinerancy.

The General Conference of 1792 was significant for another reason—the office of presiding elder was formally recognized there. The office was not new, since there had been elders in charge of districts even before the church was organized in 1784. After 1784, presiding elders were extensions of episcopal power, and in 1812 they gained formal authority to participate in the appointment-making process when William McKendree, over Asbury's objections, organized them into cabinets. In the Methodist system they have always been appointed by and served at the pleasure of the bishop. That, too, has been challenged. From the time the office was created until 1828 there was at every General Conference an attempt to change the method of selecting presiding elders to elect them. It actually passed in the General Conference of 1820, but was declared unconstitutional and eventually rejected. In almost every instance it was defeated by a very narrow margin. The issue was one that divided the preachers almost equally. I frankly wonder why the measure failed to pass. Among those who urged it were leaders in the conference such as Ezekiel Cooper, Nathan Bangs, and Nicholas Sneathen. Election was certainly more in keeping with the spirit of the times than the method they chose to follow.

Both the United Brethren and Albright's People adopted more democratic forms of church government despite their close association with the Methodists, and they used the same terms to describe it. In 1814 John Dreisbach was elected to a four-year term and designated the "Presiding Elder." Albright says, "In practice he was really a bishop for at that time there was not a higher office than his in the Evangelical Church and no authority equal to that of the conference which elected him."[7] But he was elected and served a designated term. If he was not a bishop, there is no doubt that he was the "superintendent," "overseer," or *episcopé*. "Presiding elder" was the title given to six leaders of the church prior to Seybert's election as a bishop.

Episcopacy has been a troubling office in Methodism from the beginning. Asbury and the early Methodists said they understood *superintendent* and *bishop* to be synonymous terms. Wesley disavowed a belief in apostolic succession and described Coke and Asbury as "General Superintendents"; by that he meant "overseer of the whole." Asbury explained his later use of the word *bishop* as simply more "scriptural."

And here is where the problem begins. Wesley never left the Church of England. In nobody's mind, including his own, was John Wesley a bishop. Moreover, he said that he had not varied from the Church of England "in one article either of doctrine or discipline." And yet facing the necessity of enabling the Americans under his care to become an independent church, he assumed the power of a bishop and ordained Richard Whatcoat and Thomas Vasey. Thomas Coke, who was already an ordained presbyter, was "set apart" as an "overseer of the whole," a general superintendent. Following Wesley's lead, the Christmas Conference "set apart" Asbury to be a superintendent but described it in the *Discipline* as "ordination." A case can surely be made, as Frank Baker did, for Wesley's power as a superintendent. As Baker put it, "By his extraordinary call to found and rule the Methodist societies it had been demonstrated that in function [Wesley] was the equivalent of a scriptural bishop."[8] United Methodist bishops today are "consecrated" to an office, but they act just like bishops, and we have been living in that contradiction since September 1784. It has confused us, and it has certainly led to problems in our ecumenical relations. British Methodists are today struggling with that problem as they seek to return to the Church of England, and they do not even have bishops.

Since I began to work on this topic, I have been fascinated with the route that was taken by the Evangelical United Brethren and its antecedent bodies. Despite Methodist associations, the United Brethren elected only two bishops, Christian Newcomer (1813) and Andrew Zeller (1817). At the General Conference in 1825 they discontinued the ordination of bishops altogether. If episcopacy was truly an office, as they believed it was, there was no need for persons to receive additional ordination for it. The first *Discipline* of The Evangelical Association included a form of ordination for bishops that included the laying on of hands, a Methodist practice. When, however, the Articles of Faith were revised in 1830, the practice was discontinued. In the literal sense, The Evangelical Association in its entire history never conducted an episcopal ordination; Albright died before the first *Discipline* was adopted, and Seybert was not elected until long after the ordination of bishops had been discontinued. They, too, used the terms *general superintendent* and *bishop* synonymously. The pattern in both the United Brethren and The Evangelical Association was to limit the term of superintendents to four years and to allow the possibility of reelection to an additional term or terms. In the case of Seybert an exception was made to allow him to continue as a bishop for a total of five terms. And I would be so bold to suggest that if John Wesley, a presbyter, had come to the same conclusion, United Methodism would be better off today. Let me briefly explain what I mean.

Asbury, Whatcoat, and McKendree were "itinerant General Superintendents." They itinerated throughout the connection. After 1826 the episcopacy began a gradual march toward becoming localized. Despite an agreement to change locations halfway through the quadrennium, Hedding and George presided in conferences in the North and Northeast, and Soule and Roberts presided only in the southern conferences. This trend continued until the church had established official residences for its bishops and required them to live and work in specific areas. And through these years, the areas over which they presided became smaller until today's United Methodist bishop generally presides over an area that consists of one annual conference. And not infrequently that area encompasses an entire state. In my jurisdiction, Oklahoma, Arkansas, Missouri, Louisiana, and Nebraska have only one annual conference, and Kansas is moving rapidly to join them. Despite the fact that United Methodist bishops are elected for life, we have created a variety of term episcopacy. That was accomplished simply by enacting a mandatory age for retirement and being sure that persons being considered for election were old enough to be able to serve no more than three quadrenniums. That means that persons on the average being elected to the episcopacy today are in their early fifties. It will be interesting to see what effect the slight increase in retirement age will have on the average age of persons elected in the next quadrennium. United Methodism has a form of diocesan episcopacy despite its continued adherence to the Third Restrictive Rule in the constitution that guarantees an "itinerant, general superintendency."

When the Evangelical United Brethren united with The Methodist Church in 1968, few doctrinal issues had to be solved. Maybe that was because Albert Outler had little interest in the whole enterprise. The Confession of Faith was accepted as close enough for Methodist government work. We chose to ignore doctrinal issues even though Methodism came from the English Reformation, the United Brethren from the Anabaptist wing of the continental Reformation, and The Evangelical Association from the Lutherans. But there were significant differences in matters directly related to ministry that could not be ignored. The Evangelical United Brethren elected bishops in the General Conference for a four-year term of service (of the nineteen bishops who served the Evangelical United Brethren during its separate existence, only one failed to be elected to an additional term—he died), and the Methodists elected theirs in jurisdictional conferences for life. Both The Methodist Episcopal Church and The Methodist Episcopal Church, South had first elected bishops in the General Conference, and no single act changed the nature of Methodist episcopacy more than the creation of the jurisdictional system. But that is another story. The Evangelical United Brethren proposed that in the new denomination all bishops, including those in the Central Conferences, be elected to four-year terms. The Methodists rejected this out of hand but did agree that they would require "a review of the bishops at the end of each quadrennium by a Jurisdictional Committee on Episcopacy."[9] It is, I confess, hard for me to imagine that a serious review of episcopal practice could or would take place in such a gathering. The Evangelical United Brethren were gracious in allowing bishops to serve for life. Paul Washburn was elected to a four-year term in the Evangelical United Brethren General Conference on April 23, 1968, and the next day received life tenure in his office as a United Methodist.

There was also a difference in the method of electing delegates to the General Conference. Evangelical United Brethren practice was for lay and clerical delegates to vote together; the Methodists voted separately. But the real controversy came at the point of deciding how district superintendents would be chosen. The Evangelical United Brethren, as we have already noted, had a long-standing practice of choosing presiding elders by election in the annual conferences. It appears that a number of persons involved in the negotiations from the Evangelical United Brethren side hoped that a concession on the method of electing delegates to the General Conference and giving up term episcopacy might preserve their practice of electing district superintendents. The Methodists, however, had rejected the idea in 1828 and had no intention of overturning that decision. The matter was nonnegotiable. The members of the Joint Legislative Committee were "unanimous in stating the opinion that The Methodist Church would not be able to give in to, or even to compromise, the point."[10]

I grew up in a parsonage that belonged to The Methodist Episcopal Church, South. During the early years of my life, I and any of my "preacher's kid" friends would have been able to tell you that O. P. Clark, J. O. Haynes, and Clyde Long ran the Northwest Texas Conference. They were presiding elders who moved from one district to another and stayed in the office permanently. The bishop was an obscure figure who appeared at special occasions and held the annual conference. The presiding elders oversaw the real work of the conference. They were the episcopacy in our midst. If the bishop had been truly a presiding elder who had general oversight, we would have had the United Brethren system. The United Methodist Church system understands episcopacy more in terms of administration. And so it has become. A friend of mine was the nominee for the episcopacy from his annual conference four years ago. He asked the bishop if he could be with him for two or three days to see what bishops really do. After he discovered that most of the time spent with the bishop was in discussions with lawyers who were trying to prevent a farmer from opening a pig farm next to the conference camp, he went home and took his name off the list of candidates.

Real term episcopacy also has its merits. The fact that United Methodist Church bishops are elected for life also entitles them to attend and participate in the work of the Council of Bishops. They are not allowed to vote, but they have full membership and voice in its deliberations. Bishop Frank Smith, the first president of the council when it was organized in 1940, said they made a mistake in their decision. He said they should have allowed them to vote but not to talk. The council cannot meet in separate session from the retired bishops. And now its numbers have grown to around two hundred, most of whom are retired. Because it operates by consensus and it is difficult to get its business done with large numbers, there are now suggestions being made about how to limit that number (Bishop Nolan Harmon lived to be 104 and attended the council almost up until the time he died). Term episcopacy would allow bishops to return to their annual conferences at the end of their episcopal tenure and terminate their membership in the council.

The council is also seriously considering the merits of designating one of its members as a presiding bishop. When the idea was last proposed, the Judicial Council rejected it, but it is not dead. There is nobody who can speak for the church today except for the General Conference, and there is no way between its sessions for official statements to be issued. You may remember the controversy resulting from Bishop Sharon Brown Christopher's comments at the beginning of the Iraq War while president of the Council of Bishops. She did not have authority even to appear to speak for the church or the council.

The irony to which I point is now, I hope, obvious to all, especially to those who are most familiar with the practices of the Evangelical United Brethren tradition. It would seem to me that many of those practices either have been adopted in practice or would serve us well today in The United Methodist Church. The Evangelical United Brethren had little bargaining power when the merger took place more than forty years ago, but given the shape of today's church and the issues that it faces, perhaps the Evangelical United Brethren tradition is most relevant and can step forward to give us a new vision of how to lead United Methodism in the twenty-first century. It is time to abolish the jurisdictional system. It is no longer effective and is actively ignored in most of the church. Bishops could and should be elected in the General Conference. It would make the General Council on Finance and Administration happy by saving a lot of money. Lay and clergy delegates should vote together. To provide a time of transition, the lines of the old jurisdictions could be observed so that General Conference delegates from areas that now comprise the South Central Jurisdiction could vote for bishops needed by those areas. Once elected, however, they should be assigned by the Committee on Episcopacy of the General Conference and stationed where their talents and gifts are most needed. This was attempted in 1940 when it was proposed that Arthur J. Moore, a leading bishop of The Methodist Episcopal Church, South, become bishop of the Washington, D.C., area. The former Methodist Episcopal delegates rejected the idea out of hand. But today, who can see the logic of one of the only two Hispanic bishops in the entire church, twelve years ago, being sent to Nebraska? Episcopacy has evolved almost entirely into an administrative job, as it was conceived by the Evangelical United Brethren, and this has changed the understanding of the role and work of a district superintendent. Practically speaking, the situation is what it was during my childhood when the presiding elder was the bishop on the ground.

Most of the changes I would propose can be found in the tradition and practice of the United Brethren, The Evangelical Association, or the Evangelical United Brethren. Methodism has evolved from what it was in the days when the Asburian model prevailed. Despite the Third Restrictive Rule, we no longer have "itinerant General Superintendency." Would it be too much to think of reclaiming another part of our past as we look to the future of episcopacy?

CHAPTER 9

THE PRACTICE OF LITURGY AND SACRAMENTS IN THE EVANGELICAL UNITED BRETHREN TRADITION

Kendall Kane McCabe

As a former Methodist who grew up on the Del-Mar-Va Peninsula in the mid-twentieth century, I must confess to knowing nothing about The Evangelical United Brethren Church or its traditions until I went to Yale Divinity School in 1961, and there I was fortunate enough to meet the one EUB student in residence at that time. Little did we know that seven years later we would become part of The United Methodist Church. Since then, I have been welcomed into a former Evangelical United Brethren seminary and have spent almost thirty years exploring the history, particularly the liturgical history, of my adoptive siblings. I have discovered that there are many similarities between the churches who followed a more particularly English Wesleyan track and those whose point of departure was more specifically from German Pietist origins. What they perhaps most share in common is living within the tension created by the American frontier experience between adherence to classically formulated dogmas and formulas (orthodoxy) on the one hand and an enthusiastic response to an individualistic experiential religion (revivalism) on the other. For the purposes of this chapter, I would like to call attention to some differences and changes that occur in references to liturgy and the sacraments between the Evangelical United Brethren *Discipline* of 1967 (the year prior to the Evangelical United Brethren–Methodist merger), the 1868 *Discipline* of The Evangelical Association, and the 1869 *Discipline* of the United Brethren in Christ.

Before commenting on the printed matter, however, I want to remind the reader of the wide discrepancy that can often exist between the official pronouncements of a denomination and the actual practices that are carried out in local congregations. The pronouncements may reflect official opposition or concern (and even occasional approval) about certain practices, and to that degree we may gain some insight into what is happening at the level of popular piety. Obvious disagreement about the practice of footwashing is evident in the United Brethren *Discipline* of 1869:

> Washing feet is left to the judgment of everyone, to practice or not: but it is not becoming for any of our preachers or members to traduce any of their brethren whose judgment and understanding in these respects is different from their own, either in public or private. Whosoever shall make himself guilty in this respect, shall be considered a traducer of his brethren, and shall be answerable for the same.[1]

This judgment suggests that there was wide latitudinarianism concerning liturgical practices and efforts were made to avoid contention about them. The *Discipline* functioned as a minimalist guide for belief and practice, leaving it to pastors and congregations to create their own rituals within their own contexts.

EVANGELICAL *AND* UNITED BRETHREN

The names of the denominations themselves give a hint of some of the liturgical and sacramental issues that will emerge in the process of trying to create a corporate and ecclesial identity. The Evangelical Association and the United Brethren in Christ will in less than a hundred years transform themselves into The Evangelical United Brethren *Church* (italics mine) after already changing their own names to the Evangelical *Church* and to the

Church of the United Brethren in Christ. Compare the Evangelical *Discipline* of 1868 with an adaptation of the same passage in the 1967 Evangelical United Brethren *Discipline*:

> *[1868]* This Association is...nothing else than a friendly union of such persons as wish to have not merely the form of godliness, but strive also to possess its power and substance.[2]

> *[1967]* They formally adopted the name, *The Evangelical Association*, which is, therefore, an *ecclesiastical union* [italics mine] of such persons as desire to have not merely the form of godliness, but strive to possess the substance and power thereof.[3]

This growth from friendly gathering to ecclesial identity contributed not a little to institutional schizophrenia among the Evangelical United Brethren, a condition that they carried into the union with the Methodists in 1968, a condition of which the Methodists were seemingly unaware as evidenced by their perplexity when issues soon began to be raised about such things as infant dedication, rebaptism, and the ordination of elders apart from the transitional diaconate. This unfinished business of the Evangelical United Brethren merger ended up on the United Methodist agenda.

Another indicator of differences between the two denominations is to be found in comparing the doctrinal sections of the two *Disciplines*. From their first *Discipline* in 1809, the Evangelicals adopted the Articles of Faith published the previous year in the German-language edition of the Methodist Episcopal *Discipline*. The Methodists had offered their translation to the Evangelicals and the United Brethren, but only the former took the offer seriously and incorporated large sections of it into their book, thus providing a direct line from their Articles of Faith back to the Thirty-nine Articles of the Church of England with their recognition of sacramental efficacy seen through a Calvinist lens. In the same way, the Evangelical *Discipline* incorporated large sections of the liturgical orders included in the Methodist *Discipline*, orders that were still largely faithful to the recension of the *Book of Common Prayer* sent to America by John Wesley in 1784. John H. Ness Jr. indicates that, for the Evangelicals, the *Discipline* quickly became "a doctrinal guide for ministers and church members."[4]

The United Brethren, however, included in their *Discipline* no formulae for either baptism or the Lord's Supper, but supplied a minimal text for both matrimony and the burial of the dead. One can only conclude that it was assumed the minister should be able to manage the sacraments solo, but that some help would be needed in assisting persons to maneuver through life passages. A. W. Drury, a professor in Union Biblical (later United Theological) Seminary, lamented that some pastors set greater store by the authority to solemnize marriages than to administer the sacraments:

> The church of to-day must not cease to be Christian by ceasing to be apostolic. Undoubtedly the neglect of baptism in many cases, as well as the failure to secure the full benefit of it in other cases, is due in large part to the low conceptions, weak convictions, and want of faithfulness on the part of Christian ministers. The ordaining to the ministry, while not a sacrament, is a solemn rite, and has its significance largely as conveying authority to administer the sacraments. Yet, judging by remarks often heard, many candidates for ordination think very much more of the authority to solemnize marriages than they do of the authority to administer the sacraments. On the part of many ministers, little attention is given to the subject of baptism till it is crowded upon them, and then the attention given is not intelligent or sympathetic.[5]

It is worth noting that the word *sacrament* nowhere occurs in the United Brethren *Discipline* of 1869. The Confession of Faith prefers *ordinances,* a term that is susceptible to meaning "sacrament," as its use by John and Charles Wesley indicates, but by the mid-nineteenth century in the United States was the term of choice being used by Baptists and others to distinguish their understanding of baptism and the Lord's Supper over against a sacramental one. At the delivery of the Bible in the ordination of elders, the ordinand is told to take "authority to preach the Word of God, and administer the ordinances in the Church of Christ" rather than administer the sacraments, the term used in their Methodist source.[6] The Confession of Faith states:

> We believe that the ordinances, viz: baptism and the remembrance of the sufferings and death of our Lord Jesus Christ, are to be in use, and practiced by all Christian societies; and that it is

incumbent on all the children of God particularly to practice them; but the manner in which ought always to be left to the judgment and understanding of every individual.[7]

It should be added, however, that the Evangelical *Discipline* of 1868 also scrupulously avoids the use of the term *sacrament* and speaks of baptism and the Lord's Supper specifically by name in the Articles of Faith and in the Ordinal rather than grouping them as either sacraments or ordinances.

It is evident from the United Brethren's Confession and from the Evangelical liturgical text that they share the inheritance from the Middle Ages of interpreting the Lord's Supper solely in terms of the sacrifice of Christ, a memorial of his death and passion. There is little memory of the Last Supper itself left in the event. The Confession mentions nothing about the sacred meal aspect of "the remembrance of the sufferings and death of our Lord Jesus Christ," and even the Evangelical liturgy, with all its Wesleyan influence, adroitly omits any reference to "the night in which he was betrayed" in the prayer itself, making only a brief reference to 1 Corinthians 11 in an opening rubric.

Whereas the United Brethren appear to leave the minister to create the eucharistic prayer *de novo* at each celebration, the Evangelical liturgy weaves together in one long prayer different parts taken from the Methodist rite received from Wesley. Anything intended to be shared with the congregation is assigned to the minister's solo voice. The Evangelical canon, then, adapts in order, in one prayer, sections of the General Confession, the Prayer of Consecration (with no reference to the bread and cup!), the Prayer of Humble Access, the Collect for Purity, the Vere Dignum, the Sanctus, and a brief return to both the Prayer of Consecration and the Prayer of Humble Access. In light of contemporary eucharistic practice it is worth noting that this very long prayer concludes with the Lord's Prayer recited by all as preparation for receiving Communion.

PREACHING AND THE PREACHER

The lack of a proper eucharistic prayer by the United Brethren and the exceptionally verbose one mandated by the Evangelicals points, however, to a similarity. What they have in common is the importance of the presider, one might even say the centrality of the presider, in the event. Except for some of the more radical groups growing out of the Reformation, the priesthood of all believers was a doctrine that was rarely applied to the actual offering of worship, the thing that priests are most basically expected to do. All too often the central figure of the priest at the altar simply gave way to the central figure of the preacher in the pulpit. So some attention needs to be paid to how the dominance of preaching and the preacher influenced the practice of worship and the celebration of the sacraments within the Evangelical United Brethren tradition.

It is, first of all, important to appreciate that both the Evangelical and the United Brethren denominations were rooted in the evangelical revival of the late eighteenth century where the emphasis was on proclamation of the gospel in such a way as to bring persons to repentance and amendment of life. There was a sense of urgency about saving the lost through telling the story of God's love revealed in the ministry and death of Jesus in such a way as to sway emotions and lead individuals to repent—that is, feel sorrow for their former lives—and to convert—that is, change their mode of living based on allegiance to the call of Christ on their lives. By the time of the two *Disciplines* we have under consideration, their eighteenth-century propositions had been reinforced by the New Measures of the Presbyterian Charles Finney. Finney's position as president of Oberlin College in Ohio gave him access to the large number of United Brethren in that state, so his influence would have spread far beyond his own somewhat reluctant Presbyterian colleagues who were having problems reconciling the New Measures with classical Calvinism to his more Arminian-inclined neighbors and beyond them to the Evangelicals and the Methodists.

Both the Evangelical and the United Brethren *Disciplines* (1868 and 1869) use the title "preacher" as a generic label for anyone who is called to the ministry, including the ordained, and as a specific category of laborer who is called and appointed without being ordained. More attention is given in the *Disciplines* to this unordained category than otherwise. The duties of the preacher in the United Brethren *Discipline* heavily emphasize preaching and the tasks related to it. To the question, "What are the duties of preachers?" the following answer is given:

> To preach Christ crucified, whenever they can get hearers; to form classes; to converse with the members on the spiritual condition of their souls; to administer relief, to strengthen and direct those that are afflicted and labor under temptations; to animate the indolent; to endeavor as much as possible to edify and instruct all in faith, in grace, and in the knowledge of Jesus Christ; to visit the sick on all occasions; to strive to enforce and confirm the doctrine they deliver by a well-ordered and exemplary life.[8]

And in the list of directions given to the preachers, there is the following exhortation:

> Let your business be to save as many souls as possible. To this employment give yourself up wholly. Visit those who need it; and act in all things, not according to your own wills, but as sons in the Gospel; for as such it becomes your duty to employ your time in the manner prescribed, in preaching, and visiting from house to house; in instruction and prayer, and in meditating on the word of God.[9]

The Evangelical *Discipline* reflects these same tenets[10] but at greater length with much material taken directly from Wesley and the Methodist Episcopal *Discipline* as well as with some of their own directions derived, no doubt, from experience, such as "He shall preach neither too long, nor with unabated loudness."[11]

MUSICAL STANDARDS

Particularly interesting in the light of later developments are the statements in the two *Disciplines* related to hymn singing, choirs, and instrumental music as a part of public worship. The United Brethren are told:

> We believe it is to be the duty of all the people of God to sing his praises; and to sing them in the great congregation as well as in the private circle. We therefore earnestly recommend to all our people the cultivation of vocal music, so that the singing in our

congregations may be improved. As a help to this end we advise all our people to provide themselves with Hymn Books for use in times of public and social worship. We would counsel our societies to avoid the introduction of choirs and instrumental music into their worship.[12]

It was not until the 1885 *Discipline* that the counsel against choirs and instrumental music disappeared. That was perhaps inevitable since in 1874 the church had published *Hymns for the Sanctuary and Social Worship,* with the young Edmund S. Lorenz as its music editor. That began the long relationship between the Lorenz family and the United Brethren with consequences for the sanctuary that would not have been imagined at that time. Ness, in his history of denominational publishing, refers to the demands for better music by 1891 by "the larger churches in membership and wealth, having choirs and pipe organ."[13] Middle-class aspirations were becoming increasingly apparent in the still largely rural denomination.

In 1868 The Evangelical Association was equally pious but less restrictive than its United Brethren comrades would be a year later:

> Singing has always, among the pious, constituted a part of public and private worship, and is no inconsiderable incitement to the mind; that is, if it is performed, not merely according to form and with the mouth, but also with the spirit in true devotion, to the praise and glory of God.... To confine singing in public worship to choirs, we deem, therefore, improper and injurious.[14]

BAPTISM/DEDICATION OF INFANTS

It is not unusual to be told by former Evangelical United Brethren members and former Methodists that the Evangelical United Brethren "dedicated infants" and that they had a service for it in their *Book of Ritual*. The impression often given or implied by such a statement is that the practice was a venerable one and that the liturgy was an inheritance at least as old as the Reformation. A brief review of the history of the service may bring perspective to the discussion.

There was no such service in The Evangelical Church, and a prescribed order for infant dedication first appeared in the last United

Brethren *Discipline* (1945). It was composed by order of the General Conference to supplement another piece of legislation that mandated the keeping of a Children's Membership Record. The *Discipline* stated: "Children of United Brethren parents, who have been consecrated or dedicated to the Lord, shall upon request of parents (or one parent or guardian) be enrolled on the Children's Membership Record."[15] There is no prior mention of a Children's Membership Record, so this appears to have been a means of keeping track of potential members (what Methodists at the same time called the Preparatory Membership Roll, which was a list of all baptized infants). The legislation about the Children's Membership Record said nothing about a service of dedication, nor did it require that baptized children be placed on the roll, a strange omission unless it assumed that baptism was the equivalent of dedication. The General Conference, however, passed another recommendation "that the Board of Bishops be instructed to prepare a ritual for a service of consecration or dedication of children in harmony with the provision of the foregoing item (1) under 'Children's Roll.'"[16] Still no provision was made to include baptized children on such a roll. The discussion on the floor of the Conference centered on the question of the Children's Roll. No interest at all seemed to be taken in the proposed service.[17] When a question was raised about transferring the children on that roll with their parents to another congregation, the children were referred to as "baptized." And when the new service appeared, it was headed "DEDICATION OF INFANTS (without Baptism)," again implying that infant baptism had been understood as a service of dedication. The option being offered was wet or dry dedication.

The 1945 United Brethren ritual was brief and reflects the "art of public worship" mentality that characterized much of American Protestantism at mid-twentieth century. There is an opening general statement of biblical warrants ("impressive precedent" is the term in the ritual) such as Hannah and Mary, Isaiah 40:11 and Mark 10:14. Emphasis was placed on the faith of the presenters and the environment of the local church as the setting where "this tender 'bud of promise' may blossom into a fragrant flower."[18] A permissive rubric allowed for the minister to lay hands on the child and announce the dedication with a trinitarian formula. A rosebud might also be given to "be cherished as a prophecy of unfolding life." It should be observed that this service was both longer and more involving of the congregation than was the immediately preceding order for the baptism of infants. There Mark 10:13-16 was read and the sponsors affirmed their faith and agreed to raise the children "in the nurture and admonition of the Lord." It was almost entirely individualistic in nature with little reference to the ecclesial community into which the child was being incorporated. From an ecclesiological perspective, the new dedication service was a better baptism service than the baptism service!

The first Evangelical United Brethren General Conference (1946) ordered that the United Brethren service for "Dedication of Infants without Baptism" be included in the new *Discipline*.[19] The Children's Record, which had been the occasion for the appearance of the rite in the United Brethren church, found no mention in the new *Discipline*, although a new section "Children and the Church" declared, "Children of believing parents are entitled to Christian Baptism," and referred to those who "dedicate their children to God through Christian Baptism."[20] The new service for the baptism of infants represented a quantum leap theologically and liturgically from what had been in the rituals of either of the former denominations. It clearly placed baptism within the context of the church, employed the Apostles' Creed as the historic baptismal confession of faith, and involved both sponsors and congregation in a significant way in the liturgy. Five different times in the service, reference was made to the child's being *dedicated* through baptism.

When the second Evangelical United Brethren General Conference (1950) met, the Committee on Ritual reported:

> There was a feeling in the committee that a service for the Dedication of Infants without Baptism, in an official ritual, was somewhat contradictory to the doctrine which the church was expressing in the Order for Baptism of Infants, and also to the categorical statement (*Discipline* Art. 269) that children of believing parents are entitled to Christian Baptism.[21]

The bishops submitted to committee members a new dedication service, which they included as an addendum to their report and which was approved by the General Conference for inclusion in the 1951 *Discipline*.

The forms that emerged for both infant baptism and dedication in the 1951 *Discipline* followed the same outline but varied considerably from their 1947 predecessors. The baptismal service was not as elaborate, and the dedication service lost its floral imagery as well as the parenthetic description "without baptism." While the titles appeared to distance the two services from each other as being very different acts, the contents of the services emphasized their similarity. Each service began with a trinitarian invocation and an address to the congregation. The baptismal address was a simple explanation of the place of infant baptism in the church. The dedication address was adapted from the earlier service. Then there was a Scripture reading (Mark 10:13-16) in both services. The address to the parents was the same formula in both. After the act of baptism or dedication, the concluding prayers were the same, except for the interchange of the words *baptize* and *dedicate*.

The only other significant alteration in these rituals during the brief history of The Evangelical United Brethren Church was the inclusion of more questions asked of parents, sponsors, and congregation. The same questions were included in both services. In effect, infant baptism and infant dedication became the same thing in The Evangelical United Brethren Church. The same requirements were made of those presenting the children and the same questions were asked of sponsors and congregation. Incorporation of the child into the life of the congregation was affirmed in each instance, as was the expectation that the rite would find a later fulfillment and affirmation in some sort of personal growth and commitment. It may be that regardless of what any individual's intention for the services may have been (and intent is a potent theological category), the ritual content of both infant baptism and infant dedication in the Evangelical United Brethen tradition suggests a distinction without a difference.

THE LORD'S SUPPER—1951

Until the union in 1946, there had been little change by both denominations in the way each had solemnized the Lord's Supper for a hundred years. The United Brethren permitted great variety and flexibility in their order with a minimum of prescribed text. The Evangelicals continued with their adaptation of Wesley's Sunday Service, which in its turn had been adapted from the 1662 *Book of Common Prayer*. Now, guided by the influence of the liturgical movement of the early twentieth century, the new denomination sought to create a eucharistic liturgy that would combine the best of both traditions with the fruit of those discoveries in church history and biblical theology that had made the liturgical movement possible. It first appeared in the 1951 *Discipline*.

The new service was prefaced by a rather lengthy introduction that was intended, according to the Reverend Fay Bowman, who served as secretary to the Committee on Ritual, "to be read and studied by every minister." The preface emphasizes the conservative nature of the traditional order that was chosen "to bind the church together" and "to give us the consciousness that we are a part of the church catholic." Despite the emphasis of the liturgical movement on the sacraments as celebrating the whole work of Christ rather than one aspect of it, the preface continues the inherited tradition of observing more of the imagery of the Last Supper and the passion with little regard for Emmaus or the heavenly banquet at the end of the ages. It does, however, draw on the image from the Letter to the Hebrews of Christ as both priest and victim. The Lord's Supper is still seen very much as a penitential exercise, for it is "only as the individual in penitence and faith appropriates to himself the sacrifice which Christ made for his salvation, can that salvation be made efficacious for him." In the same way, the rubrics relating to the hymn to be sung during the uncovering of the Communion vessels say that it shall be chosen from those in the Holy Communion section or "Our Savior's Passion and Death." The logic of the flow of the service is outlined in the preface, no doubt for the edification of the ministers, since when the service finally appears in the new hymnal (1957), where it may have some catechetical function for the faithful, the preface has been entirely omitted.

It is obvious from the 1951 rite that Communion weekly was not an option or at least not anticipated. The Epistle and Gospel lessons were the same at each service: 1 Corinthians 10:16-21 and Luke

22:14-19. Only if the optional "briefer form" was employed could the pastor use proper lessons for the day.

In an effort to correct their own eucharistic traditions in light of the contributions of the liturgical movement and contemporary scholarship, the compilers of the new liturgy had some difficulty separating out the essentials and probably did themselves a disservice by creating a form that was both too long and too rigid. Possibly if they had resisted the temptation to include components of the Lord's Supper from the 1935 *Methodist Hymnal*, they might have produced a service with a more obvious sequence and with more latitude for variation and the incorporation of local traditions.

CONCLUSION

The merger of the Church of the United Brethren in Christ and The Evangelical Church was an effort to realize the goal of our Lord's high priestly prayer, *ut unum sint* (that they may be one). They recognized their common heritage in German piety and their common insistence on the importance of a saving encounter with God's grace that turns one around and makes one take seriously the call to holiness. They were not ignorant of their differences, but they counted those less important than being faithful to the high calling of God in Christ Jesus. Their piety, both public and private, was focused on the One who said to take up a cross and follow him. That participation in the passion of Christ flavors their liturgical and sacramental life. Preaching for them was to enable an encounter at the foot of the cross. Baptism was a way of putting off the old self, and the Lord's Supper was the way to see and touch God's love made visible. It was intensely personal, but it was also life in community without which the individual could not be whole. And it just may be that their worship and spirituality are the reasons that three denominations—United Brethren, Evangelical, and the Evangelical United Brethren—decided to take Jesus at his word when he said, "Those who want to save their life will lose it, and those who lose their life for my sake will find it" (Matthew 16:25).

CHAPTER 10

THE PRACTICE OF MISSION AND EVANGELISM: THE MISSION TO GERMANY

Ulrike Schuler

The topic of this chapter is the practice of mission and evangelism in the Evangelical United Brethren tradition. Thus it will be helpful to say a word up front about how I understand these terms and how I believe they are used in Methodism, as well as in The Evangelical United Brethren Church and its predecessor bodies. First, *mission* as a broader term has its roots in the *missio dei* and is expressed in the trinitarian mission charge in John 20:21: "Peace be with you. As the Father has sent me, so I send you."[1] Its aim is to ensure the spreading of the gospel across the world, a commission that comes from God and that has become a global church movement, which includes simultaneously the responsibility of each individual church member called into this mission. Even though this is, ecumenically speaking, a very modern definition of mission, it seems very clearly to me to have been the basic Methodist understanding of the term from Wesley onward.

Second, *evangelism* is the reification of mission, the proclamation and explanation of the gospel. Evangelism focuses more on the personal call to individuals to follow Jesus, to experience regeneration in Christ, and to embark on a journey of transformation into the image of God. United Methodist theologian William J. Abraham captures the essential meaning of the term when he says,

"We should construe evangelism as primary initiation into the Kingdom of God."[2]

In keeping with these basic definitions of mission and evangelism, the United Brethren in Christ and The Evangelical Association understood their own calling to mission to be soteriological and, at the same time, holistic.[3] The goal of mission was not only to spread biblical knowledge (scriptural holiness), but also—as the center of evangelism—to bring about the new birth that begins the lifelong process of growing in grace whereby God's image is restored in humanity. The new faith, rooted in a healed relationship with God, leads to loving and practical action in society. Personal holiness and social holiness go hand in hand. *Diakonia* (serving others) makes it possible to experience the gospel as living grace through outreach to society. Indeed, Theodore Runyon is exactly right when he says, if orthodoxy, orthopraxy, and orthopathy—the scriptural, personally experienced and practiced faith as aspects of a Christian life—stay dynamically connected, then the Wesleyan-Methodist goal of mission to "spread Christian holiness across the nation" is achieved.[4]

THE MISSION STRATEGY OF THE UNITED BRETHREN IN CHRIST AND THE EVANGELICAL ASSOCIATION

Having noted that mission incorporates evangelism and *diakonia*, we need to consider mission strategy in detail, that is, the way in which mission is "translated" into practice. It is notable that Methodist missions in the nineteenth and twentieth centuries were closely linked to migration, to a cross-border exchange of people that promoted a cultural and spiritual exchange of influences. In this setting, Methodist missions started as home missions when people simply shared the stories of their faith with one another. People in a typical Methodist organizational structure gathered in classes and learned to pray together and talk about their progress in the faith, their growth in grace and holiness. It was natural for people to feel the need to create such classes whenever they moved to other places or countries. Classes enabled people to grow in confidence and in mutual trust so that they were able to support one another. People longed for wider connections with people of similar faith. Several classes formed a society, and societies were in contact with other societies. It is fascinating to observe how organically and dynamically those church movements as new missions emerged.

It was not until the "natural" growth of those Christian communities happened that The Evangelical Association and the United Brethren in Christ were able to establish mission societies, first as home missions focusing on evangelism in their own country and later on as foreign missions. Mission was the responsibility of the whole church, and each individual member was formed with a mission identity. In The Evangelical Association this conviction was also linguistically identifiable: each congregation was a *mission society*, which was affiliated with an annual conference that was itself part of the mission board of the General Conference, to which delegates from the annual conferences belonged. At the congregational level there were children's and women's *mission societies*, which functioned primarily to raise money for mission. In Germany, all ministers had to write *mission reports*[5] about the time they had spent in their circuit before they left for their next appointment. Every member was involved in the mission work. So it is completely correct to say that the church did not *undertake* mission—the church *was* mission.

It is also important to note that mission was initially understood to mean not mission to the heathens, but mission to all unconverted people, including the so-called nominal Christians, that is, those who were baptized but did not practice their faith. This aspect of early United Brethren and Evangelical understanding of mission can also be seen in the early Methodist churches and other revival and pietistic communities. Indeed, Wesley's often cited motto, "The world is my parish and saving souls is my vocation," shaped early Methodist missionary concern with regard to location and audience. Such a wide definition of mission caused some annoyance in the European context and gave rise to accusations of proselytizing by Methodist ministers of members of the established state churches (*Landeskirchen*).

While it is true that the United Brethren and the Evangelicals saw all people as the target audience of missions, it is also true that they focused their evangelistic efforts primarily on working-class people in rural areas of Pennsylvania and Ohio.[6] The first *Discipline* of The Evangelical Association described the movement as a plain order made up "of farmers for farmers" (*von Bauern für Bauern*). When in the course of the Industrial Revolution they expanded their work at home and abroad to persons within city boundaries, they remained focused on the working classes, that is, the industrial workers. Thus, in late-nineteenth-century Germany, they focused their efforts on the coal miners. Similarly, in the Prussia mission (*Preußenmission*) in the middle of the nineteenth century, they concentrated on spreading the gospel among the steel workers.[7]

Among the working classes in the United States and abroad, the United Brethren and The Evangelical Association developed a "very closely knit sense of community, with a distinctive spirituality." This was very important for the German settlers who had left their families and friends in their home country to come to America. United Brethren and Evangelical Association congregations gave them a feeling of togetherness and of being at home in the New World. Uprooted people gathered together in their new context experienced a "sense of connectedness."[8] They discovered a community with a family character where their native language was spoken.[9] They published a variety of materials in their "home" language, including tracts, *Disciplines*, and hymnbooks with a lot of German hymns. All of this helped people hold on to what they valued of their religious and social roots.

When the United Brethren and The Evangelical Association began to reach out to other nationalities in the United States, and later on, in mission fields, to others abroad, they did so in ways that reflected their German American rural and working-class cultural context. As O'Malley explains, this led to significant difficulties in mission, as indigenous workers sent to work in mission fields outside the United States encountered harsh resistance to the "strong Pietist-revivalist massage." O'Malley continues: "However, both denominations struggled to find ways to relate that message, which had been shaped on a rural German-American cultural ethos, to non-Christian cultures 'overseas'—including those dominated by a Protestant state-church (Germany) or by Roman Catholicism after the Reformation (the Philippines)."[10] What had been so attractive to so many German immigrants in America would prove to be a liability in "foreign" mission work, to which we now turn.

United Brethren and Evangelical Association Mission Work in Europe/Germany

Following the German revolution in 1848, there was immense immigration to the United States from Europe as people fled the revolutions and pogroms of those times. Church periodicals, such as the *Christliche Botschafter*[11] and the *Evangelical Messenger*[12] of The Evangelical Association and the *Religious Telescope*[13] as well as the German paper *Die Geschäftige Martha* (the *Busy Martha*)[14] of the United Brethren in Christ, frequently blamed the revolution on the spiritual situation following the Enlightenment. More specifically, they criticized the liberal theology being taught in German universities. In addition, these periodicals published letters from "positive" German ministers, including a speech by the German theologian Johann Hinrich Wichern concerning the need for home mission given the social circumstances created by the Industrial Revolution.[15] All of this heightened the desire among German American United Brethren and Evangelicals to support a new and growing mission movement to Europe.

The Evangelical Association celebrated its fiftieth anniversary in 1850. At that time, the members wanted to express their thanks to their forefathers' homeland and the land of the Reformation as recorded in their General Conference minutes and their periodicals.[16] A German re-emigrant and a layperson, Sebastian Kurz, who converted to Christianity in The Evangelical Association in the United States, had already written to the mission society in America in 1846 asking for a missionary to be sent to Germany.[17] By 1850, he had started class meetings in Stuttgart-Bonlanden, and he was already preaching in pietistic assemblies.[18] The mission board reflected on the information available about the situation in Germany, including Wichern's "impromptu" concerning the need for street workers and the petitions from letter writers in Germany. An effective fund-raising campaign was started—the so-called

Nicolais Zehn-Thaler-Plan—to send a missionary to Germany.[19] The campaign received an overwhelming response.

In 1850, the General Conference set up the mission in Europe[20] and using the money that had been raised sent two missionaries.[21] Initially, only one missionary, Conrad Link, and his family were sent to Germany.[22] He was welcomed in Bremerhaven by Ludwig Sigismund Jacoby and other Methodist ministers who had already opened the mission of The Methodist Episcopal Church in Germany in 1849 in Bremen.[23]

In 1865, after a long period of pressure and chicanery by the state churches, Bishop Johann Jacob Escher organized an annual conference known as the *Deutschland-Konferenz der Evangelischen Gemeinschaft*, appointing nine preachers for Württemberg, Baden, and Switzerland.[24] The mission work spread from Germany because of personal connections to friends and relatives in Switzerland in 1866, Alsace-Lorraine in 1868, and East Prussia in 1895. From its churches in East Prussia, The Evangelical Association began a mission to the German-speaking people in Latvia in 1911. All mission work in Europe was conducted exclusively in the German language by German people, a fact that distinguishes the work from the mission of The Methodist Episcopal Church in the same region.

By 1911, The Evangelical Association had societies in twenty-eight of the forty-one German city congregations. The mission progressed through the establishment of classes and Sunday schools;[25] the translation and publication of a hymnbook, the *Discipline*, and a periodical;[26] the founding of a publishing house;[27] the provision of basic Christian tracts and literature; and finally through the opening of a seminary in Reutlingen.[28] Later on, they established deaconess mother-houses, nursing care homes, hospitals, kindergartens, and other social-diaconal institutions.[29] All of this was done by The Evangelical Association in Germany.

The United Brethren mission in Germany was opened by Christian Bischoff, a former butcher, innkeeper, and cattle dealer who immigrated to the United States and was converted to Christianity by the United Brethren.[30] Bischoff started preaching in Naila, Franconia—a Catholic context without religious liberty. He soon organized classes and Sunday schools. Gradually, the mission extended north to Thuringia, Saxony, Pomerania, and Posen, but it did not develop very extensively, partly because of the frequent change of superintendents being sent from the United States.[31] There is also evidence that the United Brethren mission board had problems supporting the mission financially.[32]

Despite these problems, the mission to Germany was officially organized in 1879 as a District Mission Conference with six ministers and 235 members.[33] In 1883, a periodical, *Der Heilsbote* (*Salvation Messenger*), was published. This was followed in 1894 by a publication for evangelization called *Friedensbotschaft* (*Peace Message*). A year later, a bookstore was opened in Zeitz, followed by a printing office in 1898. In 1905, the mission was integrated into The Methodist Episcopal Church's mission, at which time it had five hundred to six hundred members.[34]

From 1881 onward, Methodist missionaries in Germany (the Wesleyan Methodists, Methodist Episcopal Church, United Brethren, and Evangelical Association) worked quite closely together. They organized preacher assemblies and discussed their mission goals and mission areas so that they would not create unnecessary problems because of overlapping work. They also organized their social activities. For example, they wrote a joint petition to the *Reichstag* (the government) in 1883, addressing temperance questions and Sunday sanctification (*Sonntagsheiligung*).[35]

In the United States, the United Brethren in Christ were much stronger than The Evangelical Association. Yet The Evangelical Association developed a lasting mission to German-speaking parts of Europe. Although the name of the church was changed twice in the United States (in 1922 to Evangelical Church and in 1946 with the union to The Evangelical United Brethren Church), the *Evangelische Gemeinschaft* kept its original name in Germany until the union with The Methodist Church in 1968. This highlights the members' ongoing understanding of themselves as a renewal movement. Even though the name changes were discussed, The Evangelical Association in Germany reflected that its original name really encapsulated its identity. It was *evangelical* insofar as it was rooted in the Protestant Reformation. It was an *association* insofar as it was a Christian society—not a denomination—inside the one church of God.

Because of the public laws, problems with property and, not least, the hostilities of the state church expressed in actions, such as refusing the sacraments to those who visited prayer meetings or services, The Evangelical Association had to apply for state recognition as soon as that was possible.[36] In 1887, it become a corporation. With the separation of state and church in the constitution of the Weimar Republic, The Evangelical Association secured corporate law in different German counties and, in 1938, for the entire German empire.

The state recognition in Württemberg in 1924 led to negotiations with the *Württembergische Landeskirche* about the opportunity to work together. These negotiations were first conducted simultaneously with The Methodist Episcopal Church in Württemberg, but they were not continued. In 1929, the dialogue led to agreements between the *Württembergische Landeskirche* and The Evangelical Association that allowed for the designation of The EA as a free church and not a sect. When questions of nationality arose (in the 1870s and during World Wars I and II), The Evangelical Association preferred to defend its Lutheran and German roots and the will to work together with the former state churches than to justify or explain its Anglo American origins and identity.

The Evangelical Association after World War II up to the Church Union in 1968

At the end of World War II, The Evangelical Association suffered a major setback in its work in Europe. It lost one-sixth of its circuit preachers; one-half of its registered members, friends, and relatives; and one-half of its Sunday school members.[37] All that remained were 161 circuit preachers; about 35,000 members, friends, and relatives; about 300 congregations and 200 preaching places; 270 Sunday schools with 16,000 members; and 1,139 stewards. In addition, The Evangelical Association suffered the loss of 42 flourishing congregations in East Prussia (later to become Poland), together with 23 church buildings and parish halls. Forty-three churches were totally destroyed, 32 were partly damaged, and 40 were superficially damaged. Moreover, the publishing house was 75 percent destroyed and its assets were placed under the control of the army of occupation because of the pastoral director's Third Reich party membership.[38] Of the eight hospitals of the diaconal work, only Bethesda in Wuppertal was undamaged, and it was requisitioned by the 77th British Rhine Army as a military hospital. Four out of the five nurses' hostels in Germany were totally destroyed. This devastation preceded a "crisis of existence, which concerned the question of their rebirth and reconstruction from the devastating effects of the recent war."[39]

Because of the union with the United Brethren in 1946, the first surveying visit of a bishop was deferred. Nonetheless, the new church united two special mission programs: the Kingdom Service Fund of The Evangelical Association and the Advance Program of the United Brethren. The result was the creation of the Kingdom Advance Program.[40] All relief and reconstruction work was undertaken for the purpose of mission, which is to say, of pervading the society with the good news of Jesus Christ. The medium or means of mission in the postwar era included all forms of practical charity alongside the more traditional means of preaching and other evangelistic forms of gospel proclamation.

Because social action easily could become activism as an end in itself, the Kingdom Advance Program was to undertake all nonreligious social action under advisement of the newly formed Evangelical United Brethren Church. In light of the church leaders of the *Bekennende Kirche* and the Western occupying powers, the churches were mostly viewed as the only authentic partners for social work. And while the progress of secularization in Germany was under way, it seemed to slow considerably in the years immediately following the war, allowing churches to play a significant part in programs of reconstruction and reconciliation.

The *Evangelische Gesmeinschaft*, in spite of being a comparatively small church in Germany (all free churches together constituted at that time about 1 percent of Protestants), became much more recognized by the main (former state) Protestant church. Besides the Kingdom Advance Program, the Protestant churches founded a relief organization known as *Hilfswerk der Evangelischen Kirchen*. It was the first time that free churches were officially included in the work of the main Protestant church in Germany. This was in part because of the ecumenical initiatives in the United States where, among others, The Methodist Church was able to give advice on how to cooperate with other free churches in Germany. It also arose out of consideration of the help that the free churches in the United States were able to give.

The *Evangelische Kirche in Deutschland* as a federation of twenty-seven *Landeskirchen* was at first annoyed by the need to distinguish between sects and free churches.[41] Nine free churches organized individual relief organizations and were later invited to join in the work of the *Hilfswerk der Evangelischen Kirchen*. Four of them—the *Methodistenkirche,* the *Evangelische Gemeinschaft,* the *Bund Evangelisch-Freikirchlicher Gemeinden (Baptisten),* and the *Bund Freier evangelischer Gemeinden,* which already had close connections through having founded a so-called *Vereinigung evangelischer Freikirchen* (Free Church Federation) in 1946[42]—together founded a *Hilfswerk Zentralausschuss der Vereinigung evangelischer Freikirchen* (central relief organization of the union of Protestant free churches), which also became part of the main Protestant relief organization.[43] These organizations helped the churches work together while still maintaining their individual identities as free churches and former state churches.

The relief organization of the *Evangelische Gemeinschaft* in connection with The Evangelical United Brethren Church in Switzerland and the United States was a phenomenal venture and something that cannot be separated from the rapid social developments and transformation following those difficult times after World War II. In both the United States and Switzerland, reconstruction and relief plans were prepared to provide immediate help at the war's end. Nevertheless, it was not easy to implement them when the end finally occurred. Germany at that time was divided into four occupation zones, making border traffic and interzone traffic difficult. Transport difficulties were further exacerbated by the ruined infrastructure. The first help given to the *Evangelische Gemeinschaft* came from Switzerland in the form of trucks carrying food, clothes, shoes, and household articles.[44] Because the direct import of aid from the United States was not at first allowed and there was no way to assure that aid would reach Evangelical United Brethren sisters and brothers in Germany, help from the mother church was sent via Switzerland.[45] In 1946, a shipload from The Evangelical Church did not reach the congregations of the *Evangelische Gemeinschaft* because of the unclear church name that it was given, namely, the *Evangelische Kirche in Deutschland*.[46]

From the spring of 1946 onward, all auxiliary food and relief aid had to be sent via the American transport organization CRALOG (Council of Relief Agencies Licensed for Operation in Germany). In addition, the church relief organization CARE (Cooperative for American Remittance to Europe) began its work at the turn of the year 1946–47, sending packages overland with food and clothes, mostly to private persons. Members of The Evangelical United Brethren Church paid for packages that were sent directly to members of the *Evangelische Gemeinschaft* or, if they knew the addresses, to congregations. Indeed, providing direct contacts was a vital part of the reconciliation work undertaken by the churches because official personal contact between persons of the occupying forces and the civil population was still forbidden.

In addition to the military administration creating problems in delivering much-needed aid, the *Evangelische Gemeinschaft* in Germany had to adjust to the new organizational structure put in place at the uniting conference of the United Brethren and Evangelical Association. "Upon union," explains O'Malley, "a single board with three divisions was formed, consisting of world mission, home mission and church extension, and women's service."[47] This reorganization led to the creation of a committee for "aid relief" that met in January 1947 to develop a reconstruction program. In June, it was decided,

1. That in recognizing the appeal from Europe, we seek to make available four barrack chapels at once, one for each of the European Conferences.
2. That special attention be given to the physical needs of our brethren to these lands, in budgeting the Kingdom Advance Program Funds.
3. That previous commitment for the binding and shipping to our German people of 300 sets of Bible stories in the German language be approved.
4. That our American representatives at the Oslo conference be urged to visit our youth in Germany after the Conferences.
5. That the following institutions be given consideration in making appropriations from the Kingdom Advance Program: Bethesda Deaconess Society, Reutlingen Seminary, Stuttgart Publishing House.[48]

This list reveals a holistic understanding of mission. Relief aid was understood as a vital part of evangelistic proclamation. The new church promptly approved the program.

Among the many projects undertaken, The Evangelical United Brethren delivered and erected wooden churches that had been designed and planned in the United States and built in Switzerland, complete with furnishings, in Berlin, Essen, Dortmund, Frankfurt am Main, Karlsruhe, Muhle, Mülheim-Speldorf, Reutlingen, Stuttgart, and Wuppertal-Barmen. This Emergency Church Program (*Notkirchen-Programm*) came to an end earlier than expected because of social progress in reconstruction, in new restrictions for urban planning, and as a result of the strengthening German economy. After 1954, wooden churches were not allowed to be built. Consequently, The Evangelical United Brethren had to find other ways to reconstruct damaged churches. Unfortunately, obtaining suitable building materials proved difficult. Thus, to rebuild destroyed churches, people did their best to improvise using recycled materials from the ruins.

The decision to use donations from the United States as far as possible in profitable and durable ventures led the church to get involved with commercial enterprises (*Wirtschaftsunternehmen*), a move that would assure future mission projects.[49] For example, the EUB Department of World Mission and the Swiss *Nachkriegshilfe* (after war aid) agreed to buy raw cotton and to sell it via Switzerland to textile companies in Germany. In this way they earned money to pay for church reconstruction in Germany, food delivery from Switzerland, church institutions, and specific mission projects. The next step involved transforming the raw cotton into clothes, towels, bedclothes, and drapes or whatever else was needed and could be sold to the congregations. The main reason for this transaction was that, before the monetary reform, the market value of raw goods was very low, and it was not possible to transfer money to Germany. With the help of these trading operations the church estimated it would obtain about twice the original monetary value of the raw goods. At the same time, church members and others could get much-needed textiles cheaper than they could in stores because there were no intermediary trade costs.

Finally, a catalog company (*Versandhaus Textilpost GmbH*) was created by a church member by order of the *Hilfswerk der*

Evangelischen Gemeinschaft. Church members from abroad bought coupons valued from five to one hundred Swiss franks, which they sent to German families who were then able to order goods according to their needs. The whole transaction was called *Dollar-Veredelungsprogramm* (dollar refining program). It was sound financial practice, as was all too evident when transactions were later forced to cease. Problems arose because of questions concerning the fairness of the trade. Customs checks investigating these complaints temporarily halted the business. Moreover, excessive demands made on ministers to participate in the sale of clothes to obtain the calculated sum needed created further problems, as did the need to find alternative credit if the money was not earned in time.

Other actions were undertaken. For example, it was well known that silk stockings were treasured by women and so were likely to be highly profitable. A kind Evangelical United Brethren tradesman in the United States donated a machine to produce these silk stockings. However, soldiers of the occupation army also traded using silk stockings, so conflict ensued here too.

Recognizing that lard could be delivered with duty prepaid, The Evangelical United Brethren literally sent tons of lard. It was intended for sale to companies first, but when the stipulated companies did not approve the deliveries, it was sent instead to congregations of the *Evangelische Gemeinschaft*. Ministers gave it to people in need after investigation by customs prohibited its sale by congregations on the grounds that it was obtained by donation. Ministers were asked to allocate it by the pound, begging for a donation of 2 DM (German mark). Donations were seldom given.

This creative response to social and political developments and the flexibility in meeting the needs of sisters and brothers above all political distinctions show, in my opinion, a deep understanding of mission as defined in the introduction to this chapter. On this understanding, mission is cross-national, ecumenical, rooted in God's love, and close to people's needs. It is also holistic in that it does not separate material and physical needs from sacred or spiritual needs. Indeed, it is amazing what members of The Evangelical United Brethren Church worldwide were able to do, even though litigation brought the entire project to an end in 1953. In 1950, the Central Conference stated that because of the

Textil-Veredelungsaktion, 1.335.404 DM were earned for the church. Between 1948 and 1957, The Evangelical United Brethren built seventy-six churches and church buildings in the three western annual conferences. They also built apartment houses along with a residential area for displaced persons and a hostel for workers. They even rebuilt hospitals as well as residences for older people and homes for leisure and for convalescing. Superintendent Richard Leger[50] summarized all of this work well, saying: "In our hearts is the memorial of brotherly help as a bright testimony in deep need and as speaking actions of the love of Jesus Christ. The faith, that is acting through love, delivered a glorious demonstration of the community of faith, of love and ministry to praise God."[51]

While The Evangelical United Brethren were working to meet the many physical and material needs after the war, they were also busy producing basic theological works and publications. They were particularly focused at this time on training ministers for the work of evangelism. To this end, they adopted the simple motto, *Each member an evangelist*. Additionally, they appointed a full-time evangelist to each conference and supported tent evangelism. From 1951 onward, this work was done in conjunction with The Methodist Church, and from 1956 onward, the *Methodistenkirche* and *Evangelische Gemeinschaft* held joint conferences for evangelism in Berlin. In 1959 the *Evangelische Gemeinschaft* started evangelistic radio broadcasting programs. At the beginning of the 1960s, both churches started worker evangelism programs.

Like the Methodist congregations in Germany, congregations of the *Evangelische Gemeinschaft* reported growth of 30 percent up to 1950.[52] "Youth for all" camp meetings led an increasing number of young people to respond to the call to become ministers.[53] Indeed, ministers in that time recognized their overriding responsibility for the young people who had effectively lost their childhood during the war and who now came back with wounded souls in need of healing. Thus the annual conferences assigned special officers to support youth work in local congregations, and they created a special board for organization and to help ensure a fast response to requests for help (*Kirchliches Jugendamt der Evangelische Gemeinschaft in Deutschland*). This work was supported by the Evangelical Youth Fellowship in the United States at multiple levels. For example, they helped organize a study exchange program and they published materials for youth leaders and for weekly meetings along with new youth hymnbooks.

Beginning in the mid- to late 1950s, the church entered a period of stagnation. By the 1960s, church membership was in decline. Despite this situation, the news that plans were under way to unite The Methodist Church and The Evangelical United Brethren Church generated real hope for many. In Germany, the dialogue about union, which had begun decades earlier, was urgently resumed. Agreement in faith, doctrine, and church structure was once again stated, and the hope of a collective missionary impact was shared. After all, cooperation still existed in the tent missions as well as in the education of ministers in East Germany.

After the General Conference in Dallas approved church union on April 23, 1968, the German Central Conference followed suit. Because of the political situation, this had to be undertaken in two parts. First, it was approved at a conference in May in Dresden for the congregations in the *Deutsche Demokratische Republik* (German Democratic Republic). Second, it was approved at a conference a week later in Frankfurt am Main for the congregations in *die Bundesrepublik Deutschland* (Federal Republic of Germany).

THE CONTINUING INFLUENCE OF THE EVANGELICAL UNITED BRETHREN IN GERMANY TODAY

The United Methodist Church is more than forty years old. From a statistical standpoint, the hopes that the union would increase the church's effectiveness in mission have gone unrealized. The *Evangelisch-methodistische Kirche* (UMC in Germany) has continued to lose members. There is some comfort perhaps to be taken in the fact that this parallels the development of other churches (excepting Pentecostal movements). It is also worth restating that, today, Methodists have a voice in the whole concert of Protestant churches. This has partly to do with the fact that many Methodists are deeply involved in ecumenical dialogue and action. It is also partly because of the fact that many Methodists are well educated and able to make a serious contribution in a country that is nowadays acknowledged as a mission field.

In my judgment, the union of the *Methodistenkirche* and the *Evangelische Gemeinschaft* was mostly successful. Even so, ministers frequently report that the former traditions can be discerned and experienced in their congregations. In particular, the following characteristics of the *Evangelische Gemeinschaft* are mentioned: (1) people are simple in their faith and in their understanding of Christian community; (2) congregations feel and behave much more as an association and have no "church" identity or loyalty; (3) congregations are ecumenically open but at the same time very firm (uncompromising) in their conviction that being Christian must be deeply rooted in personal faith and conversion; and (4) congregations focus on renewal and transformation.

Beyond these reports from the field, what is very important among the many things that the *Evangelische Gemeinschaft* brought into the union is a part of the church name. After long negotiations, the church name *United Methodist Church* was not exactly translated in Germany because of the objection of the *Evangelische Gemeinschaft*. For the authorities in Germany it was essential to include *evangelisch* in the name in order to point to the Reformation. The historical addition *methodistisch* points to the specific history and theological accent of the Methodist branch of the Reformation.

CHAPTER 11

"TRUE HOLINESS" AS SOCIAL PRACTICE IN THE EVANGELICAL AND UNITED BRETHREN TRADITIONS: A LEGACY FOR SUCCESSOR DENOMINATIONS[1]

Wendy J. Deichmann Edwards

In a humble volume titled *The Story of Red Bird Mission*, Roberta Schaeffer recounted the history of a mission project in Kentucky, begun in 1921, by The Evangelical Church. This brief narrative, published in 1980, expressed a worldview in which human history, religious faith, social practice, and the power of God intertwine in a creative dynamic of redeeming love that can be seen, felt, tasted, touched, and heard. Far from a chronology of dates, places, and names, she began: "The story of Red Bird—The Kentucky Mountain Mission... is one of deep faith in God." The mission, she wrote, "is a story of gracious outpouring of prayer and means by the church. Most of all it is a story of mountain people and those privileged to work with them, sharing together the blessed love of

Christ."[2] Schaeffer's simple and pietistic interpretation of the history of this mission and the lives it transformed exemplifies the inextricability of Christian faith, piety, and social practice that characterized the Evangelical, United Brethren, and Evangelical United Brethren (EUB) traditions in America.

The purpose of this chapter is twofold: first, to sketch the relationship between religious faith and social practice in these communions, and second, to suggest possible implications of this study for The United Methodist Church in the twenty-first century. What was it about the living faith of the Evangelicals and their counterparts in the Church of the United Brethren in Christ that prompted them to birth vital missions like Red Bird and to insist on an ambitious, missional, and often progressive social agenda while maintaining a simple, quiet, orthodox, and pietistic faith, and why does this matter today?

Much of the eighteenth-century German immigration to North America was prompted by desperately poor economic conditions following decades of war and disease of epidemic proportion in Europe. In the mid-Atlantic and upper midwestern North American context, hardworking settlers eventually established communities of religious faith and practice with some resemblance to what they had left behind in Europe, but also shaped by colonial and early national experience in the United States. The Evangelical and United Brethren faith traditions were generated by Lutheran Pietist, German Reformed, Mennonite, and Methodist influences on their founders, most notably the Reverends Philip William Otterbein, Martin Boehm, and Jacob Albright. German language and religious culture, including Pietism, factored heavily into the development of the emerging German American communities that eventually joined together into one body in 1946 and subsequently, in 1968, united with American Methodists to form The United Methodist Church.

It is no secret that attention to faith-oriented social practice has historically factored prominently in the German Pietist tradition. Begun as a renewal effort within German Lutheranism, Pietism aimed at revitalizing the life of the church and its members. Their great concern and objection were the perceived religious formalism, scholasticism, corruption, and spiritual ineffectiveness of seventeenth- and eighteenth-century Protestantism. The Pietists wanted the church to return to a pure, active, and courageous faith that would be expressed in worship and daily life. F. Ernest Stoeffler noted, for example, the "profound ethical sensitivity and...amazing emphasis upon practical piety" in the work of Johann Arndt (1555–1621), who has been widely recognized as the pioneer of Lutheran Pietism. His famous treatise, *True Christianity* (1610), was written to show "wherein true Christianity consists, namely, in the proving of true, living, active faith through genuine godliness" in the Christian life.[3]

Arndt maintained that there are two goals of the Christian life: "God-love and neighbor-love." The person of faith, in his words,

> must seek to come nearer and nearer to them, growing ever more perfect in love for God and neighbor....Christ became man so God might put a lovely visible image of this love before our eyes to show us that in this unsearchable endless divine essence He is eternal love, so that [the human] might become like the divine image of love in Christ....And, like divine and human natures in Christ, so God-love and neighbor-love cannot be separated.[4]

The figure to whom the founding of the German Pietist movement is often credited, Philipp Jakob Spener (1635–1705), revered the work of Johann Arndt as well as that of the Puritan Pietists. Most well known for his tract *Pia Desideria*, Spener wanted to reform the church through a revival of the practice of piety, including group Bible study, cultivation of spiritual life through practice and holy living, enforcement of Christian standards on candidates for ministry, and the preaching of sermons to edify believers in "faith and its effects."[5] German Pietism was, however, a broad movement for the renewal of Christianity. Stoeffler characterized adherents to this movement as Christians who "chose to regard true reformation not merely as a renewal of doctrine and ecclesiastical practice, but as a thoroughgoing renewal of man's entire life, including his social institutions."[6] In his book *Early German-American Evangelicalism: Pietist Sources on Discipleship and Sanctification*, J. Steven O'Malley traced the major sources and influences from German Pietism on the Evangelical United Brethren founders, which later dovetailed with the early Methodist carriers of Pietism to the American context.[7] These influences found expression in the distinctive doctrine, theology, and history of the Evangelical and United Brethren churches.

The doctrinal location for a theology of Christian social practice in the Evangelical and United Brethren traditions is recorded in Article XI of the Confession of Faith of The Evangelical United Brethren Church, under the heading "Sanctification and Christian Perfection."[8] It is important to note the proximity and theological linkage between justification, regeneration, good works, sanctification, and Christian perfection in the articles of the Confession of Faith.[9] They are inextricably linked as the saving work of Christ in justification flows seamlessly into the embodiment of salvation in and through the believer to others by the power of the Holy Spirit. It is here that The Evangelical United Brethren Church gave official institutional credence to the Pietist tradition's undeniable connection between faith and its practice or, in the simple but profoundly meaningful words of Johann Arndt, "Christian life."

Although there were differences between the Evangelical and United Brethren traditions when it came to application, the two German American denominations adopted similar teachings about Christian social practice. In a study booklet sponsored by the United Brethren and Evangelical churches in the two years before the denominations merged, Evangelical Bishop C. H. Stauffacher maintained:

> The Evangelical United Brethren Church inherits the belief, common to both her predecessors, that in Jesus Christ is found the cure for all our social ills, and that in him can be found salvation from the national sins that curse our society and impede the progress of the kingdom of God on earth. Therefore, true to the ideals of her common inheritance, The Evangelical United Brethren Church will have something to say about such things as leisure time, literature, amusements, gambling, temperance, divorce, race relations, slavery, the economic order, international relations, citizenship, and war.[10]

In the same volume, Evangelical Bishop J. S. Stamm added that the order of redemption, made possible by the work of Jesus Christ, is established and made effective "in the hearts and relationships of men" and women through the leadership and power of the Holy Spirit.[11]

In the early years of the United Brethren and Evangelical churches, these bodies took official positions regarding many social issues as an outworking of belief in the practice of Christian life. Temperance and Sabbath observance were strictly advocated by the Church of the United Brethren in Christ, while slavery, gambling, the use of tobacco, and secret societies were consistently prohibited. Except for reason of adultery, divorce was not allowed. The Church of the United Brethren in Christ increasingly supported the rights of women within the church, ordaining Ella Niswonger to full clergy status in 1889, a full sixty-seven years before the more culturally accommodating American Methodists followed suit. The Evangelical Church mirrored the Church of the United Brethren in Christ with regard to temperance and tobacco, and also solidly opposed slavery in any form, but staunchly declined to support the ordination of women for social reasons of their own until they were outvoted in the 1968 merger with the Methodists, who had begun ordaining women to full clergy status twelve years earlier, in 1956.

As the nineteenth century turned to the twentieth century, as the social gospel movement became more visible in North American Protestantism, the United Brethren and Evangelical churches responded, with others, to desperate areas of social crisis. Both denominations officially supported the 1908 Social Creed of the Federal Council of Churches. In 1930 the Evangelicals formed a Board of Public Morals (in 1938 renamed the Board of Christian Social Action) based on the principle that "men must be converted not simply to a personal faith in Jesus Christ, but to the program of Jesus as a method of social reconstruction." In 1933 the United Brethren Church created a Social Service Commission (renamed the Board of Christian Social Action in 1945) "to study social life and lead the church forward in the advancement of social justice."[12] Both denominations encouraged their members to become involved in civic affairs and founded numerous benevolent homes for needy children and older citizens.

The archives of both denominations are replete with examples of ways that their leaders and members applied the concept of holiness to social practice. For example, the Women's Missionary Association of the United Brethren Church issued a booklet in 1933 to encourage its members "to study some of the problems around us, and try to become aware of our duties as missionary women." The lesson contained the following prayer:

> Lord, make me quick to see
> Each task awaiting me,
> And quick to do!
> Oh, grant me strength I pray
> With lowly love, each day
> And purpose true,
> To go as Jesus went,
> Spending, and being spent,
> Myself forgot,
> Supplying human needs
> By loving words and deeds. Amen.

The lesson used prayer, hymns, Scripture, and "newspaper and magazine articles showing current conditions and need." Women were urged to study the needs of the following: migrants, "vagabond" children, "the immigrant in our midst," racial groups, and labor conditions. They were encouraged to "pray for each of these groups, and for ourselves as Christians, and the church that through us the spirit of Christ may be manifested and the Rule of God be lived." In the closing hymn, "Oh Master, Let Me Walk with Thee," the women were encouraged to dedicate themselves "to the cause of human brotherhood."[13]

Following the merger of the Evangelical and United Brethren churches, in 1946 the General Conference of the new denomination authorized a Commission on Christian Social Action, calling members "to confront the crucial issues of life in the context of evangelical faith which centered on a living, loving God who had revealed himself in Jesus Christ." The Evangelical United Brethren Church created auxiliary bodies in annual conferences and local congregations. The commission distributed study literature to encourage more serious reflection upon the opportunities and obligations of Christian people in confronting social issues and "drafted position papers for presentation to General Conference." Representatives of the commission participated in national and international ecumenical conferences on religion and race, church and state, and world order. While attention to traditional issues such as Sabbath keeping, temperance, and tobacco usage continued, greater focus was placed on matters of social justice, freedom, human rights, and peace.[14] The Uniting Conference also "endorsed a statement on social beliefs based on the positions of the two uniting churches on social issues, patterned after the statements of the Federal Council of Churches."[15]

The study material produced by The Evangelical United Brethren Church between 1946 and 1968 demonstrated a continuing commitment to the relationship between Christian faith and social practice. In his 1948 booklet titled *Christian Service*, Professor Roy D. Miller described the history of Christian practice from the early church through the present day. He wrote:

> The early church by applying two of the most basic principles of Jesus—love and inward righteousness—took care of the needs of people, especially those in their own fellowship, in the spirit of Christian charity. During the first three centuries the motivation in Christian living was love—a self-denying love, a love directed toward helping the needy, an active love centering not in words but in deeds.[16]

The following year, the leadership study booklet *Christian Training* provided the example of Jesus for "all who would learn the art of true spiritual leadership." Jesus was described by the author, Bishop Epp, as "self-forgetful to the very limit. Never did He use his divine power to personal or selfish advantage. His thoughts, his prayers, his teachings, his ministries are always for others. Here, leader of youth and men, is your perennial, perfect pattern. Learn to love and know Him and you shall grow more and more like Him."[17]

The issue of race was a prominent, if challenging, arena for applying the principles of faithful Christian life and social practice in the Evangelical, United Brethren, and Evangelical United Brethren churches. German language and the strong antislavery stances taken by the Evangelicals and United Brethren before Emancipation circumscribed the scope of their influence in the southern United States. As a result, the Evangelicals and United Brethren were spared the nightmare of division over slavery and the legacy of institutional racism that was the fate of the Methodist Episcopals following The Methodist Episcopal Church vote in 1785 to refer the ethics of the slavery issue to the states. Thus, while The

Methodist Church was administering a segregated jurisdiction of African American members as a form of compromise dictated by its reuniting conference in 1939, the Uniting Conference of the Evangelicals and United Brethren in 1946 reaffirmed positions on racial equality held consistently by both predecessor denominations. The conference commended the congregations and colleges that were practicing integration and declared:

> The Church respects human personality inherent in the people of every race, and protests against social, economic, or political discrimination based merely on racial differences. We therefore urge our members:
> 1. To encourage inter-racial fellowship.
> 2. To maintain friendly relations through the home, school and church.
> 3. To oppose all practices of racial segregation.
> 4. To keep our churches open to men of all races.
> 5. To support legislation in harmony with these convictions.[18]

The Evangelical United Brethren Church continued its intentional support for racial equality throughout the civil rights era. For example, the General Christian Social Action Committee of the denomination made the following statement at the 1954 General Conference in support of the Supreme Court's decision that declared segregation unconstitutional:

> We urge our church members to assist in preparing their communities psychologically and spiritually for implementing the Supreme Court's decision. We call upon our church members to co-operate with the authorized agencies in their communities, as effective means for accomplishing racial integration must be indivisible in character. To put this decision into effect will test the goodwill and discipline of peoples in many communities. We call upon our local churches, Annual Conferences, colleges and theological seminaries, Boards and institutions to implement this decision so that men everywhere may be lifted to new levels of social responsibility and new dimensions of human brotherhood.[19]

As an example of follow-up, in 1958 the Virginia Conference of The Evangelical United Brethren Church adopted a statement prohibiting the use of church property for "any group that in any way supports segregation or is part of a designed plan to delay integration."[20]

The Evangelical United Brethren Church included the study of race relations in its published materials from children's curricula to leadership and ministerial education. An EUB camp curriculum in 1955 included the lesson "We Are All Alike, Yet We Are Different." Using Ephesians 2:10 as a text, the workbook taught that "God has created each of us just as we are and it is His intention that every one should have equal rights and privileges when dealing with and living among others." The program encouraged discussion about "different national backgrounds, the color of our hair, our skin, our habits...our ways of expressing ourselves and...our prejudices."[21] A Leadership Education textbook for youth, young adults, and men's or women's groups published by the Otterbein Press in Dayton, Ohio, included the chapter "Who Is My Neighbor?" This program emphasized refugee relief, equality in race relations, and "the policy of respecting the [Native American] Indian as an individual and learning to know and understand his heritage and culture."[22]

In 1963 a joint declaration on race relations was issued by Evangelical Theological Seminary and United Theological Seminary stating that "the immediate months ahead may well offer an historic opportunity to build structures of justice in conformity to the moral laws of God, and the spirit of Christian charity. This calls us all in the Church to repent of our sins of prejudice and inaction and to take immediate steps to effect change." The two EUB seminaries called on "all fellow Christians to join us in the following concrete actions":

1. Examine the life of the Church, to discover and remove all practices and attitudes which deny the inclusive nature of the Church....
2. Act to direct the policies of local churches so as to create a force in each community striving for open housing, fair employment, and desegregation of facilities serving the public.
3. Send letters and telegrams to senators, congressmen, and local officials in support of civil rights legislation....
4. Support, join with, and identify ourselves with Negro citizens in their organized efforts for civil rights in every way possible.

> 5. Act personally to extend friendship to persons of all races and seek to encourage friendly contacts between the races in and out of the Church.
>
> We declare that, under God, we must act with and toward all men as the men for whom Christ died. As it was costly for him, so it may be costly for us. Words are no longer useful in this struggle unless accompanied by sacrifice and commitment.

Echoing the traditional Evangelical United Brethren understanding of true holiness as the fruit of sanctification, the seminary statement concluded with a call for the costly incarnation of love toward "every human person in the world;... once again love must become incarnate in life."[23]

One may wonder whether these statements functioned as mere rhetoric for the sake of doctrinal or theological correctness. Yet there is the story told by a young African American Baptist student named Charles Brown who enrolled at the then EUB United Theological Seminary in Dayton, Ohio, in 1959, and graduated in 1962. More recently known as the Reverend Dr. Charles Brown, who also studied at Boston University and taught on the faculties of both United and Yale, this preacher and teacher tells the story of his own amazement at the welcome, hospitality, and support he enjoyed as a student at United in the late 1950s and early 1960s when it seemed as if the whole country was exploding into violence over racial tension. Perhaps most poignant is his story of the white students who, with him, went on a seminary choir tour in the cities of the United States and who ate with him in a working-class bar because the "whites only" restaurant would not serve the African American who was a part of their student group. Something more than rhetoric moved the EUB students to practice what they affirmed—that this was the right thing to do.[24]

Similarly, the dismantling of the racially segregated Central Jurisdiction of The Methodist Church was a prerequisite placed on negotiations for the 1968 merger by The Evangelical United Brethren Church. The legacy of pietistic God-love and neighbor-love expressed in race relations for decades in the much smaller denomination was finally embraced by the larger body and by the new denomination as well.

In a 1962 article in the EUB denominational periodical, historian Dr. Arthur C. Core observed that "true pietists have been careful to teach that one does not get on in effective Christian living by a set of rules or platform.... Rather, [the pietistic witness of our tradition] says 'Expose yourself to the living Word of God.' Only he can renew the church and empower its members for the actions necessary for involvement in social matters." He concluded, "Pietism evolved as a movement determined to keep open the way to the deepest possible relationship to God in Christ through his church, and to point Christians into the pathway of true holiness and love."[25]

The implications of the legacy of the pietistic, Evangelical United Brethren heritage within United Methodism are numerous. Four in particular are worth mentioning. First, what has become of the doctrine of sanctification and Christian perfection—the matter of "true holiness"—as advocated not only by the German American Pietists, but also by John Wesley himself? If The United Methodist Church has translated this, at best, into a democratic vote by a minority of its members who are nonexpert voting delegates at each General Conference, in order to contrive and declare majority positions and policies on social issues, something has been taken away from the legacy that was left by our forebears in the faith.

Second, can our own Pietist heritage assist The United Methodist Church in overcoming its vast, searing, and distracting divisions over social practice? Can we find some worthy precedents to help us prioritize and hold fast to the value of godly love in our discourse and practice as a denomination?

Third, in the twenty-first century, are the scholars and pastors within The United Methodist Church sufficiently secure in their craft and calling to take with seriousness the dynamic, life-giving work of the Holy Spirit in prayer, regeneration, and sanctification in believers and in the church in its mission?

Fourth, in the simple, living faith of the Pietists, perhaps The United Methodist Church will find worthy precedents for a focus on what is most important to the Christian faith: the living Word of God and the salvation that is brought to the world through the incarnation, death, and resurrection of the God in Christ who is "Love itself."[26] If this becomes the case, there should be little doubt that The United Methodist Church will in fact become vitally renewed with true holiness for the life-giving mission of Jesus Christ in the world.

CHAPTER 12

WOMEN IN THE PIETIST HERITAGE OF METHODISM

Paul W. Chilcote

No examination of the Pietist heritage of Methodism could be complete without serious attention being given to women.[1] This should go without saying, but even in this new millennium, relative silence still reigns with regard to the role that women played in the Evangelical and United Brethren traditions—those strands woven together with those of The Methodist Church to form The United Methodist Church in 1968. Historians have only begun to scratch the surface of a monumental legacy that begs for careful excavation to unearth treasures long hid. This chapter will explore what scholars have recovered thus far with regard to the legacy of women and what salient themes characterize women in the Pietist heritage of Methodism.

THE PIETIST ROOTS OF WESLEYAN, EVANGELICAL, AND UNITED BRETHREN RENEWAL

Before examining some of the historiography of women in the Evangelical United Brethren heritage, we do well to remind ourselves of the rich Pietist soil into which the women of earliest Methodism in Britain and the Evangelical and United Brethren women of the early nineteenth century sank their roots. There is no need to rehearse the close connections between continental Pietism and the Wesleyan movement in England, particularly through the relationship of the Wesleys to the Moravians, all of which are well documented.[2] Little has been written, however, to demonstrate how women appropriated this important inheritance. The records demonstrate how directly Pietist influence shaped the early Methodist women. One of the few references in the Wesleyan corpus to the great Pietist figure August Hermann Francke, for example, relates directly to women. In 1763, Mary Bosanquet and Sarah Ryan established an orphanage and school for the poorest of the poor in London. John Wesley kept this model Christian community, combining vibrant personal piety and active social service, under his personal surveillance. On December 1, 1764, he expressed his optimism and great expectations concerning its progress: "M[ary] B[osanquet] gave me a further account of their affairs at Leytonstone. It is exactly *Pietas Hallensis* in miniature. What it will be does not yet appear."[3]

Wesley alludes here specifically to the famous tract of Francke in which the Pietist leader provided a historical narrative of his missional activity in Saxony.[4] He draws attention to the striking affinity, in both spirit and methodology, of the Leytonstone experiment and Francke's enterprise. Moreover, these early Methodist women exhibited all the salient characteristics of their Pietist counterparts in their emphasis on the Christian life as a life of devotion, faith as trust in Christ and not simply assent to truth, and moral courage that translates faith into action for the glory of God.[5] The Church of the United Brethren in Christ had its religious and doctrinal roots in Pietism.[6] Otterbein himself had been steeped in this tradition by his theological teachers at Herborn Academy. But Albright also expressed his spirituality in the genre of German Pietism, and there can be no question that the women of both movements drank deeply from this common well. After an examination of scholarship related to the lives and contributions of the women, therefore, I will explore how the several themes of Pietism I have identified—*prayer, faith,* and *work*—characterized the history of Evangelical and United Brethren women.

THE RECOVERY OF HER STORY

Scholars of the Evangelical United Brethren heritage have taken a number of strides forward in an effort to recover the lost history of women, but the work has only just begun, being little more than a quarter century old. It is still difficult even to identify stages in the evolution of this historiography because of to the paucity of contemporary studies.[7] Much of the work continues to revolve around the collection of data and remains compensatory in nature.

In *Conduct Becoming to a Woman*, Elaine Magalis explored the barriers to ministry and mission that impeded women, and included several inspirational stories from the Evangelical and United Brethren traditions.[8] Her study represents one of the first serious efforts to develop an interpretive framework concerning the women. Jean Miller Schmidt's groundbreaking study, *Grace Sufficient: A History of Women in United Methodism*, attempted to incorporate the EUB heritage of women into the larger Methodist historical narrative, the first panoramic history of women in the tradition.[9] But the foundational work of data collection and archival development remains a primary desideratum that will make possible a more critical, synthetic, heuristic, and therefore genuinely appreciative portrait of the women.

Finally, Donald Gorrell blazed the trail regarding to the heritage of Pietist women in Methodism. In his incisive essay "A New Impulse," in addition to demonstrating the glaring differences between the Evangelical and United Brethren traditions with regard to women, he identified two critical areas of women's leadership that emerged during the final decades of the nineteenth century and remained fixed until merger in 1968, namely, the rise and influence of *women's missionary societies* and the issue of *women's representation* in the structures of the churches.[10] In addition to these two areas of concern, the question of *women's ordination* tends to dominate the scholarship. All of these studies reveal a truly remarkable history!

THE PATH TO WOMEN'S ORDINATION

Interestingly enough, although essentially parallel to the emergence of the missionary societies, the advent of women preachers and women's ordination chronologically preceded those developments. James Will's study "The Ordination of Women" in the United Brethren heritage, published in a collection of essays concerning woman's rightful place, established the essential narrative related to the women preachers and laid the groundwork for several subsequent studies.[11] In the 1840s, even when the segregation of the sexes in worship was still the general practice of the United Brethren, women began to agitate for their rightful place in the ministry of the church. As early as 1841, L. Courtland applied for a license of preach in the Scioto Annual Conference.[12] Both her petition and that of Louisa Clemens in 1843 were denied, however, at the General Conference of 1845. In 1847 Charity Opheral received a "note of commendation" from the White River Conference, and despite its ambiguities, this note is usually considered the first annual conference license to preach granted to a woman in the Church of the United Brethren in Christ. On May 3, 1851, Lydia Sexton was the first to receive a formal quarterly license, and even after the 1857 General Conference action that prohibited such licenses for women, the requisite annual renewals seem to have been easy for her to obtain.[13] Following the disruptions of the Civil War, Maggie Thompson became the second woman to receive such a license (1874). But throughout this period occurred the preaching of other women, a group that Julia Dagenais has described as "a sisterhood of preachers." She claims, "Doubtless each of these women, about whom we know so little, had a rich story to tell—an inviting challenge to the historian."[14]

The influx of women into Union Biblical Seminary after its founding in 1871 created a circle of educated women who could move fluidly into leadership roles within the Church of the United Brethren in Christ.[15] The seminary permitted the wife of a student, Mrs. C. B. Beatty, to take classes in 1874. Perhaps her presence in the classroom prompted a serious conversation about women, because the governing body took a bold step and decided to admit women the following year (1875). There can be no question that this action prepared the way for women in ministry. The first woman graduate, Esther Balmer Sage, completed her studies in the English curriculum in 1883. Ella Niswonger was the first female student to graduate in the more rigorous regular curriculum in 1887.[16] A woman of many firsts, as we shall see, she stands out as a pioneer second to none in the quest for egalitarianism in the church. Two years later, the seminary added a new missionary curriculum, and then a deaconess curriculum, that attracted many women. These developments paved the way for the momentous United Brethren General Conference of 1889, which stands out as one of the most significant events in its history. Among many of the critical issues it addressed and upon which it acted, the ordination of women figured prominently. The debate over this question reflects and was informed by parallel developments in the Methodist Protestant and Methodist Episcopal Churches during this same period. In the end, the General Conference acted decisively:

> Not wishing to hinder any Christian, who may be moved by the Holy Spirit, to labor in the vineyard of God for the salvation of souls, it is ordered, that whenever any godly woman presents herself before the quarterly or annual conference as an applicant for authority to preach the gospel among us, she may be licensed to do so... and may be ordained after the usual probation.[17]

Within just four months, the Central Illinois Conference conferred the license to preach on both Ella Niswonger and Maggie Elliott, and on the following day, September 3, 1889, Ella Niswonger became the first ordained woman in the United Brethren heritage. Other conferences ordained women in quick succession. Jim Will compiled a listing of nearly one hundred women who were ordained by the turn of the twentieth century.[18] Of the many women in this growing fellowship, one stands out as particularly noteworthy: Minnie Jackson Goins. According to Patricia Thompson, "She may be not only the first black woman ordained in the UB Church but also the first black woman ordained in the entire United Methodist tradition."[19] Ordained in 1904, she held the position of "Evangelist at Large" in the Northwest Kansas Conference throughout her ministerial career.

Many had assumed that the 1889 General Conference action to approve the ordination of women contributed to the secession of the Old Constitution Brethren that same year. But Daryl Elliott's examination of the records led him to a different conclusion.[20] The evidence demonstrates that the ordination of women was not one of the divisive issues for the "conservative" party. Addressing this question at their own "Constitutional Convention," the "conservatives" approved the following resolution that has remained unchanged ever since: "There shall be no discrimination between men and women in the matter of granting ministerial credentials."[21] As a consequence of this action, the Michigan Conference of the "Old Constitution" church immediately licensed Mrs. S. A. Lane and Mrs. L. J. Batdorf to preach. Both women were ordained subsequently at the next General Conference, admitted to itineracy, and played an important role, along with other women, in the early years of this branch of the tradition.

Much more captive to the conservative tendencies of its German cultural inheritance, The Evangelical Association never adopted parallel legislation. Despite the fact that proponents of female preaching and ordination engaged the debate in the *Evangelical Messenger* as early as 1872, the Association doggedly maintained its prohibition of women's licensing and ordination, and the evidence seems to indicate that some leaders sought to stifle the ministry of women as Evangelicals moved forward into union with the United Brethren.[22] As Jim Will simply concluded: "In the union of the two denominations, there arose a clash of traditions."[23] In 1988, Jonathan Cooney demonstrated, however, that Evangelical United Brethren members maintained the tradition of ordaining women despite whatever prohibitive agreements may have been struck behind closed doors.[24] Not only were the previously ordained women of the United Brethren tradition permitted to retain their orders and serve in the ministry of the church, but a whole new generation of women filled the ranks as well. According to Cooney, "At least 149 women held the order of elder in some form in the Evangelical United Brethren Church. The greatest number of these were in Ohio, Indiana, Pennsylvania, and Nebraska."[25] Of these, some sixty served in the itinerant ministry. Cooney identified twenty-three women who were ordained between 1946 and 1968. "Not only were the annual conferences ordaining women," he observed, "they were actively encouraging them to prepare for ordination!"[26]

In the Evangelical United Brethren heritage, therefore, although women struggled to find a place behind the pulpits of The Evangelical Association, the fact remains that United Brethren women gained full clergy rights sixty-seven years before the same status was granted to Methodist women in 1956.

The Rise of Women's Missionary Societies

In her magisterial study of American women in mission, Dana Robert observes that "by 1900, over forty denominational women's societies existed, with three million active women, some despite sustained hostility from the men of the church."[27] According to Rosemary Keller, "Women's foreign and home missionary societies enlisted more women into service in the late nineteenth century than any type of women's organization in the country."[28] The women of the Evangelical United Brethren heritage played no small part in this amazing phenomenon and energized their respective denominations through these agencies. In her history of the Women's Society of World Service, Audrie Reber expressed a central conviction in this simple statement: "Thus the essential question is whether the church is organized for mission."[29] During the last quarter of the nineteenth century, Evangelical and United Brethren women rediscovered the central importance of mission in the life of the church and thereby embraced one of the most significant aspects of their Pietist heritage. This rediscovery permeated the church on every level and afforded women opportunities for service and influence seldom permitted before. As Jean Miller Schmidt discovered while she prepared her history of the Methodist women:

> I am finding that to understand and appreciate the real significance of the women's missionary organizations in helping to train women for leadership in the whole church (and indeed, in more public life as well), it is necessary to look at the strategic linkage between the national leadership and the working of other organizations on all structural levels of the church.[30]

In this brief chapter, space permits only the most rudimentary discussion of how these women helped organize the church for mission.[31]

At the beginning of the nineteenth century, Protestant women became increasingly interested in mission as they learned about the terrible plight of women and children around the globe from women who were beginning to enter the mission force. At a time when men continued to dominate church boards and missionary organizations, one avenue of service and action remained open to women, namely, prayer. Mary McLanachan, long-term mission educator and communicator in the United Brethren and then Evangelical United Brethren Church, celebrated the vision that gave birth to this movement in 1872:

> The organization of the Women's Missionary Association first took form in the heart and mind of one woman, Miss Lizzie Hoffman, a young school teacher in Dayton, OH. She struggled to know God's will for her life. Finally she spent a night in prayer, and near dawn the answer came as she perceived that she could enlist the women of the church in mission work.[32]

Exclusively female missionary societies began as small prayer group meetings focused on the burgeoning missionary activity of the church but rapidly expanded into powerful networks of women activated for mission in the world. Benjamin H. Niebel and Homer H. Dubs identified their primary value, particularly in light of their work and influence during the course of the First World War, pointing to four areas of service. They had value as a spiritual force in the world, as an agency for the training of Christian disciples, as a disseminator of information about the mission of the church in the world, and as a source of funding for God's mission.[33]

As was the case with regard to women's ordination, the United Brethren tradition pioneered the development of a churchwide organization by and for women. Inspired by Lizzie Hoffman's courageous vision, women established the Miami Branch Association of the Woman's Missionary Association on May 9, 1872. They drafted a constitution that then served as a model for each branch and, later, the national organization.[34] The General Conference of 1873 encouraged the expansion of this work. The women knew that they could expect resistance from certain quarters of the church, but the defense of their movement by Emeline Day in the *Religious Telescope* demonstrates the strength of their convictions and their sense of vocation. When criticized for usurping the prerogative of men, Emeline Day retorted:

> We want something or nothing. We are tired of standing in the anteroom, waiting for admittance and recognition. We are tired of asking for your sympathy or aid. We are tired of being asked

what we want. We now turn to you and ask, "What do you want?" We are ready to work with you for the Master. We come to you and say, "Give us work."[35]

She fired back this response to the charge of failing to subsume their work under that of the men:

> Whether the original Board shall put in the sickle first, or whether this new board, full of zeal and enthusiasm, shall outrun it, as did Mary of old when visiting the sepulcher, remains to be seen. We do not propose to wait for any "Board" or for any authority, save that of General Conference.[36]

If the misogynist sentiment expressed by some men remained a minority voice in the denomination, the die had already been cast by the approval of a churchwide structure for the organization by the Dayton General Conference in October 1875. Moreover, church magazines like the *Religious Telescope* continued to encourage the women, and the General Board of Missions actually promised any support the women might need.[37] In 1876 the WMA sent its first missionary, Emily Beeken, to Sierra Leone to open a school in Shenge. Hundreds of women soon followed her lead.

In 1874, Ella Yost and Minerva Strawman initiated a parallel work in The Evangelical Association but met immediate and almost insurmountable resistance. The church repeatedly turned back petitions even for the organization of local societies. Audrie Reber provides a succinct account of these developments that culminated in action during the 1880s:

> In 1882 the Board of Missions and General Conference supported the formation of women's societies in the local church in order to educate in missions and raise money for support. The pastors were urged to encourage and lead the women in their churches. The organization and mission policy remained completely in men's control. In 1883 the women began seeking support to form a national organization so that the local societies could be held together and the work could be united for greater effectiveness. In 1884 a national organization was approved but women were still to remain apart from any policy-making role. It was not until 1894 that a woman representative was finally invited to sit in the councils of the Board of Missions.[38]

"There is no doubt," therefore, as Donald Gorrell concluded, "that Evangelical women exercised less power and influence in missionary work than did their counterparts in the United Brethren Church."[39] Whereas "independence in organization typified the United Brethren Woman's Missionary Association... Evangelical women were affected by their dependent and auxiliary relationship to the male Board of Missions."[40]

The women's renewed concern for the mission of the church and the communication of this vision led to two other critical developments related to women toward the close of the nineteenth century that can only be touched upon briefly here. First, women launched their own periodicals—the women's missionary magazines. In 1882, the United Brethren Woman's Missionary Association began publication of the *Women's Evangel*. An editorial in the very first issue "graphically presented the challenge each denomination gave to women in their churches."[41] It continued:

> Many centuries have passed since the command was given to women, "Go and tell that Jesus has risen," but not till this century (the latter part of it) have Christian women come together with one mind and heart to roll away the stone from the living sepulcher.... Christian women of all ranks and denominations, let us join hands in one endeavor—with one thought, one prayer, one motto, one voice,—*The women of all lands for Jesus*.[42]

Four years later the Women's Missionary Society's *Women's Messenger* began serving the Evangelical constituency. In 1892, when division within The Evangelical Association led to the formation of the United Evangelical Church, Elizabeth Krecker was elected to lead women's mission work under a new Woman's Home and Foreign Missionary Society, which launched *Missionary Tidings* that same year.[43] According to Magalis, these missionary magazines "not only helped thousands to identify with the missions cause, they made money.... These journals were to be found in parlors and drawing rooms, in parsonages and churches throughout the country. Women read them avidly and, through them, participated vicariously in the work of the missionaries."[44]

Second, Dana Robert has argued that "the cultural and theological attitude of the women's missionary movement at the beginning of the twentieth century was characterized by its motto:

'Woman's work for woman.'"[45] This motto reflects a pervasive emphasis on the need to improve women's lives both at home and around the world.[46] The provision of medical care in pregnancy and childbirth, therefore, as well as the care of children in well-baby clinics, typified the women's work, and perhaps no more dramatically than through the emerging role of *deaconesses*.[47] According to Behney and Eller, "impressed by similar movements in other American denominations, the [United Brethren] General Conference in 1897 gave official approval for deaconess service, embracing visitation, evangelization, and humanitarian Christian efforts."[48] The Evangelical Association followed suit in 1903. In the early twentieth century the churches developed more formal structures for deaconess education and work leading to licensure and consecration. While the deaconess movement enlarged the sphere of activity for women, some men viewed it as a clear alternative that kept women out of the ordained ministry. Neither the history of the deaconess movement within this tradition nor the way in which women navigated the complexity of such attitudes has been investigated thoroughly. Despite the fact that the deaconess movement never developed into a significant force within the Evangelical and United Brethren traditions as it did in the parallel Methodist bodies, this forgotten story, in other words, needs to be reclaimed.

The women's societies influenced the church on every level. Space prohibits a discussion of the complex history of these organizations from the closing decade of the nineteenth century and through the mergers and consolidations necessitated by divisions within the life of the church and subsequent unions in the twentieth century.[49] The institutional histories are fairly well known even though a coherent narrative that seeks to place these developments in a more fully textured cultural and social context remains to be done. Less known are the stories of the women themselves—leaders like Ella Yost, Minerva Strawman Spreng, Susan Bauernfeind, Sarah Dickey, Mellie Perkins, Mrs. W. H. Hammer, Elizabeth Krecker, Justina Lorenz Showers, and Mary McLanachan[50]—who not only shaped the institutions they led but the denominations they loved. As Audrie Reber has demonstrated, "The women became so apt at raising [money] that the opportunities for participation in policy-making were bound to follow."[51] But their contribution far exceeded finances. Participation and leadership in the societies opened the door to ecumenical relations and educational endeavors and inculcated a missional spirituality in the life of the church.

Mrs. W. H. Hammer championed the cause of a Woman's Missionary Society in The Evangelical Association and gave devoted service to its expansion throughout the denomination. She coined the motto "A Woman's Missionary Society in every congregation and every woman a member." Seldom in its history had a vision become such a reality in the life of the church.

THE QUEST FOR EQUAL REPRESENTATION FOR WOMEN

Before exploring some of the salient themes related to the Pietist women, it remains only for us to survey briefly a third issue, namely, the quest for equal representation for women in the institutional life of the church. Donald Gorrell demonstrated that with regard to this issue, the Evangelical and United Brethren traditions represent a study in contrasts.[52] As early as 1883, women were admitted as delegates to annual conference sessions in the Church of the United Brethren in Christ.[53] The revised Constitution of 1889 gave women even greater status and power within the structures of the church. In addition to the privilege of ordination, women were accorded the right to "be elected as lay delegates at all levels of the church."[54] In 1893, Mattie Brewer of Lower Wabash and Mrs. S. J. Staves of Des Moines participated as the first two women delegates to General Conference.[55] In their Quadrennial Address, the bishops affirmed that "several conferences have chosen to send as delegates esteemed women from among them. These Christian women are here to-day accorded this highest representative trust in the Church, and are welcomed unchallenged to sit with us in the highest council of the denomination."[56] These actions paved the way for women clergy to find a place and voice at General Conference as well, and at the turn of the century the great woman of firsts, Ella Niswonger, took her seat as the first ordained woman at the General Conference of 1901. As in other areas of church life, The Evangelical Association delayed action in this arena. Women, in fact, were not seated at General Conference until the eve of anticipated union with the United Brethren in 1946. Mrs. Edward Stukenberg and Irene Haumersen served as delegates not only to their final Evangelical Conference, but to the Uniting Conference of the same year. So in the quest for equal representation, the United Brethren led the way, just as in the case of ordination, preceding Methodist action by thirteen years.

Women in the Pietist heritage of Methodism, and particularly among the United Brethren, pioneered in women's ordination, the development of women's missionary and deaconess societies, and the rights of women in the institutional life of the church. Rosemary Skinner Keller identified the primary legacy of the women attached to each of these movements:

> Through drives for ordination and laity rights for women, persons sought to appropriate the ministries of women in clerical functions and in the mainstream governance and decision-making of the churches on an equal basis with men. Women's missionary societies sent the first single female missionaries into the field and provided major funding for all mission work. Deaconess societies trained the first female professionals in the church who served as home and foreign missionaries and assistants to pastors. They were separatist groups "for women only," resulting essentially in a "sphere of their own," and set apart from general decision-making and clerical rights and responsibilities.[57]

SALIENT THEMES

The faithful disciples of Christ we have encountered in this brief survey of women in the Pietist heritage of Methodism left behind a remarkable legacy that ought to be known and celebrated. As I have worked through this material and encountered many remarkable stories of faith and perseverance, three salient themes have surfaced time and time again that are linked intimately with the Pietist heritage in which these women stood: *prayer, faith,* and *work*. Elizabeth Krecker offers a vision of how these primary elements are held together in the lives of authentic Christians:

Earnest prayers, coupled with faith and effort, will do wonders. Let us never forget our dependence upon God. Let us have more prayer in connection with our work.... if we can believe "that there is power in Christ for the production of holiness—I mean holiness of life and character... we shall do for our age something that is well worth doing."[58]

To illustrate these themes as personally and directly as I can, I would like to elevate the life and witness of three women representing the United Brethren, Evangelical, and United Evangelical branches of the family tree. After providing a vignette of each witness, I will draw from their writings, and those of several other women, to paint a portrait of the *spirituality, faithfulness,* and *missional* vision of these remarkable women.

VIGNETTES

Sarah Dickey (1838–1904) was born near Dayton, Ohio, on April 25, 1838.[59] Her mother died when she was eight years of age, so she was placed with hardworking farm relatives who had little concern for her thirst for education. At sixteen she took matters into her own hands, began to attend school, received her teacher's certificate, and taught for the next seven years (1857–63) in country schools near Dayton. Driven inward by the painful experiences of her childhood, she relied heavily on the inner promptings of dreams and visions. In 1858 she joined the Church of the United Brethren in Christ and felt compelled increasingly to serve as a missionary in Africa. The church's rejection of her application opened the door for her to direct her missionary zeal in an unexpected direction.

In 1863 she accepted an invitation to staff a United Brethren Freedmen's School in Vicksburg, Mississippi. Liberated by Union forces only months earlier, as many as "thirty thousand freed slaves, ragged and bewildered, swarmed the streets and crowded into bullet-ridden buildings; in some places six at a time could be found living in dingy, windowless huts no more than a few feet square."[60] A new vision began to emerge of a life work among the freed slaves of the South, and Sarah laid plans to fulfill her new dream. At the end of the war she returned north and applied for admission to Mount Holyoke Female Seminary in South Hadley, Massachusetts, one of the premier centers of education for women at that time. She completed the four-year course, despite tremendous financial hardship, and was one of thirty-eight out of the original class of one hundred to graduate in 1869.

"Burdened with debt but armed, she felt, with a divine commission to establish in the South a school like Mount Holyoke," as Helen Griffith observes, "she returned to Mississippi."[61] She taught for a year in a school established by the American Missionary Association in Raymond, but eagerly launched into a venture of her own early in 1871 at nearby Clinton. Living in the home of a leader in the African American community, and amid threats from the Klan and the ostracism of neighbors, Sarah recruited an integrated board of trustees and ultimately chartered her own school in 1873. Two years later, after having secured appropriate facilities, she opened Mount Hermon Female Seminary, a boarding school for "Negro" girls. Two months later a white mob killed her friend and supporter, Charles Caldwell, who had offered her hospitality from the outset of the work.

Sarah remained undaunted in her efforts to bring education to the least advantaged, and "Mount Hermon girls" became teachers in "Negro" elementary schools throughout the state. She may have raised as many children as she taught, her institution functioning as much like an orphanage as a school, and when Clinton closed its only facility for black children, she took those who were displaced as day scholars at Mount Hermon. Concerned about the condition of housing for many of the families she served, Sarah borrowed money to purchase additional land near the school and subdivided this property for those families who wished to build on land of their own. The residents of Dickeyville, as it came to be known, benefited from Sarah's vigilant care and concern for their well-being. Sarah was ordained by the United Brethren in 1896 and died eight years later in her beloved Clinton.

Sarah Dickey's contemporary *Elizabeth Overholtzer Krecker* (1844–1903) was born of sturdy Huguenot stock on a Lancaster County farm in Pennsylvania on August 1, 1844.[62] Reflecting on those early years when she was known as "Little Lizzie," Elizabeth attributed her faith to the influence of her parents:

> It seems to me the greatest blessing with which God in His infinite goodness has favored me is pious parents who early inculcated the doctrine of the religion of Jesus Christ into the minds and hearts of their children. All other blessings under the guidance of my heavenly Father center around this greatest of all. It is because I was born of pious parents, who early taught me to lisp the name of Jesus that I cannot remember when that sweet sound first reached my ear.[63]

Following the untimely death of her mother, and recognizing her remarkable abilities, Elizabeth's extended family provided for her education, making it possible for her to attend Union Seminary, the predecessor of Albright College. After several experiences of teaching "in the prairie" upon graduation, she returned home in autumn 1864, finding new opportunities to teach in her native state. The young teacher met Frederick Krecker, a dedicated physician, whom she married in April 1867, and immediately started a family. The year 1876 brought a remarkable turn of events to this fairly typical "professional" family when Dr. Krecker responded to an inner call to serve as a missionary in Japan.

The Kreckers' life in Tokyo energized Elizabeth, and she quickly bonded to the women and children she served. In 1880 the family moved to Tsukiji where Elizabeth encountered the poorest of the poor and thus commenced her work, alongside her husband, in the Tokyo slums. Only three years later, on April 26, 1883, Elizabeth's husband succumbed to a malignant form of typhus, and she was left alone with four children and a burgeoning ministry. Two and a half years later, she returned to the United States determined not to abandon mission but to build bridges around the world by committing herself to its promotion at home. Encouraged by the vision and work of Minerva Strawman Spreng, she quickly became a critical force within the newly conceived Woman's Missionary Society of The Evangelical Association and gained a reputation as the "Francis Willard of Women's Mission."[64] In 1888 she was elected organizer of the Woman's Missionary Society and, when division came to The Evangelical Association in 1892, was appointed to direct the women's work under the Woman's Home and Foreign Missionary Society of the United Evangelical Church, a position she held until her death.

A snapshot of one year, 1897, provides a glimpse of her indefatigable labors. In that one year she visited forty-one cities, held seventy-five meetings, gave eighty-nine addresses, and organized twenty-two auxiliaries.[65] A Methodist Episcopal bishop, who had witnessed her missionary work firsthand, described her as "the finest woman missionary he had ever met."[66] She died on November 16, 1903, just twelve miles from the farmstead where she was born.

Service in Japan binds Elizabeth to *Susan Bauernfeind* (1870–1945), the first single woman missionary sent overseas by the Woman's Missionary Association of The Evangelical Association.[67] Sailing from San Francisco, she arrived at her final destination in Tokyo, Japan, on October 10, 1900, a far cry from the log house in which she was born thirty years earlier and the Minnesota farm on which she was raised. She served faithfully for forty-three years as an ambassador of reconciliation among a people she would come to love dearly. According to Patricia Thompson, "Susan was talented and versatile, excelling as a linguist, an evangelistic missionary, a teacher, a social worker, an administrator, and an organizer."[68] Having been invited to speak about the Christian faith to teenage girls in a nearby mill, Susan opened a social center in Japan's largest cotton-spinning factory in 1902. She established her home in Koishikawa and started a Sunday school program there that evolved over time into the Koishikawa Evangelical Church, formally organized that same year. With her encouragement and support, the church became totally self-supporting by 1916, the first such achievement in the denomination.

Absolutely convinced of the wisdom embodied in the strategy to move new communities of faith from dependency to self-sufficiency, she poured her energies into the cultivation of indigenous evangelists. To this end, she established Tokyo Bible School in 1904. In the early 1920s the program expanded to include men, and the school boasted an enrollment of as many as two hundred students. In 1910 the death of a mother in childbirth led to the foundation of Aisenryo (Dormitory of the Spring of Love) Orphanage for homeless girls. Lowell and Betty Messerschmidt recall how, when the great earthquake of September 1, 1923, devastated Tokyo, Susan "led the 52 orphans out of the city to safety."[69] This courageous act earned for her one of two national recognitions related directly to her ministry, personally presented to her by the emperor of Japan.

Susan returned to the United States in March 1941 upon the recommendation of the government and never returned to her adopted home. Throughout the course of the war, she traveled across the country with a message of reconciliation. After the Japanese surrender, firsthand accounts from her coworker Lois Kramer, who had been interned in Japan during the war, left Susan devastated. The Messerschmidts recall her address based on Habakkuk 2:13-14, "The toil of the nations ends in smoke," of October 27, 1945, to the Evangelical Theological Seminary community and afford this vivid account:

> "The smoke of the burning," she stated, "speaks of the folly of hatred." She told the hushed congregation that two hundred and fifty churches in Tokyo had been destroyed while only thirty remained. She called the roll of those whom she knew to be among the casualties. She continued, "I am grateful to God that it was my privilege to spend so many years in Japan and win so many to Christ. Those who have gone on to glory through fire are with Him. They served and loved and now live victoriously with the Lord. Those who remain are courageous and taking a new lease on life. God will strengthen the Church of Christ in Japan through these faithful. They need our prayers."[70]

Later that night, Susan Bauernfeind died, many have claimed, of a broken heart.

PRAYER

These women, like their Pietist forebears, viewed the Christian life as a life of devotion. Prayer anchored their lives, provided the impetus for their extraordinary acts of courage, and sustained them in the journey toward the fullest possible realization of their humanity. Barbara Troxell and Patricia Farris have identified holistic spirituality as one of the significant contributions of women to the renewal of the church.[71] Nothing could be more true of the women who stand in the Pietist heritage. "If our Woman's Missionary Society is to do any great work," claimed Elizabeth

Krecker, "it must be done largely by prayer."[72] In a letter in which one of Susan Bauernfeind's converts of Koishikawa reflects upon his mother in the faith, he simply confesses, "She was an amazing woman of prayer." Among the many handwritten volumes to be found among the Susan Bauernfeind Papers in the Center for the Evangelical United Brethren Heritage, one consists of meditations and prayers that reflect her holistic spirituality. On November 9, 1939, at the Boshi Home in Koriyama, she shared her reflections on the importance of mothers who pray, based on Proverbs 22:6. Her cryptic notes include the following insights:

> Much said about bringing up children—teaching children—teachers, etc., but when all is said and done, there never was, there is not and never will be a better teacher than the mother.
> Reason: She knows her child best. She loves her child best.
> Hannah an ideal mother. Child Samuel given to the Lord. Ex. Syrophonecian woman. Matt. 15:27 Mark 7:28 Simplest of dramas—two persons and a chorus.
> The woman had faith. She was in earnest. She had an aim. Not discouraged by delay.
> Christ's love is liberal but it must be sued. Christ's love is wise. It keeps knocking until we become love-sick for Him.
> Faith strengthened by continued prayer.
> Ps. 6:8 Tears have a tongue & language that our Father knoweth. The only language of a baby is, weeping. Mother understands.[73]

Prayer, as we have seen, was central to the women's missionary societies. Not only did prayer give rise to the development of this movement; women practiced prayer in their common life in these significant groups. In her introduction to "Prayer in Mission," Audrie Reber referred to a frequently quoted statement in the publications of the women: "When we depend on money, we get what money can do. When we depend on organization, we get what organization can do. When we depend on program and education, we get what they can do. But when we depend on prayer, we get what God can do."[74] Virtually all the societies developed Spiritual Life Programs. Fellowships of Prayer sprang up in the various branches and united the women in one great "chain of prayer." Elizabeth Krecker emphasized the importance of prayer in virtually all her annual presidential addresses. She encouraged and inspired women to pray. Her words inspire us still today:

Let this be a year of believing prayer. Let us set apart time and give ourselves to this part of our intercessory work. It will lead into the fellowship of that compassionate heart of his that led to call for our prayers. It will elevate us to the insight of our regal position as those prayers will count for something with the great God in the advancement of his kingdom. It will make us feel how really we are God's fellow-workers on earth to whom a share in his work has in downright earnest been entrusted. It will make us partakers in the soul travail, but also in the soul satisfaction, as we know how, in answer to our prayer, blessings have been given that otherwise would not have come.[75]

A prayer by Vera Blinn expresses in poignant fashion many of the convictions about the life of prayer shared by the women:

For the daily task, a little too big and a little too hard for my present ability, and for the daily increase of power that comes to meet it.
For the opportunity to give that makes me richer.
For the privilege of service that proves me not worthless in the world.
For the unspeakable honor of working with Thee and meeting some need Thou hast of me—which I cannot understand, but can believe.
For the generous share of happiness which Thou hast given me; but more for joy, which Thou wouldst not limit, as Thou wouldst not limit obedient and loving service.
For the certainty learned from experience that Thou dost hear and answer the cry of need, and therefore that Thou wilt accept the thanksgiving of an eager, grateful heart—dear Lord and Father, I thank Thee. Amen.[76]

FAITH

As Minerva Strawman Spreng, a founder of the Woman's Missionary Society, lay on her deathbed in 1924, she left those in her hearing, and those who have ears today, an enduring testimony. "Tell them not to be afraid to attempt big things for God," she admonished. "Tell them to be faithful and keep at it!"[77] As she cared for the displaced and marginalized victims of racism in the Reconstruction South, Sarah Dickey was fond of saying, "Trust in

Christ." In the face of what often seemed to be insurmountable obstacles and impervious barriers, women put their trust in Christ. Women in the Pietist heritage of Methodism understood faith as trust in Christ, and that well-founded trust led them to accomplish great things for God. As Elizabeth Krecker prayed: "Teach me to yield myself up to thee so fully that thou wilt not only guide and support me but act by me, think through me, and live in me."[78] Elsewhere she paints a portrait of the life of faith:

> It is not creeds or constitutions or organizations in themselves that spread our Lord's precious gospel, but individual lives which are read as living epistles by all men. Let us learn more and more to love and serve, to carry comfort and consolation to homes where sorrow has come; to rejoice with those who rejoice and weep with those who weep. Let us ever seek the beautiful spirit of love that seeketh not her own, that will give and ask nothing because the heart is possessed by God. Let it be said of us . . . that we are great in our "love for God and humanity." Let the fundamental will, the propelling, motive force of all be love. "Love that serves, love that sacrifices itself, love that so sacrifices itself that it lays down life in order that the recipient of it may enter into life.". . .
> Nothing but waiting at the throne,—keeping the heart under the eyes of the Lamb, to be again and again penetrated by his Spirit—will put the soul into the condition in which it is a meet instrument to impart the light and power of God to others.[79]

In the early years of her work in Japan, Susan Bauernfeind entrusted herself and those she loved to Christ, believing that an amazing harvest would come from the seeds she had the privilege to sow. In the midst of the Second World War, she reflected on the fruit of her labor, and in a prose poem titled "Looking into the Heart of Japanese Christians" she celebrated the faithful whom she counted among her friends:

> When those missionaries who have suffered imprisonment since Pearl Harbor tell us of the steadfastness of the native Christians under very trying conditions; when they say that the best work America ever did for the millions of Japan was the giving them the Gospel because that has created a bond that can never be broken, and is absolutely indestructible, that gives us a glimpse into the heart of the Japanese Christians.

> When missionaries are imprisoned and the food is insufficient, Christians who have only too little for themselves and their families go out to search for suitable food for their teachers who are imprisoned, and beg for permission to take it to them, risking life itself to do so; when the food may consist only of a few extra eggs or pickled radishes, that is looking into the heart of Japanese Christians.[80]

She had the rare privilege of seeing her trust in Christ reflected in the loving action of those she sought to serve.

WORK

Finally, women in the Pietist heritage of Methodism possessed the moral courage to translate their faith into action for the glory of God. One of the words scattered across the pages of the women's writings is *coworkers*. Whether helping to establish the course of a missionary society, determining how best to teach the children of freed slaves, or developing social services in industrial Japan, these women viewed their brothers and sisters as coworkers in God's great mission in the world. In the meditation "Workers Together," shared with the Women's Missionary Society in Koriyama, Bauernfeind illustrated how partnership with God and one another strengthens the bond of Christian love:

> Standing alone, often discouraged. Every Christian needs Christian fellowship.
> Giving up means going backward.
> W.M.S. members—workers. Every Christian is a worker. Trained or not.
> Yokotasan bringing in others.
> God used Andrew. He brought Peter.
> Jabatasan bringing Fujisakisan. Not alone—worked with God—God with us.
> W.M.S. women one aim, one faith, therefore strong.[81]

The women were united together in a common mission. They lived out their faith with integrity, working together for the restoration of God's rule in the lives of all people.

In Elizabeth Krecker's address for New Year's Day in 1898 she offered this poignant vision of a missional church and its vocation in God's world:

> We want our people to regard their association with the church not merely as a means of enjoying religious privileges, but as an entrance into activity for spreading a knowledge of God.... We do not want our church to be a stagnant pool of water, but a flowing river, that nourishes the plains through which it passes. No missions mean[s] stagnation, missions stand for Christian activity. The missionary spirit is the spirit of life; the non-missionary spirit is the lifeless, the motionless, the death-spirit. The non-missionary dwells upon itself, upon the one congregation, the one pastor, the one conference, the one country; the missionary spirit sees beyond the conflicts of one individual soul, beyond one church edifice, beyond one conference. It can take in all the world of souls into its large heart and mind. And paradoxical as it may seem, the missionary spirit, while dwelling on others, is a greater power in the higher growth of self than the non-missionary spirit, which makes self its object. We need not set apart a portion of ourselves and, as it were, label it "Missionary Department." Let the missionary be our state of being, our general attitude, our spirit. We want our church to be one grand, great mission, we want every aspect of its work to glow with a halo of missionary interest, we want every member to be missionary.... Then, indeed, the church would be able to fulfill her function of functions, her peculiar function of evangelizing the world.[82]

Women in the Pietist heritage of Methodism left behind a legacy of prayer, faith, and work. Their story must not be forgotten, for it is a treasure much too valuable to be left in the past. Frances Schneider enables us all to pray in gratitude for the lives and witness of these coworkers in the faith:

> Dear Heavenly Father,
> We feel surrounded by a great cloud of witnesses, all those faithful ones who have gone on before. In the midst of them we see Jesus, high and lifted up.
> We thank You, God, for sending your Son into the world to be our Savior.
> Thank You, Lord, for calling women as well as men, to be your disciples. We are grateful for the opportunity of sharing in

your work. Forgive us when we have been weak like Peter, and self-centered like Judas.

We thank You, God, for sending your Son into the world to be our Redeemer.

In the midst of life's changing scenes, You are the Changeless One, the same yesterday for our mothers, the same today for us, the same tomorrow for our children.

You are "the solid foundation that cannot be shaken."

We thank You, God, for sending your Son into the world to be our Companion.

Thank you, Lord, that this is not the end of the road. May this be a broad new highway on which we can run faster with the Good News of Jesus Christ.

We pray in His name. Amen.[83]

AFTERWORD

THE EVANGELICAL UNITED BRETHREN TRADITION AND THE FUTURE OF UNITED METHODISM

William J. Abraham

A book devoted to the contribution of The Evangelical United Brethren Church to the future of Methodism is long overdue. Yet I confess immediately that the task of writing an afterword for such a volume is a daunting one. My roots are neither in The Evangelical United Brethren Church nor in United Methodism, so I lack the benefit of being an insider. In addition, my study of the EUB tradition is hopelessly thin to the point of being nonexistent. Moreover, my experience within United Methodism, that is, predominantly in Texas, has reinforced my ignorance of the EUB tradition. To be sure, I have known as a scholar that The Evangelical United Brethren Church was critical in the formation of The United Methodist Church. However, in more than twenty years of living in the bowels of United Methodism at the seminary, conference, and national levels, the references to The Evangelical United Brethren have been so sparse that it would be easy for me to think that the *United* in *United Methodism* is simply a generic notion that stands for unity rather than specifically for the EUB tradition. One thinks of the old quip I first heard from Albert Outler that "United

Methodists are as united as Free Methodists are free." *United* in this instance has nothing to do with the EUB; it has morphed into a generic notion of unity without any content; this is how it is understood in much of United Methodism.

Over against this, I want to say immediately that what little exposure I have had to the EUB tradition has not only strangely warmed my heart; it has filled me with enthusiasm. When I gave the Heck lectures at United Theological Seminary in 2007, I felt immediately at home in the atmosphere of warm piety, honest conversation, unpretentious ecclesiality,[1] and serious scholarship. I felt as if I were much closer to Methodism as I knew it growing up in Ireland compared to my typical experience in The United Methodist Church. Furthermore, I treasure my copy of S. J. Gamertsfelder's *Systematic Theology* and hope one day to give it the attention it deserves.[2] Finally, I have found a natural kinship with those students and scholars (few though they are) who have explicitly identified themselves in their roots with the EUB tradition. So on a personal level I approach the EUB tradition with a hermeneutic of generosity rather than a hermeneutic of suspicion. I am fully convinced that it is imperative that United Methodism take far more seriously than it has done to date the role that the EUB tradition ought to have had in United Methodism's formation and its immediate past history. The chapters presented in this superbly crafted volume provide an excellent foundation from which to begin that too-long delayed task.

But how should we proceed at this point? How should we articulate a suitable agenda for the future? One way to frame the core issue would be to ask this question: What difference would it have made over the years if we had really paid attention to the EUB vision and practices of spirituality, doctrine, theology, evangelism, social ministries, polity, liturgy, sacraments, education, epistemology, and the like? Regrettably, it is not possible to take up this agenda in any detail simply because we lack the vital historical work on the nature and content of the EUB tradition, and because very few of us have assimilated what is actually available to the degree needed. However, if we lower the bar and recast the issue in terms of future developments, perhaps we can make progress. Can we not say that even a cursory knowledge of the EUB tradition yields a network of resources that should be pivotal in any future expression of United Methodism? Surely we can. Necessarily my choice of resources will reflect my normative theological and ecclesial commitments, but initially the heart of my thesis can be put on a postcard: *United* Methodism needs to take much more seriously the Pietist dimensions of its history.

To speak in this manner is to invite ridicule in most academic and ecclesiastical circles. Pietism is so readily dismissed as anti-intellectual, escapist, and emotional that folk will naturally be repelled by this thesis. It will not help to add, as I now do, that what is at stake here is the "Pietism of the lower order," that is, the old-fashioned, unreconstructed Pietism of the originating fathers of the Evangelical United Brethren rather than the "Pietism of a higher order," that is, the Pietism of Schleiermacher and Kant. So I acknowledge at the outset that my thesis is initially a hard pill to swallow. Everything hinges here on what we mean by Pietism, so let's get beyond the vulgar stereotypes and explore my thesis more carefully.[3] I propose we look at Pietism, as mediated through the EUB tradition, as involving three elements: a general vision of Christianity, a particular approach to doctrine, and a distinctive attitude to missionary policy.[4] In, with, and through all of these I want to press for a future that takes with radical seriousness the work of the Holy Spirit breathing through the length and breadth of United Methodism.

Permit one more preliminary comment. It is very appropriate that we engage in this kind of reflection forty-plus years into the history of The United Methodist Church. Even so, we must approach our quarry with due caution and realism. For one thing, United Methodism is still in the grip of the legacy of Albert Outler, who was the foremost architect of The United Methodist Church. Whatever appropriate noises he may have made on occasion, Outler showed no real interest in assimilating the gifts of the EUB tradition. Folk from the EUB tradition should not take this personally, for Outler pretty much despised the whole of the Methodist tradition beyond Wesley. He was so preoccupied with the sources of Wesley and so keen to impose his own theology (dressed up as a reading of Wesley) on the whole church that it served his interests to inhibit any serious engagement with the whole sweep of Methodist tradition and practice.[5]

For another consideration, United Methodism is presently so taken up with the uncritical adoption of passing cultural and theological fads that it scarcely has the time or inclination to look again at its own radically diverse roots as symbolized by the EUB tradition. I welcome, for example, the interest in all things emerging. But it is astonishing to me that some United Methodists can seriously believe that the theological obscurantism and vagaries of disillusioned fundamentalists can really represent more than a catalytic curiosity as we reach for truly effective resources for the future. Furthermore, it is clear that United Methodism faces challenges that not even the best in the EUB tradition can meet successfully. The challenges, for example, of unity, or of finding ways actually to make robust disciples, cut very deep; they will require radically new and additional resources.

Finally, we must honestly face the fact that The Evangelical United Brethren Church and its predecessors have their own unique network of vices that should be eschewed. The Mennonite strain, for instance, could easily reinforce the commitment to a version of facile pacifism that is no match for the challenge of terrorism or even for the conventional vicissitudes of contemporary politics.[6] So as we proceed, we are not in search of some handy labor-saving device that will eliminate the need for comprehensive evaluation of the whole life of The United Methodist Church.

The core thesis already announced is this: *United* Methodists need to take much more seriously the Pietist dimensions of our history. More specifically, I propose that the EUB embodiment of Pietism has much to teach United Methodism in the way it handled its vision of the Christian life, in its explicit confessionalism, and in its attitude to missionary work. Let me begin with the matter of the Christian life.[7]

United Methodism as a whole is obsessed about the doctrine and practice of the Christian life. As I read the tradition, this was the case within Methodism from Wesley onward. It is true of his canonical sermons. And it is true of the initial internal transformations of the tradition in the holiness tradition, in revivalism, in the social gospel tradition of the late nineteenth and early twentieth centuries, and in existentialism. The obsession with the doctrine and practice of the Christian life is also visible in the current interest in "feel-good" Christianity, in liberation theology, in the desire to uphold both evangelism and social justice, and in the making of disciples for the transformation of the world. All of these enthusiasms reveal a tradition preoccupied with the Christian life. Where Eastern Orthodoxy has been obsessed with worship, and where Roman Catholicism has majored on authority, Methodists have been preoccupied with living the Christian faith. In this we display our Pietist origins, for the hallmark of Pietism is precisely the appropriation of the gospel, not just as doctrine or ritual, but as something personal, inward, applied, active, and living. Our origins in Pietism show themselves most conspicuously at present in our renewed interests in spirituality and in our long-standing enthusiasm for social causes. Truth be told, however, the commitment to social causes really carries the day. It is this element in the Christian life that predominates. We are still very nervous about the personalistic dimensions of the Christian faith. Consult on a regular basis the webpage of the *United Methodist Reporter* and you will find the headlines are overwhelmingly devoted to social work. Examine the priorities recently engineered by the bishops and the Connectional Table at the General Conference of 2008 and you will see that two out of the four priorities are taken up with social issues.[8] Consider the change in the mission statement to "make disciples of Jesus Christ for the transformation of the world" and you will note that the addition of the last qualification finally settled the matter for the foreseeable future. We are not so much Pietists of a higher order as Pietists with a social agenda.

Our critics want to dismiss this partiality for social action as apostasy and sentimental liberalism. I do not, for the issue is one of genuine balance in the faith or fullness of faith rather than unfaithfulness or heresy. But there is a deep problem that our critics are missing, and I think that the EUB tradition can help us fix it. Pietism with its missionary zeal, its educational interests, its care for poor persons, and (in some cases) its political radicalism was clearly a social agenda. However, it was first and foremost an agenda driven by the classical interests of the human agent in personal salvation from sin. That element is missing as a characteristic feature of contemporary United Methodism. This absence is reflected in the fact that I would be astonished to find a story of deep conversion on the webpage of the *United Methodist Reporter*. It is also reflected in the fact that our vision of evangelism has shifted to that of making disciples. This is entirely appropriate in its own right, but when it is harnessed to the transformation of the world, it betrays a shallow triumphalism that promises more than it can deliver and immediately signals a priority in the life of discipleship that is theologically flawed. Imagine the consternation if we said something like this: the making of disciples of Jesus Christ for the healing of our souls. This would be seen as hopelessly reductionistic; yet few notice the reductionism of the amended mission statement.[9]

Against all this it will be pointed out that I am ignoring the remarkable rediscovery of the Wesleyan theology of prevenient, justifying, and sanctifying grace. Does not this important development, enshrined in the fresh reading of Wesley's canonical sermons over the last generation, suggest that I am cherry-picking the evidence to bolster a weak case? On the contrary, this development allows me to articulate my worry even more forcefully. Where we have retrieved the personalistic side of our Pietist heritage, we have done so in the language of theological abstraction, reducing it to a grandiose thesis about "responsible grace" that lacks the bite and specificity of the tradition.[10] The same applies to the worry about whether we should speak of an *ordo salutis* or a *via salutis*. We do not really know what to do with repentance, faith, justification, new birth, the witness of the Spirit, and entire sanctification. The ascetic theology represented by these concepts is a dead letter.[11] The hymns that capture them are archaic and surreal. The struggles, dynamic, and drama of conversion that they open up are utterly foreign to us. As a result, we are saddled with superficial and unstable spiritualities that can quickly be displaced by a suffocating social and political moralism. We reduce sin to the various sins of exclusivism, sexism, racism, and other capital evils, and we fail to plumb the depths of the human predicament. In these circumstances we should not be surprised when we end up riddled with moral triumphalism and unable to convert folk in any deep way to Jesus Christ as Lord and Savior.

This is precisely where the EUB tradition can offer medicine. Bishop Thomas Bowman's *The Great Salvation*, for example, provides splendid access to the particularities of the spiritual life that mirrors the classical Wesleyan tradition.[12] Drawing on the pioneers of Methodist theology, like John Fletcher and Richard Watson, he notes: "Although we as a Church are not Methodists in name, we nevertheless belong to the great Methodist family."[13] More important, Bowman provides an articulation of the foundational Wesleyan themes that is robust, friendly, irenic, and rhetorically attractive. The concepts I mentioned earlier (repentance, faith, justification, new birth, the witness of the Spirit, and entire sanctification) are not simple concepts, as the theological debates they have evoked in the history of the church show. Nor is it easy to come to terms with them existentially, as the testimonial literature that unpacks them in living experience reveals.[14] This is where Bowman's work is a little jewel of exposition. Clearly, Bowman has found a way to reproduce the tradition with clarity, confidence, and charity. This includes his treatment of the doctrine of entire sanctification, a topic that occupies almost half of the volume. Frankly, reading this material is a tonic compared to the insipid, abstract, and even scholastic treatment one finds in the current literature within United Methodism;[15] this is Pietism at its very best and strongest. United Methodism needs to relearn both the theology at stake and the art of making it a living option for itself and the whole church of Jesus Christ.

The EUB tradition was also at its best in its ability to keep alive the wider theological doctrines without which Pietism will degenerate into all sorts of folly and ecclesial malpractice. We can see this initially in its treatment of its Confession of Faith.[16] Scholars have long noticed that the Confession of Faith is a much more contemporary document than the Articles of Religion. I do not know the full story here, but it is clear that the Evangelical United Brethren were sufficiently interested in their canonical doctrines to revise them. The canonical doctrines were living elements of the faith; they were not archaic or merely landmark documents. To put the issue sharply, The Evangelical United Brethren Church was utterly clear that it was a confessional church. This is not a pedantic issue, for one of the besetting sins of Pietism is to become so anthropocentric, so focused on human agents and their feelings, dispositions, and actions, that it loses its theological bearings and then degenerates into rationalism, legalism, and moralism. The central concepts that caught the attention of Pietism make no sense outside the deeper canonical theism of the church; once you lose the latter, the concepts undergo transpositions in which they take on a whole new life of their own. In the case of Christian Wolff and Immanuel Kant, you get a theologically barren rationalism.[17] Schleiermacher, as "a Pietist of a higher order," ended up inventing his own brand of post-Christian theology that caused a third schism in the church. At a popular level Pietism degenerates into a loveless judgmentalism and legalism. The Evangelical United Brethren Church appears to have weathered these temptations remarkably well. It did so by acknowledging that it was a confessional church, by revisiting its confession, and by keeping in mind the close relationship between its central concerns and the deep doctrinal heritage enshrined in its Confession of Faith.

Compare this with what has happened to doctrine within United Methodism. Under the tutelage of Albert Outler, United Methodism came to reject any idea of being a confessional church.[18] In fact the aversion to doctrine went as far as dropping the term *doctrine* from the official *Book of Discipline* of the new church. The very idea of being a confessional church was ridiculed. To this end, a bogus distinction between being a conciliar as opposed to a confessional church was invented, ignoring the obvious fact that most, if not all, conciliar churches are also confessional. Indeed one purpose of church councils is to canonize creeds, confessions, and articles of religion.

Much was at stake in the rejection of United Methodism as a confessional church. For one thing, we can see that Outler and many of those who followed him were deeply alienated from the corporate faith of their communities. The casual way in which the matter of canonical doctrine was handled is astonishing. No serious attention was given to the issues at stake because the folk involved behind the scenes knew that an impending commission would finesse the debate by developing a new creed or by inventing a whole new way of thinking about doctrine. Equally, there was a massive effort to make a confused and totally inadequate epistemology of theology the primary marker of United Methodism. What made one a United Methodist doctrinally speaking was not the actual canonical doctrines of the predecessor communities as enshrined in the canonical and constitutional commitments (the Articles of Religion and Confession of Faith) but commitment to the quadrilateral of Scripture, tradition, reason, and experience. In addition, we were saddled with constitutional questions about

AFTERWORD

what happened in 1968 that remain unresolved as a matter of historical investigation. The debate about the status of Wesley's *Sermons* and *Explanatory Notes on the New Testament* in United Methodism rumbles on with both sides informally claiming certainty. Interestingly, when we factor in the EUB tradition, we now have to ask whether the constitution of The Evangelical United Brethren Church was violated when the *Sermons* and *Explanatory Notes* were added, for nothing like this material was constitutive of the EUB position. Outler himself was so sure of his ground after 1972 that he believed that given that doctrine was last reviewed in 1808, it would not need to be addressed for another one hundred and fifty years.[19] He totally ignored the EUB tradition at this point; it simply did not appear on his radar screen. What is most tragic in this whole story is that the delicate way in which The Evangelical United Brethren Church appropriated its doctrines was simply ditched in favor of a vision of theological method that eviscerates the epistemic diversity that is crucial to theology proper.[20]

Happily, we are now beginning to come to terms with the mess that we are in doctrinally. We now have a firm grip on the distinction between doctrine and theology. The former is the specific teaching proposed or adopted; the latter is the activity of theological reflection that results in particular doctrines or teaching. We have also come to terms with the significance of canonization of doctrine, that is, the formal adoption of particular doctrine by a community. Ecclesial communities, rather than simply individuals or professional theologians, commit themselves publicly to hold this or that doctrine or set of doctrines. Communities also develop conventions and mechanisms for securing or changing these doctrines. This case was made with some force and success by the Confessing Movement; happily the General Conference of 2008 has at long last appointed a standing commission to take up questions of doctrine.

We are also beginning to see the pivotal place of doctrine in the life of the church, for what we do in ministry is intimately connected to what we believe together about creation, sin, redemption, and the whole gamut of themes that show up in systematic theology. Most important, we are relearning that both doctrine and theology are intimately connected to the life of faith. While there is a proper place in theology for standing back, for keeping a critical distance, there is also a proper place for prayer, for spiritual discipline, and for the life of holiness. The intimate connection that exists between doctrines of the Christian life and living the Christian life extends into the heartlands of theology. Properly understood, theology is closely related to spiritual formation.[21] The good news at this point in the journey is that there is a real chance that the EUB vision and appropriation of canonical doctrine can be visited and explored with a view to moving forward in doctrinal renewal.

I turn last to the topic of the work of mission. I have already touched on this in the earlier section that calls for a renewed emphasis on the personalistic dimension of the Christian life. There my point was that we talk a lot about a balance between personal faith and social action but that we lack the language and conviction to give voice to the element of personal faith. I proposed there that the EUB tradition can help us get beyond the theological abstractionism and scholasticism that have befallen us. Here my concern is much more mundane. We need to open up to more spontaneous and creative ways of engaging in mission, letting local congregations and laity take the lead in forming groups and practices to implement the full range of missionary activity.

Let me approach the issue abruptly. In more than twenty years of service in seminary and my annual conference, I have heard next to nothing about the work of our church in overseas mission. No doubt some of this is my fault; I have not Googled the General Board of Global Ministries consistently to keep up with what is happening. However, this is only half of the story. The other half of the story is that we have handed the work of mission over to the general agencies of the church and they have gone off and done the work for us and without us. Whatever the detailed reality, the appearances and impressions are clear. First, the bulk of our missionary work is humanitarian in orientation; it is not directed at planting new churches, nor is it directed to the salvation of souls. Second, the work sidelines the natural desire for local churches and laity to be involved in the work of mission, most especially the work of conversion and church planting. We appear to suffer from the conventional problems that gave rise both to Methodism and to the pioneering founders of The Evangelical United Brethren Church. We are suffocated by centralized institutionalism and we have no real interest in the personalistic dimensions of the Christian faith. It is as if the wheel has come full circle; we have traveled back in time to the nominalism and institutionalism of Anglicanism and the Reformed tradition. If we fall foul of the party line and the party system in mission, we are ignored or demonized; we have no space for diverse ways of doing the work of mission.

It takes only a glance at the lives of Jacob Albright and Philip Otterbein, not to speak of John Wesley and the early Methodists, to know that they faced the same kind of straitjacket in mission. They improvised as best they could for the sake of the salvation of souls. They met in private houses, in barns, and in the open fields. They worked across congregational lines. They invented relevant forms of catechesis and practices of spiritual formation. With fortitude and intellectual prudence they bore the offense of demonizing criticism from establishment leaders. They rediscovered the importance of fellowship, informal conversation, and a catholic spirit. They creatively borrowed from past and present innovations. They appreciated the critical importance of good order, of the gifts of the church down through the ages, and of the need for efficient organization. They were well aware of the poisonous effects of sectarianism and separation. Yet they also went out in fear and trembling to reach people for Christ and to provide them with the essentials of the gospel. They knew that if the established churches failed to spread the gospel in faithful and realistic ways, then eventually the stones would cry out. So they invented ways to circumvent and supplement the conventional ministries of the traditional churches.

Over the last decade United Methodism has begun to face up to the need to recapture something of this spirit. The widespread talk of being a movement rather than a church, although literally nonsense, is attempting to put words to the reality on the ground. The creation of volunteers in mission and the provision of ways to give to ministries through special projects outside United Methodism within the General Board of Discipleship are clearly a step in the right direction. Local churches are paying their franchise fees to the denomination but then going a second and third mile to reach out in mission overseas on their own.[22] The existence and success of the Mission Society are astonishing developments over the last generation. Yet we have a long way to go. The reaction to the Mission Society officially has been a tragic farce. The idea that there can be only one sending mission agency is a big mistake, reflecting theological intolerance and carnal fears about competition for funds. We remain hidebound by a parochial and uncharitable mentality that is extremely reluctant to consider helping indigenous mission churches overseas outside United Methodism in the grinding work of evangelism and church planting.[23]

I do not want to be misunderstood at this point. There are no problem-free situations, so we should be charitable with respect to past performance. Developing missional practices that give a much stronger mandate to innovate on the part of local churches and groups of laity will bring their own vices and challenges. There are very important theological, cross-cultural, and sociopolitical issues to be explored in depth as we move into the future. However, we should be crystal clear that we cannot continue in mission with a mentality of business as usual. Looking again at the EUB tradition can help us be open to new initiatives and practices as we move into a new day.[24]

Let me conclude with a final comment. My central thesis has been that *United* Methodism needs to take much more seriously the Pietist dimensions of its history. I have proposed that the EUB embodiment of Pietism has much to teach United Methodism in the way it handled its vision of the Christian life, in its explicit confessionalism, and in its attitude to missionary work. My concluding comment is this: in pursuing this agenda, we must ever keep in mind that for Pietists all this work must be soaked in a radical openness to the work of the Holy Spirit. The gifts of the Evangelical United Brethren are charisms of the Holy Spirit. They by no means exhaust the charisms of the Spirit in the life of the church, but they are vital charisms whose rejection bespeaks a narrow ingratitude that calls for repentance and renewed faith. This means that their reception is not an inert, casual affair; reception itself will require the wisdom of the Spirit. Locating the gifts of the Evangelical United Brethren in the work of the Spirit also mandates us to be open to all the gifts of the Spirit that have been given to the church catholic. This deep work of renewal is a long-haul, cross-generational project that requires patience, gratitude, and fortitude.

APPENDIX

EVANGELICAL UNITED BRETHREN WOMEN'S TIMELINE

Paul W. Chilcote

The following timeline isolates important events related to women in the histories of The Evangelical Association (EA), The Evangelical Church (EC), the United Evangelical Church (UEC), the Church of the United Brethren in Christ (UB), and The Evangelical United Brethren Church (EUB). The issue of inclusion/exclusion, of course, makes this a very subjective document, not meant to be definitive in any way, but suggestive of the enormity of the place, roles, and influence of women in these traditions.

1839—first local woman's missionary society organized in Immanuel Evangelical Church in Philadelphia (EA)
1841—Sister S. Copeland petitioned Scioto Conference for a license to preach (UB)
1843—Louisa P. Clemens petitioned Scioto Conference for a license to preach (women's petitions dismissed by General Conference of 1845) (UB)
1847—Charity Opheral petitioned White River Conference for a license to preach; received a "note of commendation to liberate to public speaking" (UB)
1851—Lydia Sexton granted the first quarterly license to preach by Iroquois Circuit of Illinois Conference (continued to be easily

obtained, even after 1857, but never elevated to annual conference licentiate) (UB)

1857—General Conference passed resolution prohibiting preaching licenses for women (UB)

1859—Upper Wabash Conference issued Lydia Sexton a "letter of recommendation to preach" (UB)

1862—Mrs. J. K. Billheimer begins missionary service in Sierra Leone (UB)

1869—Lydia Sexton appointed as first woman chaplain in the United States (Kansas State Prison) (UB)

1872—Lizzie Hoffman begins promotion of a churchwide women's missionary association (UB)

1872—first women's missionary organization formed in the Miami Conference (presided over by Mrs. T. N. Sowers) (UB)

1872—first statement supporting women's right to preach appeared in the *Evangelical Messenger* (EA)

1874—Mrs. C. B. Beatty permitted to attend classes as first woman student at Union Biblical Seminary (UBS) (UB)

1874—Maggie Thompson granted quarterly conference license to preach (first since Sexton) (UB)

1874—Emma Yost and Minerva Strawman promote women's missionary societies (EA)

1875—UBS took formal action to admit women (UB)

1875—Woman's Missionary Association organized by nine annual conferences (UB)

1875—Department of Young Women founded by Mrs. T. N. Sowers (UB)

1875—Sarah Ann Dickey founded Mount Hermon Female Seminary in Clinton, Mississippi, for "Negro girls" (UB)

1876—Maggie Thompson received "letter of recommendation" from Indiana Conference (UB)

1876—Emily Beeken begins service as first Woman's Missionary Association missionary to Sierra Leone (UB)

1878—Evangelical women petitioned to start local women's missionary societies (EA)

1880—Minerva Strawman's petition granted to start local women's missionary societies (EA)

1882—*Women's Evangel* launched (UB)

1883—first woman, Esther Balmer Sage, graduated from UBS (UB)

1883—Women's Missionary Society (WMS) founded (EA)
1883—Constitution approved for Young Women's Bands (UB)
1883—Miami Conference admitted first women delegates (UB)
1884—WMS constitution approved (under direction of Minerva Strawman Spreng) (EA)
1886—*Missionary Messenger* launched (EA)
1887—first unmarried woman, Ella Niswonger, graduated from UBS in the regular curriculum (UB)
1888—East Ohio Conference admitted women delegates (UB)
1889—General Conference approved both licenses to preach and ordination for women (UB)
1889—Ella Niswonger becomes first woman ordained elder with full clergy rights in Central Illinois Conference (UB)
1890—Maggie Thompson Elliott ordained (UB)
1891—Visa Bell ordained (UB)
1891—women of minority UEC met to organize Women's Home and Foreign Missionary Society (UEC)
1892—Ellen Runkle King ordained (UB)
1892—division of Evangelical Association led to two separate Women's Missionary Societies (EA)
1892—Minerva Strawman Spreng organized and elected president of the Woman's Missionary Association (to 1924) (EA)
1892—Elizabeth Krecker elected to lead women's mission work under the Woman's Home and Foreign Missionary Society with formation of UEC (UEC)
1892—*Missionary Tidings* launched (UEC)
1893—first women lay delegates seated at General Conference, Mrs. Mattie A. Brewer (Lower Wabash) and Mrs. S. J. Staves (Des Moines) (UB)
1895—Mrs. Hartman (St. John's, Oregon) seated as first female member of a UEC annual conference (UEC)
1896—Sarah Dickey ordained (Miami Annual Conference) (UB)
1897—General Conference approved deaconesses (UB)
1898—women martyred in Sierra Leone (UB)
1900—Susan Bauernfeind becomes first woman appointed to Japan as the first single woman missionary appointed to a foreign mission (Japan) by the Evangelical Association (EA)
1901—Ella Niswonger becomes first woman seated as ministerial delegate to General Conference (UB)

1901—Ethel Bookwalter Burtner becomes first woman graduated from UBS in missionary curriculum (UB)

1902—Susan Bauernfeind founded Koishikawa Church, the first church to become self-supporting in Japan in 1916 (EA)

1903—Evangelical Association approved deaconesses (EA)

1904—Susan Bauernfeind founded Tokyo Bible School (EA)

1904—Minnie Jackson Goins becomes first African American woman ordained (Northwest Kansas) (UB)

1908—first women graduated from UBS in newly created deaconess curriculum, Flora C. Kitzmiller and Hannah Buhan Sharp (UB)

1909—Woman's Missionary Association became part of the General Board of Missions (UB)

1912—Woman's Missionary Association changed name to Women's Missionary Association (UB)

1915—Mellie Perkins, UB deaconess, founded Edith McCurdy Mission School in Santa Cruz, New Mexico (UB)

1918—*Women's Evangel* renamed the *Evangel* (UB)

1921—Red Bird Mission founded (EA)

1922—Woman's Missionary Society and Women's Home and Foreign Missionary Society united to form the Women's Missionary Society of The Evangelical Church (EC)

1922—The *Evangelical Missionary World* launched with the merger of the *Missionary Messenger* and the *Missionary Tidings* (EC)

1944—Ruth Dietzel appointed first general secretary of the newly formed Christian Service Guild (for employed women) (EC)

1946—first women lay delegates, Mrs. Edward Stukenberg (Illinois) and Irene Haumersen (Wisconsin), seated at General Conference (EC)

1946—women informally denied ordination in the newly organized Evangelical United Brethren Church, but local exceptions abound up to merger in 1968 (EUB)

1946—Justina Lorenz Showers elected first president of newly established Women's Society of World Service, merging predecessor women's missionary organizations (EUB)

1947—*World Evangel* replaced predecessor women's missionary magazines (EUB)

1950—first Quadrennial Convention of the Women's Society of World Service held in Indianapolis (EUB)

NOTES

1. The Pietist Background of The Evangelical United Brethren Church

1. F. Ernest Stoeffler, *The Rise of Evangelical Pietism* (Leiden: E. J. Brill, 1971), 1.

2. Carter Lindberg, ed., *The Pietist Theologians: An Introduction to Theology in the Seventeenth and Eighteenth Centuries* (Malden, Mass.; Oxford, England; Victoria, Australia: Blackwell Publishing, 2005), 2.

3. D. Philipp Jakob Spener, *Auffrichtige Übereinstimmung mit der Augsp. Confession, Zu nöthiger vertheidigungseiner reinen lehr/von ihm selbst entgegen gesetzt der sogennanten Christ-Lutherischen Vorstellung* (Frankfurt: Johann David Zunner, 1695), 114–15.

4. Stoeffler, *Rise of Evangelical Pietism*, 23.

5. Quoted in A. W. Drury, *History of the Church of the United Brethren in Christ* (Dayton, Ohio: Otterbein Press, 1924), 145.

6. Hernn D. Philipp *Jakob Speners Theologische Bedencken und andere Brieffliche Antworten* (Halle: Verlegung der Waysen-Hauses, 1712), 4:266–67. See also K. James Stein, *Philipp Jakob Spener: Pietist Patriarch* (Chicago: Covenant Press, 1986), 81.

7. See Ted Campbell, *The Religion of the Heart: A Study of European Religious Life in the Seventeenth and Eighteenth Centuries* (Columbia: University of South Carolina Press, 1991), 2–3.

8. *Kompendium Der Kirchengeschichte* (Tübingen: Verlag von J. C. B. Mohr Paul Siebeck, 1960), #106, 395.

9. Peter Erb, trans. and ed., *Johann Arndt: True Christianity* (New York: Paulist Press, 1979), 13–14.

10. Johannes Wallmann, "Johann Arndt (1555–1621)," in Lindberg, *The Pietist Theologians*, 27.

11. Stoeffler, *Rise of Evangelical Pietism*, 8.

12. Edward Farley, *Requiem for a Lost Piety: The Contemporary Search for the Christian Life* (Philadelphia: Westminster Press, 1966), 123.
13. Donald Bloesch, *The Crisis of Piety*, 2nd ed. (Colorado Springs: Helmers and Howard, 1988), 31.
14. Dale Brown, *Understanding Pietism*, rev. ed. (Nappanee, Ind.: Evangel Publishing House, 1978, 1996), 24–25.
15. Lindberg, *The Pietist Theologians*, 12.
16. Brown, *Understanding Pietism*, 20.
17. "Pietism as a Movement of Revival," *Covenant Quarterly* 33, no. 3 (Aug. 1975): 3.
18. "Das Herz Bilden: Ertrag des Bildungsgedankens bei Spener für die heutige Zeit," in *Nicht nur fromme Wünsche: Philipp Jakob Spener neu entdeckt* (Frankfurt am Main: Spener Verlag GMBH, 2000), 106–10.
19. Gary Sattler, *Nobler than the Angels, Lower than a Worm: The Pietist View of the Individual in the Writings of Heinrich Müller and August Hermann Francke* (Lantham, Md., and London, England: University Press of America, 1989), 129–30.
20. Heinrich Schmid, quoted in Horst Weigelt, "Interpretations of Pietism in the Research of Contemporary German Church Historians," *Church History* (The American Society of Church History) 39, no. 2 (June 1970): 237.
21. Quoted in John T. McNeill, *Modern Christian Movements* (Philadelphia: Westminster Press, 1954), 74.
22. Drury, *History of the Church of the United Brethren in Christ*, 95–107.
23. J. Steven O'Malley, *Pilgrimage of Faith: The Legacy of the Otterbeins* (Metuchen, N.J.: Scarecrow Press, 1973), 77.
24. Cited in Drury, *History of the Church of the United Brethren in Christ*, 57–58.
25. A. W. Drury, trans. and ed., *Minutes of the Annual and General Conferences of the Church of the United Brethren in Christ, 1800–1818* (Dayton, Ohio: UB Publishing House, 1897), 10.
26. O'Malley, *Pilgrimage of Faith*, 94–104, 180.
27. Arthur C. Core, ed., *Philip William Otterbein: Pastor, Ecumenist* (Dayton, Ohio: Board of Publication of The Evangelical United Brethren Church, 1968), 87.
28. Raymond W. Albright, *A History of The Evangelical Church* (Harrisburg, Pa.: Evangelical Press, 1942), 24–25.
29. James Bemesderfer, *Pietism and Its Influence upon The Evangelical United Brethren Church* (Harrisburg, Pa.: Copyright by the author, printed at the Evangelical Press, 1966), 62.
30. Albright, *A History of The Evangelical Church*, 27–44; Karl Heinz Voigt, *Jacob Albrecht: Ein Ziegelbrenner wird Bischof* (Stuttgart: Christliches Verlagshaus, 1997), 39–87.
31. J. Bruce Behney and Paul H. Eller, *The History of The Evangelical United Brethren Church* (Nashville: Abingdon Press, 1979), 147, 183.

32. *Proceedings of the Twenty-third General Conference of the United Brethren in Christ* (Dayton, Ohio: UB Publishing House, 1901), 28.

33. Brown, *Understanding Pietism*, 33.

34. "Die Gerechtigkeit Jesu Christi: eine frucht der Wiedergeburt," in *Der hochwichtige Articul von der Wiedergeburt* (Franckfurt am Mayn: In verlegung Johann David Zunners, 1696), 805.

35. *Herrn D. Philipp Jakob Speners Theologische Bedencken und andere Briefliche Antworten* (Halle: Verlegung des Waysen Hauses, 1715), 3:304.

36. "Wiederholung der Wiedergeburt,"in *Der hochwichtige Articul von der Wiedergeburt*, 952.

37. Albert C. Outler and Richard P. Heitzenrater, eds., *John Wesley's Sermons: An Anthology* (Nashville: Abingdon Press, 1991), 336.

38. A brief and thoughtful survey of the theological shift in American Protestantism is provided by Donald W. Haynes in "Finding Our Way—after a Costly Detour," *United Methodist Reporter* (Dallas, Tex.: UMR Communications), May 2, 2008, 17a.

39. *Nicodemus or a Treatise Against the Fear of Man, Wherein the Causes and Sad Effects Thereof Are Briefly Described with Some Remedies Against It*, trans. Anton William Boehm (London: J. Downing, 1709), 10–25.

40. Ibid., 112.

41. Ibid., 123.

42. Ibid., 82–83.

43. Ibid., 112, 120, 122, 125, 127.

44. Ibid., 113.

45. Rueben P. Job, *Three Simple Rules: A Wesleyan Way of Living* (Nashville: Abingdon Press, 2007), 54.

46. A. J. Lewis, *Zinzendorf: The Ecumenical Pioneer* (Philadelphia: Westminster Press, 1962), 66.

47. Abram W. Sangrey, ed., *Christian Newcomer: His Life and Journal* (Lancaster, Pa.: Published by the Philip William Otterbein District, East Pennsylvania Conference, The United Methodist Church, 1996), 66, 83, 95, 103, 105, 201, 209, 210.

48. *History of the Church of the United Brethren in Christ* (Dayton, Ohio: Vonneida and Sowers, 1860–61), 1:247.

49. *On the Journey Home: The History of Mission of The Evangelical United Brethren Church, 1946–1968* (New York: General Board of Global Ministries, 2003), 188.

2. Martin Boehm, Philip William Otterbein, and the United Brethren in Christ

1. Pietism had a great influence on the religious culture of colonial German Americans. See F. Ernest Stoeffler, *Continental Pietism and Early American Christianity* (Grand Rapids: Eerdmans, 1976).

2. Spener, considered the father of Lutheran Pietism, published *Pia Desideria* (*Pious Wishes*) in 1676, which served as a manifesto for reform among Lutherans with Pietist sympathies. Pietism was a movement that understood Christianity to be primarily about piety (faith and action) rather than doctrinal orthodoxy. The more radical Pietists, among whom Pastorius associated, were convinced that true Christianity could exist only outside the established church.

3. Barbara Heck and Philip Embury, the founders of Methodism in New York, were part of this migration. They went first to Ireland, where they became part of Wesley's Methodist connection.

4. Schlatter resigned his pastorate in 1755, working full time to establish schools. The project, partly funded by the Society for Promoting Christian Knowledge (SPCK), was unpopular because it included teaching English. In 1757 he abandoned it and accepted a chaplaincy during the French and Indian War.

5. Pietism, broadly defined, shaped the type of evangelical religion that influenced the leaders of the revival, including Puritans like Jonathan Edwards, Dutch Reformed clergy like Theodorus Frelinghuysen, and Anglicans like George Whitefield.

6. Martin Boehm, manuscript interview, transcribed by Henry Boehm, Drew University, Methodist Collection, Madison, New Jersey.

7. Henry G. Spayth, *History of the Church of the United Brethren in Christ* (Cincinnati, Ohio: Published at the conference office of the United Brethren in Christ, 1851), 28–29.

8. Because of various readings of the term *ministry* in Henry Boehm's interview with his father, there is some discrepancy among historians about when Boehm was selected pastor. A. W. Drury, *History of the Church of the United Brethren in Christ* (Dayton, Ohio: Otterbein Press, 1924), 97, cites the earlier date of 1756. Spayth, *History*, 31, writes that the event happened in 1758. Historian Martin G. Weaver, *Mennonites of Lancaster Conference* (Scottdale, Pa.: Mennonite Publishing House, 1931), 103, follows Spayth.

9. Spayth, *History*, 28.

10. Ibid.

11. Boehm, manuscript interview, Madison, New Jersey. The significance of Nancy Keagy needs to be further researched.

12. Spayth, *History*, 28–29.

13. Ibid., 29–31.

14. Ibid.

15. Ibid. Interestingly, Spayth does not report Boehm speaking of a new birth.

16. Ibid.

17. Weaver, *Mennonites*, 103. Drury, *History of the Church of the United Brethren in Christ*, 207.

18. Boehm, manuscript interview, Madison, New Jersey.

19. Spayth, *History*, 32. Whitefield's fifth preaching tour had taken him to Maryland in December 1754 and Virginia in January 1755. See George Whitefield, *Works of the Reverend George Whitefield* (London: Edward and Charles Dilly, 1771), 3:113–16.

20. Charles Henry Smith, *The Story of the Mennonites* (Berne, Ind.: Mennonite Book Concern, 1941), 573–74.

21. Martin Boehm, manuscript interview, Madison, New Jersey.

22. Ibid.

23. Ibid.

24. Drury, *History of the Church of the United Brethren in Christ*, 101.

25. Testimonial to Otterbein, trans. Arthur C. Core, Otterbein Collection, United Methodist Church Archives, Madison, New Jersey. His near relative and "godfather was Philip William Keller, steward to the court of Nassau-Dillenberg."

26. Certificate of Ordination and Recommendation, translation, Otterbein Collection, United Methodist Church Archives, Madison, New Jersey.

27. Before these clergymen's arrival, there were "four pastors to serve a German Reformed population of thirty thousand." See J. Steven O'Malley, *Pilgrimage of Faith: The Legacy of the Otterbeins* (Metuchen, N.J.: Scarecrow Press, 1973), 168–69.

28. Spayth, *History*, 21.

29. Letter from Rieger, Otterbein, Stoy, DuBois, and others (Nov. 28, 1753), translation, Otterbein Collection, United Methodist Church Archives, Madison, New Jersey. See also Petition of the Lancaster Congregations to the Trustees of the Charity Schools. Dec. 28, 1754, copied from *Life of Dr. Wm Smith*, 1:90. Records, Lancaster Reformed Church, Otterbein Collection, United Methodist Church Archives, Madison, New Jersey.

30. Contract of Officers of Lancaster Congregation with Masons to Build a New Church at Lancaster, Feb. 26, 1753, Otterbein Collection, United Methodist Church Archives, Madison, New Jersey.

31. Lancaster was not far from the radical Pietist Ephrata Community. O'Malley has noted, "This was a peak period in the history of the Ephrata cloister, and their influence had frequently penetrated the city of Lancaster.... Even Otterbein's library at this time included a copy of the sectarians' Berleburg bible." See O'Malley, *Pilgrimage of Faith*, 169. The First Great Awakening also reached central Pennsylvania, especially through the Moravians after Whitefield's 1740 evangelistic tour. See Charles H. Maxson, *The Great Awakening in the Middle Colonies* (Chicago: University of Chicago Press, 1920), 123. See also O'Malley, *Pilgrimage of Faith*, 168–69. Whitefield's sixth evangelistic tour began at the end of May

1754 and coincides with Drury's date for Otterbein's conversion. See Arnold Dallimore, *George Whitefield* (Edinburgh: Banner of Truth, 1980), 2:367. Whitefield was in Philadelphia for the month of August. See Whitefield, *Works,* 3:99–101.

32. A. W. Drury, *The Life of the Rev. Philip William Otterbein: Founder of the Church of the United Brethren in Christ* (Dayton, Ohio: UB Publishing House, 1890), 68. "This is the date given in some papers left by Mr. Spayth."

33. Ibid.

34. Ibid.

35. Elmer T. Clark, ed., *The Journal and Letters of Francis Asbury* (Nashville: Abingdon Press, 1958), 2:753–54.

36. Agreement between Otterbein and his Lancaster congregation signed about 1757, translation of German transcription by Scott Kisker, Records, Lancaster Reformed Church, Otterbein Collection, United Methodist Archives, Madison, New Jersey.

37. Frederick Shaeffer was converted by Otterbein while he was at Lancaster and eventually became a United Brethren minister. See John Lawrence, *The History of the Church of the United Brethren in Christ* (Dayton, Ohio: Vonnieda and Sowers, 1860), 1:139.

38. Records, Lancaster Reformed Church, Otterbein Collection, United Methodist Archives, Madison, New Jersey.

39. Records, Tulpehocken Area, Otterbein Collection, United Methodist Church Archives, Madison, New Jersey.

40. O'Malley, *Pilgrimage of Faith,* 173.

41. Spayth, *History,* 23–24. Lawrence, *History,* 1:147.

42. P. W. Otterbein, "Heilbringende Menschwerdung und die Herrliche Sieg Jesu Christi Ueber den Teufel und Tod Vorgestellt," trans. Ehrhardt Lang, Otterbein Collection, United Methodist Archives, Madison, New Jersey.

43. Ibid.

44. Ibid.

45. Ibid.

46. Records, Frederick, Maryland, Otterbein Collection, United Methodist Church Archives, Madison, New Jersey. On April 19, 1762, he married Susan LeRoy, the daughter of a French Huguenot who had immigrated in 1754. See Susan LeRoy Otterbein, Otterbein Collection, United Methodist Church Archives, Madison, New Jersey.

47. O'Malley, *Pilgrimage of Faith,* 178. Here Otterbein's Great Meetings were first called "sacramental meetings"—their style influenced by the love feasts at the cloister.

48. John Bowen, *Robert Strawbridge and the Rise and Progress of Methodism on Sam's and Pipe Creeks, Md., from the year 1764* (Westminster, 1856), 9–11.

49. Drury, *History of the Church of the United Brethren in Christ,* 112.

50. Records, York, Pennsylvania, Otterbein Collection, United Methodist Church Archives, Madison, New Jersey.

51. W. E. Musgrave, *The Church of the United Brethren in Christ: Teachings and Progress* (Huntington, Ind.: Church of the United Brethren in Christ, Dept. of Christian Education, 1945), 4.

52. Drury, *History of the Church of the United Brethren in Christ*, 101. "At the time of the meeting at Isaac Long's barn, a Virginia preacher was present; and as all could not be accommodated in the barn, he preached... to an overflow meeting in the orchard. It is related that a shower of rain came on during the meeting, and that this preacher was the last to leave the ground."

53. Spayth, *History*, 41.

54. Ibid.

55. Lawrence, *History*, 1:170–71.

56. Drury, *History of the Church of the United Brethren in Christ*, 89.

57. Ibid., 102. "The historic mode of baptism with the Mennonites was by pouring, and only adults were recognized as proper subjects. The Reformed baptized by sprinkling, and insisted on infant baptism. There is some likelihood that that 'Virginia preachers' baptized by immersion."

58. Boehm, manuscript interview, Madison, New Jersey. This evangelistic work continued despite the death of Otterbein's wife a year later, in April 1768. See Susan LeRoy Otterbein, Otterbein Collection, United Methodist Church Archives, Madison, New Jersey.

59. A familiar friend, "River Brethren," in John Winebrenner, ed., *History of All the Religious Denominations in the United States* (Harrisburg, Pa.: John Winebrenner, 1848), 553. "Out of these social circles, was organized the Religious Association, now commonly known the River Brethren."

60. Anonymous, *U.S. Census, Religious Bodies* (1936), 12:1:329, quoted in David T. Jones, *Early Components of the Church of the United Brethren in Christ* (Hamilton, Ohio: Hamilton Printing Co., 1956), 7.

61. Minutes of the Coetus, 1770, cited in J. H. Dubbs, "Otterbein and the Reformed Church," *Reformed Quarterly Review* 31 (Jan. 1884): 114. His pulpit was filled in his absence by members of the Reformed coetus.

62. Clark, ed., *Asbury Journal and Letters*, 1:105. An interesting account of Schwope is found in Asbury's *Journal* for Nov. 22, 1772:

> Went about two miles to preach at Mr. Durbin's and met with a German minister, Mr. Benedict Swope, who heard me preach at both places. We had some conversation about the ordinances administered by Mr. Strawbridge. He advanced some reasons to urge the necessity of them and said Mr. Wesley did not do well to hinder us from the administration of them. I told him they did not appear to me as essential to

salvation [and that it did not appear to be my duty to administer the ordinances at that time].

See ibid., 1:54. There is a tradition that a German minister ordained Strawbridge. If the tradition is true, the minister was likely Benedict Schwope. See Bowen, *Robert Strawbridge*, 9.

63. Churchbook, in Spayth, *History*, 45.

64. Clark, ed., *Asbury Journal and Letters*, 1:114.

65. *Minutes of the Association of Reformed Congregations of Maryland, Records of Itinerant Ministries: Krieders Ref Church [St. Benjamin's] Carroll County, MD*, Otterbein Collection, United Methodist Church Archives, Madison, New Jersey.

66. Ibid. The Association met on Oct. 2, 1774, again at Pipe Creek; June 12, 1775, at Frederickstown; Oct. 15, 1775, at Baltimore; and June 2, 1776, at Hagerstown. There was also a meeting scheduled for Oct. 20, 1776, in Canawacke.

67. Churchbook, in Spayth, *History*, 48–49.

68. Ibid., 46–54.

69. J. B. Wakely, *The Patriarch of One Hundred Years; being reminiscences, historical and biographical of Rev. Henry Boehm* (New York: Nelson and Phillips, 1875), 30.

70. Boehm, manuscript interview, Madison, New Jersey.

71. Wakely, *Patriarch*, 20.

72. John Firth, *Experience and Gospel Labours of the Rev. Benjamin Abbott; to which is annexed A Narrative of His Life and Death* (Philadelphia: D. & S. Neall, 1825), 71.

73. Wakely, *Patriarch*, 19–20.

74. Clark, ed., *Asbury Journal and Letters*, 1:444.

75. Ibid., 1:460–61. In May 1784 at Stevens City, Virginia, after he had "raged and threatened the people, and was afraid it was spleen," Asbury consoled himself "that Mr. Otterbein, a worthy German minister, had done the same a little time before."

76. Clark, ed., *Asbury Journal and Letters*, 1:512–13. Otterbein had already begun to adapt some methods of the English-speaking revivalists. At Great Meetings "Otterbein held at times conferences with the preachers who were present." At these conferences lay preachers "were accepted by one or another of the [ordained] preachers and by them designated to the preacher's office." See "Historical Statement," *Discipline of the United Brethren in Christ*, 1815.

77. "Historical Statement," *Discipline of the United Brethren in Christ*, 1817.

78. J. Bruce Behney and Paul H. Eller, *History of The Evangelical United Brethren Church* (Nashville: Abingdon Press, 1979), 56.

79. Wakely, *Patriarch*, 30.
80. Clark, ed., *Asbury Journal and Letters*, 2:128–29.
81. Samuel S. Hough, *Christian Newcomer: His Life, Journal and Achievements* (Dayton, Ohio: Church of the United Brethren in Christ, 1941), 43.
82. Clark, ed., *Asbury Journal and Letters*, Aug. 24, 1800, 2:245, emphasis mine.
83. A. W. Drury, ed., *Minutes of the Annual and General Conferences of the Church of the United Brethren in Christ, 1800–1818* (Dayton, Ohio: UB Publishing House, 1897), 9–10.
84. Ibid., 10–12, emphasis mine.
85. Ibid.
86. Ibid., 12–14. "Then shall another always be chosen in his stead. This is the wish of both and all of the preachers present unanimously consent and are agreed that it be thus."
87. Clark, ed., *Asbury Journal and Letters*, 2:400.
88. Drury, ed., *Minutes of the Annual and General Conferences*, 12–14.
89. Ibid., 17–18.
90. Boehm, manuscript interview, Madison, New Jersey.
91. Drury, ed., *Minutes of the Annual and General Conferences*, 19.
92. Clark, ed., *Asbury Journal and Letters*, 2:572.
93. Ibid., 3:403–4. See also Drury, *History of the Church of the United Brethren in Christ*, 808–10.
94. Clark, ed., *Asbury Journal and Letters*, 1:406.
95. Drury, *History of the Church of the United Brethren in Christ*, 810–11.
96. Boehm, manuscript interview, Madison, New Jersey.
97. "Letter to the English Methodists," signed by Christian Newcomer, May 25, 1811, in Drury, *History of the Church of the United Brethren in Christ*, 814.
98. Clark, ed., *Asbury Journal and Letters*, 2:697.
99. Ibid.
100. Drury, *History of the Church of the United Brethren in Christ*, 816.
101. Ibid., 818.
102. Ibid., 819.
103. Clark, ed., *Asbury Journal and Letters*, 2:710–11.
104. Hough, *Christian Newcomer*, 158–59.
105. Ibid., 161–62. Otterbein reportedly said, "I have always considered myself too unworthy to perform this solemn injunction of the Apostle, but now I perceive the necessity of doing so before I shall be removed."
106. Ibid., 162–63.
107. Ibid., 163. Newcomer wrote in his journal for Nov. 24, 1813, "I returned home, where I found a letter from Baltimore, informing me that old father William Otterbein had departed this life, on the 17th of November,

1813, aged 87 years, 5 months, and 14 days. He is called to his everlasting home, where he rests from his labors and his works will follow him."

108. Behney and Eller, *History of The Evangelical United Brethren Church*, 107.

109. Ibid., 108.

110. Ibid., 107.

111. David T. Jones, *Early Components of the Church of the United Brethren in Christ* (Hamilton, Ohio: Hamilton Printing Company, 1956), 5, wrote that those who formed the United Brethren "had in common: (1) their differences with their parental denominations. All were 'irregulars' or 'dissenters' to a greater or lesser degree, regarding the parental denominations as cold and formal and as having lost the vital spark of religion; (2) each individual sensed his 'lost state' (*Verlohrnen Zustand*); and (3) each joyfully experienced 'all Spirit and Life' (*alles Geist und Leben*) in spiritual rebirth."

112. The UBC and The Evangelical Association (Albright's People) eventually merged in 1946 to form The Evangelical United Brethren Church. This church then merged with The Methodist Church in 1968 to form The United Methodist Church.

3. Jacob Albright and The Evangelical Association

1. J. Steven O'Malley, "The Distinctive Witness of the Evangelical United Brethren Confession of Faith in Comparison with the Methodist Articles of Religion," in Dennis M. Campbell, William B. Lawrence, and Russell E. Richey, eds., *United Methodism and American Culture: Doctrines and Discipline* (Nashville: Abingdon Press, 1999), 69. See also O'Malley's *John Seybert and the Evangelical Heritage: Biographical and Personal Reflections on a Life Touched by Godliness* (Lexington, Ky.: Emeth Press, 2008) and *Early German-American Evangelicalism: Pietist Sources on Discipleship and Sanctification* (Lanham, Md.: Scarecrow Press, 1995).

2. The basic history is J. Bruce Behney and Paul H. Eller, *A History of The Evangelical United Brethren Church*, ed. Kenneth W. Krueger (Nashville: Abingdon Press, 1979). For the founding period, also consult Cecil Pottieger, *Jacob Albright beyond the Blue Mountain* (Lansdale, Pa.: the author, 1953), and his "Jacob Albright in Monroe County, [Pa.]," *Annals of Eastern Pennsylvania, Journal of the Historical Society and the Commission on Archives and History of the Eastern Pennsylvania Conference of The United Methodist Church* 3 (2006): 19–26.

3. Behney and Eller, *History of The Evangelical United Brethren Church*, 73–75.

4. Ibid., 76–79.

5. This membership estimate and others in this chapter are from

Sylvanus C. Breyfogel, *Landmarks of The Evangelical Association, Containing All of the Official Records of the Annual and General Conferences from the Days of Jacob Albright to the Year 1840* (Reading, Pa.: Eagle Book Printing, 1888).

6. Paul Eller, *These Evangelical United Brethren* (Dayton, Ohio: Otterbein Press, 1957), 46.

7. Albright's ordination certificate is given in full in Raymond W. Albright, *A History of The Evangelical Church* (Harrisburg, Pa: Evangelical Press, 1942), 66, and in the account of the conference and ordination in Behney and Eller, *History of The Evangelical United Brethren Church*, 75–76.

8. Albright, *A History of The Evangelical Church*, 84.

9. As a tribute to Albright, a chapel was erected near the cemetery in 1850 and rebuilt in 1860. The chapel was designated a Heritage Landmark of the UMC in 1968.

10. *Glaubenslehre und allgemeine Regeln christlicher Kirchen-Zucht und Ordnung der sogennanten Albrechts-Leute... zum Druck befördert von George Miller* (Reading: Degdruckt bey Johann Ritter und Comp., 1809).

11. *Lehre und Zuchtordnung der Bischöflich methodistenkirchen Kirche: aus dem Englischen übersetzt, auf anrathen der Ehrw. Bischofs Asbury und der Philadelphischen Conferenz, unter der Anweisung von Henrich Böhm, zum Druck befördert* (Lancaster, Pa: Gedruckt bey Henrich und Benjamin Grimler, 1808); the copyright was dated Jan. 12, 1808; a German translation of the 1804 Methodist Episcopal Church *Discipline* but not published until the spring of 1808, before the 1808 General Conference convened and an updated 1808 MEC *Discipline* was published.

12. The following year Ignaz Romer published a commentary on the book of Revelation: *Das Geheimniss der Bosheit bis auf den Grund aufgedekt: nebst Anzeige des Ruttungsmittels der Kirche: in einer Erklarung der Offenbarung Jesu Christi an Johannes* (*The Mystery of Evil Uncovered to its very Depths, besides a notice of deliverance of the Church in an Explanation of the Revelation of Jesus Christ to [Saint] John*) (Lancaster, Pa: Bey Henrich und Benjamin Frimler, 1809).

13. "Von der Christlichen Vollkommenheit," *Glaubenslehre...1809*, pt. 6, 37–42. For full English text see *The Doctrine and Discipline of The Evangelical Association* (New Berlin, Pa.: George Miller for The Evangelical Association, 1832). For interpretation see Kenneth E. Rowe, "Christian Perfection in the Evangelical Church Book of Discipline," *Methodist History* 18, no. 1 (Oct. 1979): 68–72, and O'Malley, "The Distinctive Witness," 69.

14. *Auf Anrathen des. Ehrw. Bischofs Asbury und der Philadelphischen Conferenz, unter der Anweisung von Henrich Böhm and Druck befördert.*

15. *Minutes of the Methodist Conferences from the First Held in London by the Late John Wesley A.M. in the Year 1744* (London: John Mason, 1862),

1:81; Frank Baker, "Doctrines in the Discipline," *Duke Divinity School Review* 31, no. 1 (Winter 1966); 55–59.

16. Hezekiah J. Bowman, *Voices on Holiness from The Evangelical Association* (Cleveland, Ohio: Publishing House of The Evangelical Association, 1882), 17; Ralph K. Schwab, in his 1922 University of Chicago doctoral study *The History of the Doctrine of Christian Perfection in The Evangelical Association* (Menasha, Wis.: Collegiate Press, 1922), 18, notes Miller's dependence on Boehm's translation of the MEC *Discipline* but does not mention Romer; nor does he speculate on the origin of the first eleven paragraphs. Two other sources do not deal with the matter of the origin of the Evangelical statement on perfection: J. Wesley Corbin, "Christian Perfection and The Evangelical Association through 1875," *Methodist History* 7, no. 2 (Jan. 1969): 28–44, and William H. Naumann, "Theology and German-American Evangelicalism: The Role of Theology in the Church of the United Brethren in Christ and The Evangelical Association" (PhD diss., Yale University, 1966).

17. *The Doctrines and Discipline of The Methodist Episcopal Church in America, with Explanatory Notes by Thomas Coke and Francis Asbury* (Philadelphia: Printed by Henry Tuckniss for John Dickins, 1798), 185.

18. *Lehre und Zuchtordnung*, 11. Although the introduction is unsigned, Boehm in his autobiography credits Romer with having prepared it. Henry Boehm, *Historical and Biographical of Sixty-four Years in the Ministry* (New York: Carlton & Porter, 1865), 178.

19. O'Malley, "Distinctive Witness," 69.

20. George Miller, *Kurze beschreibung der würkenden Gnade Gottes bey dem erleuchteten evangelishen prediger Jacob Albrecht* (Reading, Pa.: Johann Ritter, 1811).

21. George Miller, *The Life of Jacob Albright*, trans. and ed. James D. Nelson (Dayton, Ohio: Center for the Evangelical United Brethren Heritage, 1985), 3. Excerpted in Russell E. Richey, Kenneth E. Rowe, and Jean Miller Schmidt, eds., *The Methodist Experience in America: A Sourcebook* (Nashville; Abingdon Press, 2000), 108.

22. George Miller, *Kurze und deutliche Lehren zum Wahren und Thätigen Christenthum, aufgesetzt in der reinen absicht zu Gottes Lob und sum nutzen der menschheit* (Reading, Pa.: Gedruckt von John G. Jungman, 1814). A second, improved (*zweite und verbesserte*) edition was published in 1844 with a new title: *Das Thätige Christenthum, oder kurze und deutliche Lehren zur Beförderung wahrer Gottseligkeit* (New Berlin, Pa.: J. C. Reisner für die Evangelische Gemeinschaft, 1844). The work was reprinted many times in German, and at least one translation into English, 1871, survives.

23. *Die kleine biblische Catechismus zum Gebrauch aller Gottliebenden Seelen*, trans. John Dreisbach (New Berlin, Pa.: G. Miller, 1809); 2nd ed. (New Berlin, Pa.: Miller and Niebel, 1818).

24. James Kirby, Russell Richey, and Kenneth Rowe, *The Methodists*

(Westport, Conn.: Greenwood Press, 1996), 169–70. Methodist Bishops Asbury and Coke commended the catechism in their 1798 annotated *Book of Discipline*.

25. The standard history of this form of German American hymnody is Don Yoder, *Pennsylvania Spirituals* (Lancaster, Pa.: Pennsylvania Folklife Society, 1961). See also Terry Heisey, "Singet Hallejah! Music in The Evangelical Association, 1800–1894," *Methodist History* 28, no. 4 (1990): 237–51.

26. William W. Orwig, *History of The Evangelical Association* (Cleveland: Charles Hammer for The Evangelical Association, 1858), 59.

27. Elmer T. Clark, ed., *The Journal and Letters of Francis Asbury* (Nashville: Abingdon Press, 1958), 2:399.

28. Ibid., 2:477.

29. Ibid., 2:550.

30. On the language question, see Edward F. Ohms, "The Language Problem in The Evangelical Association," *Methodist History* 24, no. 4 (July 1987): 222–38; Paul F. Blankenship, "Bishop Asbury and the Germans," *Methodist History* 4, no. 3 (April 1966): 5–13; and Paul F. Douglass, *The Story of German Methodism* (Cincinnati: Methodist Book Concern, 1939), 78–79.

31. This version of the encounter was published in the *Evangelical Messenger*, Feb. 21, 1855, 28, while Dreisbach was editor. The fullest version of the Dreisbach-Asbury encounter was published three years later in Orwig, *History of The Evangelical Association*, 1:56–57. For a third version see Reuben Yeakel, *History of The Evangelical Association* (Cleveland: Evangelical Publishing House, 1894), 1:108–9. Dreisbach's journal covering this period was extant until at least 1894 but since has been lost.

32. Asbury to Jacob Gruber, July 7, 1814, *Journal and Letters of Francis Asbury*, 3:504. Original autograph letter, Lovely Lane Museum and Archives of the Baltimore-Washington Conference, UMC, Baltimore, Maryland. The late 1950s translator of Asbury's letter conveniently indicated the inability to decipher the words *deceitful apers*, leaving only a dash in the printed text to signal missing words, perhaps not wanting to derail the Methodist-EUB union. Conversations between The Evangelical United Brethren Church and The Methodist Church regarding church union began in earnest in 1958. However, the words *deceitful apers* are quite clear to this examiner of the original autograph letter.

33. Other sources say the conference convened at the Dreisbach farm in Union County or in the home of Henry Eby in Lebanon, Pennsylvania.

34. *Doctrine and Discipline of The Evangelical Association together with the Design of their Union, translated from the German* (New Berlin, Pa.: Printed by Geo. Miller for The Evangelical Association, 1832), 107–11; the first *English* Evangelical *Discipline*. The rite was revised in 1880, adding the

Lord's Prayer at the end of the Confession and restoring additional text from the Methodist service but keeping the fivefold "shape" of the 1817 rite. In the 1900 revision, portions of the Sursum corda are added to the General Confession, and to the post-Communion prayer are added portions of the concluding Gloria in excelsis of the Methodist rite.

35. The many editions/reprintings of the popular Evangelical hymnal *Geistliche Viole* included German translations of popular English-language hymns, such as Charles Wesley's "A Charge to Keep I Have" ("Ein Werk ist mir vertraut") and "Jesus, Lover of My Soul."

36. Conference resolution cited by Albright, *A History of the Evangelical Church*, 185.

4. The Theological Heritage of Pietism

1. James O. Bemesderfer, *Pietism and Its Influence upon The Evangelical United Brethren Church* (Harrisburg, Pa.: Evangelical Press, 1966), where a balanced survey of major Pietist figures is presented, although he acknowledges which ones exercised more influence on the EUB founders.

2. The present author has exemplified such an approach in *Pilgrimage of Faith: The Legacy of the Otterbeins* (Metuchen, N.J.: Scarecrow Press, 1973).

3. This follows the tripartite division of the Heidelberg Catechism, which develops these three motifs in 129 questions and answers, involving an exposition of Decalogue, Apostles' Creed, and the Lord's Prayer. In orthodox schools, these questions were addressed as formal categories of discursive thought; at Herborn, they were interpreted chronologically and developmentally, with reference to how they are appropriated by pilgrims looking toward the full salvation embodied in the answer to question one: "That I wholly belong to my faithful Savior Jesus Christ." See *Heidelberg Catechism* (Philadelphia: United Church Press, 1963), first published 1563 in the Palatinate.

4. On Ramus, see Walter J. Ong, *Ramus, Method, and the Decay of Dialogue* (Cambridge: Harvard University Press, 1958). In his syllogism, a personal witness to truth replaced a formal minor premise, leading to an existential rather than a formal conclusion to the argument.

5. O'Malley, *Pilgrimage of Faith*.

6. See A. W. Drury, *The Life of Rev. Philip William Otterbein* (Dayton, Ohio: UB Publishing House, 1884), 36.

7. Philip William Otterbein, "Letter concerning the millennium," in Arthur Core, ed., *Philip William Otterbein: Pastor, Ecumenist* (Dayton, Ohio: EUB Board of Publication, 1968), 102.

8. The definitive treatment of the radical Pietists is Hans Schneider, *German Radical Pietism*, no. 22 in the Pietist and Wesleyan Studies Series, ed. J. S. O'Malley (Metuchen, N.J.: Scarecrow Press, 2007).

9. See Jonathan Strom, "Problems and Promises of Pietism Research," *Church History* 71, no. 3 (September 2002): 536–53.

10. Chief among these events was the Thirty Years' War (1618–48), in which more than a third of the population of the German Holy Roman Empire was killed. The war also resulted in the massive destruction of property. More than a century would be required for the empire to recover to prewar population levels.

11. Reitz had been trained under Cocceian influence at Bremen, particularly the local pastor, Theodore Untereyck, and the author of the *Hymns of the Covenant*, Joachim Neander. See Schneider, *German Radical Pietism*, 26.

12. The text (untranslated) appeared as *Unparteyische Kirchen- und Ketzer-Historie/Von Anfang des Neuen Testaments Biss auf das Jahr Christi 1688* (Frankfurt: Fritsch, 1699–1700); 2nd ed. (1729).

13. Johann Arnold, *Die erste Liebe der Gemeinden Jesu Christi*, 1696 (Frankfurt a.m., 1711–12), as found in Stähelin, *Die Verkundigung des Reich Gottes* (Basel: Verlag Friedrich Reinhardt, n.d.), 5:256, author's translation. The text of his principal historical study (untranslated) appeared as *Unparteyische Kirchen- und Ketzer-Historie/Von Anfang des Neuen Testaments Biss auf das Jahr Christi 1688*.

14. Arnold, "Concerning Perfection in Christ," bk. 3, chap. 15, as found in Stähelin, *Die Verkundigung des Reich Gottes*, 5:277.

15. Especially Weigel, Jacob Boehme, and Rosicrucianism. See Schneider, *German Radical Pietism*, 46n56.

16. Philadelphianism came to expression in the thought of Johann Wilhelm and Johanna Eleonora Petersen, and its imprint was felt in Horch, the historians Reitz and Arnold, and their advocate, the court preacher Conrad Broske, among others.

17. Grete Möller, "Föderalismus und Geschichtsbetrachtung im XVII. Und XVIII. Jahrhundert," *Zeitschrift für Kirchengeschichte* 50 (1931): 231.

18. *Mystische und Prophetische Bibel/das ist Die ganze Helige. Schrifft/Altes und Neues Testaments/Auffs neue und auch dem grund verbessert/samft Erklärung/Der fürnehmsten Sinnbilder und Weissagungen/Sonderlich Des H.Lieds Salomons und der Offenbarung J.C./Wie auch/Denen fürnehmsten Lehren/bevoraus die sich in diese letzte Zeiten schicken* (Marburg: Gedruckt den Joh. Kürzner/Univers. Buchhandlung, 1712), chap. 2, n.p. All translations are those of the author.

19. Ibid.

20. *Heidelberg Catechism*, Q. 54.

21. Song of Songs 2:10-13 (NIV), cited in Horch, *Mystische und Prophetische Bibel*, preface to Acts 1, n.p.

22. Schneider, *German Radical Pietism*, 152.

23. Schneider observes that this would erase the boundaries between

canonical and apocryphal writings, emphasized by Luther, despite the fact that the editor elsewhere presupposes the literal sense of the text. Ibid., 153.

24. The uniting emphasis of the Otterbein-Boehm movement was preceded by Zinzendorf's abortive efforts to develop a "congregation of God in the Spirit" under Philadelphian influence in 1741–42.

25. Stahlschmidt's *A Pilgrim's Trip over Water and Land* recounts his experiences with both Tersteegen and Otterbein. See selections in J. Steven O'Malley, *Early German-American Evangelicalism* (Lanham, Md.: Scarecrow Press, 1995), 107–36.

26. See the designation of Seybert as radical Pietist in Scott Kisker, "Radical Pietism and Early German Methodism: John Seybert and The Evangelical Association," *Methodist History* 37, no. 3 (April 1999): 175–88; see also J. Steven O' Malley, *John Seybert and the Evangelical Heritage: Biographical and Personal Reflections on a Life Touched by Godliness* (Lexington, Ky.: Emeth Press, 2008).

27. See Schneider, *German Radical Pietism*, 151–54.

28. "Protocol of the United Brethren in Christ," Sept. 25, 1800, and Sept. 23, 1801, as found in Core, *Philip William Otterbein*, 120.

29. Their name, *Evangelische Gemeinschaft*, was adopted at their first General Conference in 1816, when the name changed from the Newly Formed Methodist Conference (1809). Before that, they were known simply as Albright People (*Albrechts Leute*).

30. Connections between European Philadelphians and New Prophets ran deep in colonial Pennsylvania, since they were at the vanguard of continental immigrants into that colony beginning in the late seventeenth century and continuing into the early eighteenth century.

31. On the 1789 confession, see *Disciplines of the United Brethren in Christ*, pt. 1, 1814–41, ed. A. W. Drury (Dayton, Ohio: UB Publishing House, 1895), 1–3, and "The Constitution and Ordinances of the Evangelical Reformed Church of Baltimore, Maryland, 1785," in Core, *Philip William Otterbein*, 109–14.

32. Philip William Otterbein, "The Salvation Bringing Incarnation and Glorious Victory of Jesus Christ over the Devil and Death" (Lancaster, 1760), as reprinted in O'Malley, *Early German-American Evangelicalism*, 19–41.

33. See Core, *Philip William Otterbein*, 77–90.

34. A. W. Drury, *History of the Church of the United Brethren in Christ* (Dayton, Ohio: UB Publishing House, 1924), 266.

35. See J. Bruce Behney and Paul H. Eller, *History of The Evangelical United Brethren Church* (Nashville: Abingdon Press, 1979), 73, 81, 83, 139, 148.

36. See *Journal of Christian Newcomer* (John Hildt, 1830). Seybert's jour-

nal remains unpublished; for a study of his life see J. Steven O'Malley, *John Seybert and the Evangelical Heritage: Biographical and Personal Reflections on a Life Touched by Godliness* (Lexington, Ky.: Emeth Press, 2008); these ecstatic practices among the Inspired are discussed in Schneider, *German Radical Pietism*, 122.

37. Schneider, *German Radical Pietism*, 123.

38. See Behney and Eller, *History of The Evangelical United Brethren Church*, catechisms: 89, 142, 301, 344; hymnals: 61, 74, 89, 110, 144, 160, 181, 245, 271, 304, 343, 374.

39. *Doctrines and Disciplines of The Evangelical Association* (Cleveland: Evangelical Publishing House, 1897).

40. See the discussion of Hochmann von Hochenau found in Schneider, *German Radical Pietism*, 39.

41. John J. Esher, *Christliche Theologie*, 3 vols. (Cleveland: Evangelical Publishing House, 1889–99).

42. See J. Steven O'Malley, *On the Journey Home: The Mission History of The Evangelical United Brethren Church, 1946–68* (New York: General Board of Global Ministries, The United Methodist Church, 2003).

43. Reginald Ward, *The Protestant Evangelical Awakening* (New York: Cambridge University Press, 1992), 230. For more on Tersteegen, see O'Malley, *Early German-American Evangelicalism*, 143–232.

44. These hymns include his "Come, children, let us set forth, for the evening draws nigh" (*Kommt Kinder, lasst uns gehen*) sung in early Evangelical camp meetings and adapted by Johannes Walter, the early Evangelical hymn writer, in what became one of the most beloved early Evangelical choruses; see Reuben Yeakel, *History of The Evangelical Association* (Cleveland: Evangelical Publishing House, 1894), 1:449.

45. Gerhard Tersteegen, *Sermons and Hymns* (Kingsport, Tenn.: Harvey and Tait, n.d.), 2:53.

46. Ibid.

5. Doctrine and Theology in the Church of the United Brethren in Christ

1. In his exhaustive study of EUB doctrine and theology, William Henry Naumann identifies three major periods in the development of United Brethren and Evangelical doctrine and theology: (1) 1800–1841, the period of the formation and fixing of faith and characteristic emphases; (2) 1841–89, the period of dialectic between standards of the first period and practical problems that arose as the sect became a denomination; and (3) 1890–1930, the period that focused attention on transdenominational movements of liberalism, higher criticism, fundamentalism, and ecumenism. See his "Theology and German-American Evangelicalism: The

Role of Theology in the Church of the United Brethren in Christ and the Evangelical Association" (PhD diss., Yale University, 1966). The Isaac Long barn incident (the Longs were all Mennonite) occurred between 1766 and 1768, most likely 1766; the conference in Baltimore occurred at the parsonage in 1789; the first regular annual conference met in 1800; the first General Conference met in 1815. There was a growing use of the UB name from 1813 to 1881, when the name was formally adopted in 1890. In a 1942 denominational promotional pamphlet, "The Church of the UB in Christ: Origin-Purpose-Program," Ulsie Perkins Hovermale, editor and compiler, describes the UB as "an American Church" and "one of America's oldest religious denominations" and claims, "The Church of the UB in Christ was the first new denomination founded in the US."

2. A. W. Drury, *History of the Church of the United Brethren in Christ* (Dayton, Ohio: Otterbein Press, 1924), 808–9.

3. Naumann, "Theology and German-American Evangelicalism," 407.

4. J. A. Weller, "The Relation of the Sunday School to the Church," in Jonathan Weaver, ed., *Christian Doctrine: A Comprehensive View of Doctrinal and Practical Theology* (Dayton, Ohio: UB Publishing House, 1890), 555, 559.

5. Drury, *History of the Church of the United Brethren in Christ*, 552, 559, 669, and T. J. Sanders, "Our Educational Policy," *Quarterly Review* 8 (1897): 27.

6. J. Steven O'Malley, *Pilgrimage of Faith: The Legacy of the Otterbeins* (Metuchen, N.J.: Scarecrow Press, 1973). Also see his *Early German-American Evangelicalism: Pietist Sources on Discipleship and Sanctification* (Metuchen, N.J.: Scarecrow Press, 1996).

7. O'Malley, *Pilgrimage of Faith*, 191.

8. James Bemesderfer, *Pietism and Its Influence upon The Evangelical United Brethren Church* (published by author, 1966).

9. O'Malley, *Pilgimage of Faith*, 189–90.

10. There are seven major sources to define United Brethren doctrine and theology: (1) "Confessions of Faith," found in the *Disciplines of the UB Church in Christ, 1814–1841*, ed. A. W. Drury (1895), and the *Disciplines* of 1873, 1877, 1881, 1885, 1889 (the first germs can be found in the Rules of 1785 for Otterbein's church in Baltimore); (2) there were many theologically minded churchmen who wrote, but there is a paucity of books and scarcity of theologians who were generally acknowledged as representative of the denomination, with the exceptions of Bishop Jonathan Weaver, "whose books served as denominational standards" and who had "no rivals," who wrote *Christian Doctrine*, and *Practical Comments on the Confession of Faith* (1892), and *Christian Theology* (1900), and his most able successor A. W. Drury, *Outlines of Doctrinal Theology, with Preliminary Chapters on Theology in General and Theological Encyclopedia* (Dayton, Ohio:

Otterbein Press, 1914/1926), both of whose theology has been described as "conservative, biblical pietism," and who only marginally reckoned with the newer scientific knowledge and newer theological positions; (3) the Bonebrake professors of theology, including Lewis Davis (1872–85), Landis (1886–91), Drury (1892–1930), Etter (1891), Howe (1931–38), and J. Bruce Behney (1939–46); (4) a ninety-seven-year-old church magazine called the *Religious Telescope*, 1834–1930; (5) a journal called the *Quarterly Review of the UB in Christ*, 1890–1910; (6) Bonebrake Theological Seminary's *Bulletins and Catalogues*, 1872–1946; and (7) five histories of the United Brethren, including Spayth (1841), Hanby (1850), Lawrence (1861), Berger (1897), and Drury (1924).

11. See, for example, E. B. Kephart, *Apologetics or A Treatise on Christian Evidences* (Dayton, Ohio: UB Publishing House, 1901). Kephart discusses such topics as the need for revelation, Scripture, inspiration of Scripture, miracles (two chaps.), facts, Christ, prophecy, Scripture and history, superiority of Christianity, and objections answered.

12. A. W. Drury, "The Visible Church: Its Organization and Government," in Weaver, *Christian Doctrine*, 429.

13. Naumann, "Theology and German-American Evangelicalism," 381–82.

14. For a discussion of the pragmatic nature of theology, see Tyron Inbody, "Methodism and Pragmatism: Promise or Peril?" *Quarterly Review* 25, no. 3 (Fall 2005): 274–91.

15. A. W. Drury, "Our Confession: Its History," *Quarterly Review* 3 (1892): 34.

16. Paul Eller, *These Evangelical United Brethren* (Dayton, Ohio: Otterbein Press, 1957), 120.

17. "Our Confession of Faith" (no author listed, apparently Etter), *Quarterly Review* 2 (1891): 373–74.

18. The thirteen articles are the triune God, creation, person and work of Jesus Christ, Holy Spirit, Holy Bible, church, sacraments, fallen humanity, justification, regeneration, sanctification, Christian Sabbath, and resurrection of the dead, which form the outline for the *Quarterly Review* series of articles on the Confession of Faith in which the denomination attempted to describe what is most characteristic of UB doctrine.

19. In his editorial announcing the series of essays on the thirteen articles of the Confession of Faith, J. W. Etter says, "Why we have existed for over a hundred years without a catechism is more than I can understand." *Quarterly Review* 2 (1891): 367–68.

20. Daniel Berger, *History of the United Brethren in Christ* (Dayton: United Brethren Publishing House, 1897), 216.

21. A. W. Drury, *The Life of Rev. Philip William Otterbein: Founder of the Church of the United Brethren in Christ* (Dayton, Ohio: UB Publishing

House, 1884), 210, 250, 297, 300. E. W. Curtis, "Philip William Otterbein," *Quarterly Review* 8 (1897): 249: "The truth of history is that we are not Methodists.... We are UB with an origin distinct." For a discussion of where the UB and the MEC differed, see Naumann, "Theology and German-American Evangelicalism," 423-25.

22. Curtis granted that "a want of organization seems to be one of the principal weaknesses of the general movement." "Philip William Otterbein," 249.

23. Drury, *Life of Philip William Otterbein*, 205, 299, 302, 304.

24. Wayne Clymer speaks of "our lifelong preoccupation with our identity" and the "desire to be unique and to belong to a unique church" growing out of a strong feeling of inferiority. "A Footnote on Uniqueness," *UTS Bulletin* 60, no. 2 (March 1961): 31.

25. James Nelson, "EUB Piety and Hymnody," in Robert Frey, ed., *The Making of an American Church: Essays Commemorating the Jubilee Year of the EUB Church* (Lanham, Md.: Scarecrow Press, 2007), 157.

26. G. M. Mathews, "Why I Am a United Brethren in Christ," *Quarterly Review* 7 (1896): 37.

27. J. P. Landis, "The Triumph of Christianity," *Quarterly Review* 8 (1897): 12.

28. George Miller, "The Economics of Jesus," *Quarterly Review* 9 (1898): 297. For a discussion of the UB involvement in the social gospel movement, and the relation of UB revivalism and commitment to the social gospel, see Naumann, "Theology and German-American Evangelicalism," 387, 398, 405, 408-11, 419.

29. Naumann, "Theology and German-American Evangelicalism," 389.

30. Eller, *These Evangelical United Brethren*, 112-13.

31. Drury, *History of the Church of the United Brethren in Christ*, 446.

32. See Otterbein's sermon in Arthur Core, *Philip William Otterbein: Pastor, Ecumenist* (Dayton, Ohio: Otterbein Press, 1960), 77.

33. *Religious Telescope* 1, no. 18 (Aug. 26, 1835): 70.

34. J. Bruce Behney and Paul H. Eller, *The History of The Evangelical United Brethren Church* (Nashville: Abingdon Press, 1979), 161-62. On the explanatory amendment, see Berger, *History of the Church of the United Brethren in Christ*, 306-8.

35. Weaver, *Christian Doctrine*, 160, 164, 167.

36. William Reese, "Depravity," *Quarterly Review* 4 (1893): 150.

37. James Will, "The 1962 EUB Confession of Faith," in Frey, *The Making of an American Church*.

38. Core, *Philip William Otterbein*, 83-85.

39. I. K. Statton, "Justification," in Weaver, *Christian Doctrine*, 256, 260.

40. M. R. Drury, "Justification," *Quarterly Review* 4 (1893): 242.

41. Ibid., 245.

42. O'Malley, *Pilgrimage of Faith*, 120, 125, 142.

43. Marion Drury, *Our Catechism: A Manual for Christian Teaching for Use in the Families, Sunday School, Junior Societies, and Juvenile Missionary and Temperance Organizations of the United Brethren in Christ* (Dayton, Ohio: UB Publishing House, 1897), 33. The structure of pt. 2 closely parallels the three-part structure of the Heidelberg Catechism.

44. L. Bookwalter, "Consecration," in Weaver, *Christian Doctrine*, 275.

45. A. W. Drury, *Outlines of Doctrinal Theology*, 139–40. Ironically, while the Evangelicals put greater stress on doctrine, they had no creedal component on sanctification but introduced to the Articles of Faith a sixteen-paragraph addendum. The United Brethren had an entire article in their Confession of Faith but refused to commit to any one view alone, each view true to the experience of some persons, from sanctification as the moment of regeneration to sanctification as a gradual work to an instantaneous second work; J. S. Mills, "Mysticism in the United Brethren Church," *Quarterly Review* 9 (1898): 136.

46. C. J. Kephart, "Sanctification," in Weaver, *Christian Doctrine*, 301, 305.

47. George Holt, "Sanctification," *Quarterly Review* 4 (1893): 249.

48. Drury, *Life of Philip William Otterbein*, 303. Part of the source of this egalitarianism, loose organization, and lack of discipline (compared to the Methodists) was "the circumstances of a German people in a country prevailingly English.... The aversion of the German mind, too, to a thorough discipline, with which Luther in his time had to contend, lingered with the Germans of America." As in Luther's time the Germans were impatient in putting their necks under a yoke, so in this case the Germans were not favorably inclined to a formal discipline, but were shaped by the spirit of opposition to order and discipline. Drury, *History of the Church of the United Brethren in Christ*, 257, 317–18.

49. *Religious Telescope* 1, no. 2 (Jan. 14, 1835): 1.

50. Berger, *History of the Church of the United Brethren in Christ*, 221.

51. Elmer O'Brien, "Ecumenism: Past, Present, and Future," in Frey, *The Making of an American Church*, 182.

52. Apart from the Reformed tilt toward a democratic view of the church, and Anabaptist egalitarianism, a more important influence was the emergence of the new, voluntary forms of association that had become characteristic of the eighteenth century. O'Malley, *Pilgrimage of Faith*, 135.

53. Drury, *History of the Church of the United Brethren in Christ*, 320.

54. A. W. Drury, "Polity of the UB Church," *Quarterly Review* 3 (1892): 268–70.

55. Ibid., 268.

56. Berger, *History of the Church of the United Brethren in Christ*, 195–96.

57. Drury, "Polity," 269.

58. J. B. Kanaga, "Divergent Tendencies of Church Polity and Life," *Quarterly Review* 9 (1898): 138.

59. J. B. Kanaga, "Divergences in Church Polity," *Quarterly Review* 7 (1896): 79.

60. Drury, "Polity," 267.

61. Donald Gorrell, "The EUB Understanding of Ministry," in Frey, *The Making of an American Church*, 37.

62. Behney and Eller, *The History of The Evangelical United Brethren Church*, 115.

63. Bemesderfer, *Pietism and Its Influence upon the Evangelical United Brethren Church*, 83.

64. James Stein, "The Road to Johnstown," in Frey, *The Making of an American Church*, 16.

65. Eller, *These Evangelical United Brethren*, 70.

66. They were reassured that infants were not damned because they were members of the invisible church by virtue of the atonement of Christ; since they were passive in their transgressions, so they were passive in their relation to the atonement, which is suspended when they come of age. D. N. Howe, "Christian Baptism: Its Nature and Design," in Weaver, *Christian Doctrine*, 194; L. Bookwalter, "The Lord's Supper," *Quarterly Review* 4 (1893): 44.

67. Marion Drury, *Our Catechism*, 32.

68. Kendall McCabe, "The Dedication of Infants: A Ritual History," *Telescope-Messenger* 5, no. 1 (Winter 1995): 2.

69. Will, "The 1962 EUB Confession of Faith," 57, 61.

70. John Harnish, *The Orders of Ministry in The United Methodist Church* (Nashville: Abingdon Press, 2000), 36–40.

71. Thomas Frank, *Polity, Practice, and the Mission of The United Methodist Church* (Nashville: Abingdon Press, 2006).

72. Behney and Eller, *The History of The Evangelical United Brethren Church*, 55, 106, 110.

73. Elmer O'Brien, "The EUB Celebration, November 1996," in Frey, *The Making of an American Church*.

74. See, for example, Petition 81122 submitted to the 2008 General Conference of the UMC regarding five specific areas of inclusiveness or exclusion affecting our mission to make disciples. The fifth area is "the proper use of the name," namely, United Methodist and not Methodist. The petitioner claims that this misuse declares "the marriage was a pretense" and was "a hostile corporate takeover." Then the petitioner lists more than a dozen "serious betrayals of the spirit of union and inclusiveness," including glorifying Wesley and Asbury while ignoring Otterbein, Boehm, and Albright; abandoning EUB institutions, such as Westmar

College and Otterbein Press; making "repeated attempts to close United Theological Seminary"; removing the EUB hymnal from circulation, including only two EUB hymns in the 1989 *United Methodist Hymnal;* and so on. "These are not petty acts to be ignored and forgotten. They exclude and offend part of our membership."

75. Harnish, *The Orders of Ministry in The United Methodist Church,* 41.

76. Gorrell, "The EUB Understanding of Ministry," 40.

77. Frank, *Polity, Practice, and the Mission of The United Methodist Church,* 177.

78. Harnish, *The Orders of Ministry in The United Methodist Church,* 40, 119, 143–44.

79. Ibid., 19, 20, 41.

6. Doctrine and Theology in The Evangelical Association/Church

1. See John Seybert, *Journal,* trans. J. G. Eller, 2:7–9 (Saturday, June 29, 1822; Friday, July 5, 1822). Ibid., 5:60 (Friday, June 26, 1829). Cf. Joseph Harlacher, *Journal,* trans. J. G. Eller, 81 (Sunday, Nov. 17, 1833).

2. On one occasion he wrote in his *Journal,* 3:41 (Friday, Dec. 30, 1825): "Roop requested that I have prayer with them and as I prayed the power of God came upon us so that the servant girl who also was present was weeping very bitterly." Cf. *Journal,* 2:7 (Wednesday, June 26, 1822).

3. "Ein Kind Gottes braucht...keine Beweisgrunde mehr dasz Christus Gott sei, es fuhlt inn in seiner Seele, als lebendige Gotteskraft." *Der Christliche Botschafter* 2 (July 1837): 49; *Der Christliche Botschafter* is hereafter cited as *CB.*

4. In the very first issue of the *CB,* "Ein Wink an Prediger," *CB* 1 (Jan. 1836): 4, warns against relying on "Kopf-Wissenschaft" without "das Herz voll von der Liebe und Gnade Gottes."

5. Don Yoder has written about the folk hymns and choruses that were an integral part of the Bush-Meeting Dutch—the United Brethren, The Evangelical Association, the Church of God, and groups they produced "by schism and example." See *Pennsylvania Spirituals* (Lancaster, Pa.: Pennsylvania Folklife Society, 1961), 12.

6. Ibid., 349, 354–56. Walter also published the first hymnbook of the denomination in 1810. Dreisbach wrote at least thirty-five hymns in German and others in English, compiled a songbook in 1821, and edited many of the official hymnbooks of the church. See Raymond W. Albright, *A History of The Evangelical Church* (Harrisburg, Pa.: Evangelical Press, 1942), 277.

7. Seybert, *Journal,* 11:36 (July 8, 1840); Albright, *A History of The Evangelical Church,* 228.

8. Albright, *A History of The Evangelical Church,* 209.

9. See "Ursachen des Unglaubens," *CB* 6 (Jan. 1, 1841): 3. Cf. Thomas

Buck, "Fall des Menschen," *CB* 1 (Feb. 1836): 9. Cf. "Hasslichkeit und Schrecklichkeit der Sunde," *CB* 1 (Nov. 1836): 86.

10. Camp meetings were begun in The Evangelical Association in 1810. Albright, *A History of The Evangelical Church*, 99. Also see *CB* 3 (Aug.–Sept. 1838): 58–59, 66–67.

11. Ammon Stapleton, *Annals of The Evangelical Association of North America and History of the United Evangelical Church* (Harrisburg, Pa.: Publishing House of the United Evangelical Church, 1900), 165. Also see Paul H. Eller, "Revivalism and the German Churches in Pennsylvania, 1783–1816" (PhD diss., Dept of Church History, University of Chicago, 1933).

12. Joseph Harlacher, *Journal*, trans. J. G. Eller, 86–87 (Dec. 14, 1833). John Dreisbach wrote that he "had long conversation with Zimmerman, a miller, and father in this home. My purpose was to convince him of the genuine Christianity, and that we, by grace, can overcome all sin and live holy lives, if we could please our God." See *Day Book*, trans. J. G. Eller, 4:5 (June 13, 1815).

13. Disagreement over how to express this conviction was a contributing factor to denominational schism.

14. John Arndt, *True Christianity*, ed. William Jaques (London: Booth and Co., 1815), 1:345.

15. Albright, *A History of The Evangelical Church*, 94. Family worship, like private devotions, also was promoted. A sermon by Wesley on family worship was used in *CB* (Oct. 15, 1840): 153–54. See "Die Kenntnisz der Heilige Schrift," *CB* (Sept. 1, 1840): 134. Also see *CB* 5 (June 15, 1840): 95.

16. Albright, *A History of The Evangelical Church*, 57. See Allen H. Zagray, "John Seybert's Use of the Bible" (BD thesis, Evangelical Theological Seminary, 1957).

17. *Der kleine biblische Catechismus* (Dritte Auflage; Neu-Berlin, Pa.: Salomon Miller und Henrich Niebel, 1818).

18. One such defense was a well-written series of articles that criticized rationalists for their scorn of the sacredness and venerability of the Bible. See Jacob Vogelbach, "Rationalismus, Vernunftglaube, Unglaube," *CB* 4 (July 1829): 50–51.

19. Albright, *A History of The Evangelical Church*, 55, 58.

20. See "Beweise der Gute GOttes aus den Werken der Schopfung," *CB* 2 (May 1837): 40; "Weisheit GOttes in dem ganzen Zusammenhang der Natur," *CB* 2 (Nov. 1837): 85; and Joseph Harlacher, "Der Schöpfer," *CB* 6 (July 1, 1841): 97–98.

21. Evangelicals were in step with a pervasive viewpoint of nineteenth-century revivalistic groups: the conviction that the beliefs and practices of the mass of ordinary people are the most important and reliable. See Timothy L. Smith, *Revivalism and Social Reform in Mid-Nineteenth-Century America* (New York: Abingdon Press, 1957), 9.

22. Albright, *A History of The Evangelical Church*, 68–69; J. Bruce Behney and Paul H. Eller, *The History of The Evangelical United Brethren Church* (Nashville: Abingdon Press, 1979), 87–88.

23. The focus on ministry in German was also reinforced by an unfortunate schismatic movement in 1831 led by an English-speaking minister. Albright, *A History of The Evangelical Church*, 221.

24. He served as publisher from 1820 to 1827, edited the *Evangelical-Messenger* for four years, published a catechism, and purchased the first printing press with his own money.

25. "Kurze Beweiszfuhrung fur die Gottheit Christi," *CB* 2 (July 1837): 49–51.

26. George Miller, *Practical Christianity* (Cleveland: Evangelical Association, 1871), 57.

27. Reuben Yeakel, *Jacob Albright and His Co-Laborers* (Cleveland: Publishing House of The Evangelical Association, 1883), 134.

28. In his *History of The Evangelical Association* (Cleveland: Evangelical Publishing House, 1894), Reuben Yeakel comments that "most likely Walter would not have become such a powerful preacher, if he had first passed through one of the theological schools *of that time.*" See Albright, *A History of The Evangelical Church*, 62–65. The widespread lack of formal education is probably one reason most contributors to the church press did not sign their names. They did not want to flaunt their abilities in the faces of those who had not had educational opportunities.

29. W. W. Orwig, *History of The Evangelical Association* (Cleveland: Charles Hammer for The Evangelical Association, 1858), 134.

30. Samuel P. Spreng, *The Life and Labors of John Seybert* (Cleveland: Lauer and Mattill, 1888), 227.

31. Reuben Yeakel, *Bishop Joseph Long* (Cleveland: Publishing House of The Evangelical Association, 1897), 194.

32. Also favored were Arndt's predecessors, August Francke's *Fear of Men*, Johann Rambach's *Meditations and Contemplations on the Suffering of Our Lord and Saviour Jesus Christ*, and Gottfried Arnold's *Portraits of the First Christians*. See James Orville Bemesderfer's "Pietism and Its Influence upon The Evangelical United Brethren Church" (STD diss., School of Theology, Temple University, 1966).

33. George Miller, *Practical Christianity*, 156; *CB* 4 (March 1839): 17–19.

34. Yeakel, *History of The Evangelical Association*, 1:101.

35. Richard Watson was an English Methodist and systematizer of Wesleyan doctrines. A sizable part of his *Institutes* is devoted to the amassing of evidences for the truth of the Christian revelation. The mood of Butler and Paley continued to prevail throughout much of the nineteenth century, even after the threat of deism was long gone.

36. Albright, *A History of The Evangelical Church*, 213.

37. Schlieszlich wunschen wir aber doch einen Jeden noch zu erinnern,

dasz ohne die Salbung des heiligen Geistes und die gottliche Ausrustung von Himmel, alles Studieren und alle Wissenschaften in der ganzen Welt ihn nicht tuchtig machen das Predigt-Amt zu verwalten; weszhalb wir Jedem rathen, vor allem Andern, die unumganglich notwendige Gnade, Salbung und Weisheit zu seinem Berufe, von Gott zu erbeten (*CB* 9 [March 1, 1844]: 37).

38. This was supported by the assurance that nature was on their side, which was part of the evidence-centered theology to which Evangelicals were devoted. In this pre-Darwinian period these people who lived close to nature had little difficulty believing that nature was a certain proof of God's existence and benevolence to humans. Albright often observed his regular devotional habits out-of-doors. Albright, *A History of The Evangelical Church*, 91. John Seybert, almost constantly outdoors because of his incessant travels, could be rhapsodic about God's natural revelation. Seybert, *Journal*, May 1, 1822, 1:103–4.

39. See Leland Scott, "Methodist Theology in the Nineteenth Century" (PhD diss., Department of Religion, Yale University, 1955), xvii, 21.

40. Ralph Kendall Schwab gives a detailed account of this extensive discussion and the conflicts that arose around it in *The History of the Doctrine of Christian Perfection in The Evangelical Association* (Menasha, Wis.: George Banta Publishing Company, 1922). Schwab concludes that "it took until 1871 for the official Wesleyan doctrine of Christian perfection, backed by the authoritative use of ecclesiastical organization and the discipline, to finally conquer the German heritage of the church on this doctrine. And since 1871, although firmly established, the doctrine of Christian perfection has gradually fallen into desuetude" (110). From the nineteenth century into the twenty-first century many Evangelicals have given leadership to the interdenominational holiness camp meeting event.

41. John Dreisbach, "Our Higher School Institutions," *Evangelical Messenger*, Dec. 26, 1855, 204; the *Evangelical Messenger* is hereafter cited as *EM*. See Behney and Eller, *The History of The Evangelical United Brethren Church*, 85–91, for a profile of Dreisbach's education.

42. "Why Are There Not More Candidates for the Ministry?" *EM*, Dec. 13, 1865, 394.

43. Seybert, Clewell, Spreng, and countless others considered the infidel a formidable foe. The infidel was a straw man that served the churches' self-interest as an enemy to rally their forces in self-defense. See Martin Marty, *The Infidel* (New York: Meridian Books, 1961), 12.

44. T. G. Clewell, "The Germans—How to Reach Them," *EM*, Aug. 23, 1860, 132–33; Sept. 6, 1860, 140.

45. T. G. Clewell, "Biblical Institutes," *EM*, April 15, 1869, 116. The appearance of articles and books giving evidence of learning was another

sign of rising theological interest. Most noteworthy was a ten-volume set known as the Evangelical Normal Series, published in 1884–85 for lay study.

46. Roy B. Leedy, *The Evangelical Church in Ohio* (Harrisburg, Pa.: Evangelical Press, 1959), 132.

47. Albright, *A History of The Evangelical Church*, 266.

48. Behney and Eller, *The History of The Evangelical United Brethren Church*, 211–12. The name was changed in 1910 to Evangelical Theological Seminary. A second school was opened in 1903 at Albright Collegiate Institute. Ibid., 303.

49. Anton Huelster, *Die Seelenlehre* (Cleveland: Verlag von der Evangelischen Gemeinschaft, 1875), vii. See also his "The Importance of Religious Culture," *EM*, April 6, 1871, 105.

50. Sydney E. Ahlstrom, "Scottish Philosophy and American Theology," *Church History* 24 (Sept. 1955): 268.

51. Ibid., 267.

52. At the time Evangelicals began to extend their reading beyond the Bible, the hymnbook, and the *Discipline*, they felt the greatest kinship with Methodist writers, who had already come to some appreciation of Scottish philosophy. See Scott, "Methodist Theology in the Nineteenth Century," 93–94, 189.

53. Thomas Reid, Dugald Stewart, Sir William Hamilton, and James McCosh, "The Pastoral Office—III," *EM*, July 8, 1869, 209–10; editorial note in *EM*, Feb. 26, 1874, 68.

54. Both were devotees of the Scottish philosophy.

55. See Ahlstrom, "Scottish Philosophy and American Theology," 261. Also see T. G. Clewell, "Faith Versus Folly," *EM*, April 5, 1860, 52.

56. Anton Huelster, "The Millennium," *EM*, Sept. 19, 1866.

57. Anton Huelster, "The Relation of Science to Religion," *EM*, Nov. 1, 1881, 2.

58. See S. P. Spreng, "The Latest Edition of Beecherism," *EM*, Aug. 1, 1882, 241.

59. Ahlstrom, "Scottish Philosophy and American Theology," 267.

60. Francis P. Weisenburger, *Ordeal of Faith: The Crisis of Church-Going America, 1865–1900* (New York: Philosophical Library, 1959), 71.

61. See William H. Naumann, "Theology and German-American Evangelicalism: The Role of Theology in the Church of the United Brethren in Christ and The Evangelical Association" (PhD diss., Yale University, 1966), 152–71.

62. Anton Huelster, Review of *Biology*, by Joseph Cook, *EM*, Dec. 6, 1877, 389.

63. John Dillenberger and Claude Welch, *Protestant Culture* (New York: Charles Scribner's Sons, 1954), 198–206.

64. Paul H. Eller, *These Evangelical Brethren* (Dayton, Ohio: Otterbein Press, 1950), 117.

65. Some of these were H. C. Sheldon at Boston University; Milton Terry at Garrett; Olin Curtis at Drew; Charles Briggs, William Adams Brown, and A. C. McGiffert at Union Theological Seminary; Henry Churchill King and Frank Hugh Foster at Oberlin; William Newton Clarke at Colgate; Levi Payne at Bangor; George B. Foster at Chicago; and Preserved Smith at Lane Seminary.

66. *The Evangelical*, June 24, 1901, 196–97. *The Evangelical* is cited hereafter as *TE*.

67. M. A. Martin, "Dr. James M. Gray and the Ministers on the Pacific Coast," *TE*, Dec. 24, 1919, 11.

68. Correspondence with Harold P. Scanlin, president of the Historical Society of the Evangelical Congregational Church, June 6, 2008.

69. Naumann, "Theology and German-American Evangelicalism," 266–313.

70. H. B. Hartzler, "Alarming and Humiliating," *TE*, March 5, 1919, 7.

71. Stevens rejected the substitutionary theory of atonement. See Roland Bainton's explanation of Steven's theological viewpoint in *Yale and the Ministry* (New York: Harper & Brothers, 1957), 179–80. Critical of the penal satisfaction theory of the atonement (Systematic Theology, [Cleveland: C. Hauser, 1913], 274–79), Gamertsfelder preferred to talk about Christ's death as substitutionary suffering (Systematic Theology, [Harrisburg, Pa.: Evangelical Publishing House, 1921], 289–94).

72. *TE*, June 26, 1889, 205.

73. See William H. Naumann, "Solomon J. Gamertsfelder, Theologian," *Telescope-Messenger* (Center for the Evangelical United Brethren Heritage, United Theological Seminary) 18, no. 1 (2008): 1–5.

74. *EM*, Sept. 12, 1906, 10; *EM*, Sept. 19, 1906, 10.

75. Naumann, "Theology and German-American Evangelicalism," 228–65.

76. Ted A. Campbell, "Progressive Evangelicalism: The Theological Matrix of Garrett-Evangelical," *AWARE* (Winter 2005): 2–3.

77. "Address of the Bishops," *TE*, Oct. 11, 1898, 322.

78. "Perkasie Park Bible Conference," *TE*, July 30, 1903, 484.

79. A. E. Hangen, "Avoiding Extremes," *TE*, Aug. 15, 1922, 4–5.

80. *General Conference Journal of The Evangelical Church*, 1926, 213–14.

81. W. H. Bucks. "The Second Coming of Christ," *EM*, July 26, 1916, 4–5.

82. John S. Stamm, "The Theological Teaching of The Evangelical Church" (master's diss., Dept. of Systematic Theology in the Graduate Divinity School, University of Chicago, 1926), 2.

83. Ibid.

84. Newell J. Wert, "Spiritual Vitality of the Evangelical United

Brethren Heritage," in *The Making of an American Church*, ed. Robert L. Frey (Lanham, Md.: Scarecrow Press, 2007), 7.

7. The Confession of Faith

1. For evidence in support of this claim, see Jason E. Vickers, *Invocation and Assent: The Making and Remaking of Trinitarian Theology* (Grand Rapids: Eerdmans, 2008), chap. 1.

2. For evidence that it was in fact used in such settings, see J. Steven O'Malley, "The Distinctive Witness of the Evangelical United Brethren Confession of Faith in Comparison with the Methodist Articles of Religion," in *Doctrines and Discipline: United Methodism and American Culture*, ed. Dennis Campbell et al. (Nashville: Abingdon Press, 1999), 55–78.

3. See Stephen Prothero, *Religious Literacy: What Every American Needs to Know—and Doesn't* (New York: HarperOne, 2008).

4. For the link between Christian doctrine and a well-ordered and good life, see Ellen Charry, *By the Renewing of Your Minds: The Pastoral Function of Christian Doctrine* (New York: Oxford University Press, 1999).

5. This is not to say that the Articles of Religion should be read in this way or that the original framers of the Articles (Methodist and Anglican) intended such a reading. It is simply to say that the progression of the Articles suggests such a reading, whereas the progression of the Confession mitigates against it.

6. For a recent work that is critical of sacrificial theories of the atonement, see J. Denny Weaver, *The Non-Violent Atonement* (Grand Rapids: Eerdmans, 2001). For a more appreciative understanding of sacrifice by a United Methodist theologian, see Andrew Sung Park, *The Triune Atonement: Christ's Healing for Sinners, Victims, and the Whole Creation* (Louisville: Westminster John Knox Press, 2009).

7. See especially, Norman Wirzba, *Living the Sabbath: Discovering the Rhythms of Rest and Delight* (Grand Rapids: Brazos Press, 2006).

8. Episcopacy and Ordination

1. J. Bruce Behney and Paul H. Eller, *The History of The Evangelical United Brethren Church* (Nashville: Abingdon Press, 1979), 289.

2. Raymond W. Albright, *History of The Evangelical Church* (Harrisburg, Pa.: Evangelical Press, 1942), 85.

3. Samuel P. Spreng, *The Life and Labors of John Seybert: First Bishop of The Evangelical Association* (Cleveland: Lauer and Mattill, 1888), 198.

4. Albright, *History of The Evangelical Church*, 68.

5. Paul F. Blankenship, "Bishop Asbury and the Germans," *Methodist History* 4, no. 3 (1966): 10–11.

6. Lee (1938), 176–77.
7. Albright, *History of The Evangelical Church,* 110.
8. Frank Baker, *John Wesley and the Church of England* (Nashville: Abingdon Press, 1970), 263.
9. *Official Proceedings of the General Conference of The Evangelical United Brethren Church,* 1966 (Dayton, Ohio: Otterbein Press, 1967), 717.
10. Ibid., 715.

9. The Practice of Liturgy and Sacraments in the Evangelical United Brethren Tradition

1. *Discipline of the United Brethren in Christ* (1869), 16–17.
2. Ibid., 8.
3. Ibid., 14.
4. John H. Ness Jr., *One Hundred Fifty Years: A History of Publishing in The Evangelical United Brethren Church* (Dayton, Ohio: EUB Board of Publication, 1966), 14.
5. A. W. Drury, *Baptism* (Dayton, Ohio: UB Publishing House, 1902), 31–32.
6. *Discipline of the United Brethren in Christ* (1869), 64.
7. Ibid., 16.
8. Ibid., 36.
9. Ibid., 37.
10. Ibid., 57–64.
11. Ibid., 58.
12. Ibid., 109.
13. Ness, *One Hundred Fifty Years,* 401.
14. *Discipline of the United Brethren in Christ* (1869), 27.
15. Ibid., 28.
16. *Minutes of the 1945 General Conference,* 570.
17. Ibid., 214–16.
18. *Discipline of the United Brethren in Christ* (1945), 251.
19. *Minutes of the 1946 General Conference,* 300.
20. *Discipline of the United Brethren in Christ* (1945), 103.
21. *Program, Reports, Memorials and Rituals,* 369.

10. The Practice of Mission and Evangelism

1. This mission theory (*missio dei*), in which not the church but God is the subject of the mission, has been widely accepted since it was endorsed by the World Mission Conference in Willingen, Germany, in 1952.
2. William J. Abraham, *The Logic of Evangelism* (Nashville: Abingdon Press, 1989), 13.
3. This is, of course, an ideal type. There have been aberrances in the history of Methodist mission and evangelism.

4. Theodore Runyon, *Die neue Schöpfung. John Wesleys Theologie heute* (Göttingen: Vandenhoeck and Ruprecht, 2005), 61.

5. That tradition was cultivated in Germany until the church union in 1968. These reports are important for our German Central Archives in Reutlingen. Insofar as the ministers filled them out accurately, they provide a good picture of the mission developments of congregations.

6. See the map in J. Steven O'Malley, *On the Journey Home* (NewYork: General Board of Global Ministries, The United Methodist Church, 2003), 10. Also see the statistics on page 15.

7. Ibid., 12.

8. Ibid., 13.

9. While there were also a few English-speaking conferences in The Evangelical Association, German was the main conference language up to 1920. The situation changed after World War I when the German language was discouraged in American society.

10. O'Malley, *On the Journey Home*, 32.

11. *The Christliche Botschafter* is The Evangelical Association's main periodical. It is a good, informative source where news from Germany, letters, mission reports, and all important information about the church were published. It is the longest-running German published church newsletter (published 1836–1946) in the United States.

12. This English periodical was published from 1848 until 1946.

13. This English periodical was first published in 1834.

14. This monthly German periodical began publication in 1841. It was discontinued in June 1846. From 1846 to 1848 it was published as *Der Deutsche Telescope* (the *German Telescope*). In 1849 the name *Die Geschäftige Martha* was restored, before being changed in 1851 to *Der Fröhliche Botschafter* (the *Joyful Messenger*).

15. Johann Hinrich Wichern (1808–81) was a theologian and founder of the *Innere Mission* (home mission) of the German state churches, an agency of the Prussian government to reform prisons.

16. See, for example, "Ein Vorschlag und Plan, um einen Missionar nach Deutschland zu schicken," *Christliche Botschafter* 22 (Nov. 15, 1849): 173.

17. Sebastian Kurz (1789–1868) immigrated in the early 1830s to the United States. He became a member of The Evangelical Association in Pennsylvania; re-emigrated in 1845 to Bonlanden, Württemberg, and started class meetings; and wrote letters that were printed in the EA periodical *Der Christliche Botschafter*. Kurz later became a colporteur of The Methodist Episcopal Church.

18. There were several similar applications to the mission society. The one written by Sebastian Kurz was twice printed in the *Christliche Botschafter* 20 (Oct. 15, 1846) and 3 (Feb. 2, 1850): 21.

19. For a detailed description, see Ulrike Schuler, *Die Evangelische Gemeinschaft. Missionarische Aufbrüche in gesellschaftspolitischen Umbrüchen* (Stuttgart: 1998) [emk studien 1], 124–27. Nicolai's plan is printed in *Christliche Botschafter* 22 (Nov. 15, 1849): 170–71.

20. Resolution made on Sept. 9, 1850, in Pittsburgh. Noticeable is the broader goal: the beginning is in Germany but the mission goal is Europe!

21. Jäckel printed the list of all names of donors: Ruben Jäckel, *Geschichte der Evangelischen Gemeinschaft. Bd. 2:1850–75* (Cleveland: Lauer and Mattill, 1895), 255.

22. Johann Conrad Link (1822–83) immigrated to the United States in 1836–37, becoming a member of the EA and minister of the West Pennsylvania Conference. In 1850, he was appointed as missionary to Germany. Link became, together with Johannes Nikolai (1818–1912), the second sent missionary, the founder of The Evangelical Association in Germany. After some disagreements, Link left the EA in 1865, becoming a Baptist minister. See Karl Heinz Voigt, "Johann Conrad Link," in *Biographisch-Bibliographisches Kirchenlexikon*, vol. 5 (1993), columns 92–94.

23. Ludwig Sigismund Jacoby (1813–74) was educated in a Jewish tradition, converted to the Lutheran Church, immigrated to the United States, became a minister of The Methodist Episcopal Church with the special appointment to work with Germans, was sent to Germany in 1849 to found a Methodist mission there, founded a tract house and seminary, and in 1871 returned to the United States. See also Karl Heinz Voigt, "Ludwig Sigismund Jacoby," in *BBKL*, vol. 2 (1990), columns 1418–42.

24. Johann Jacob Escher (1823–1901) was born in Baldenheim, Alsace, France. His family immigrated to the United States (Warren, Pennsylvania) in 1832. The family members' lives were revolutionized in an awakening caused by Johannes Seybert's preaching. The family moved with sisters and brothers of The Evangelical Association to Northfield, Illinois, and founded an EA congregation, where Escher became a Sunday school teacher. In 1849, he was accommodated into the newly founded EA Illinois Conference. In 1847, he was ordained as a deacon and, in 1849, as an elder. In 1862 Escher founded a training center for ministers (Plainfield College, later Northfield College, that moved to Naperville in 1870); he became secretary of the Sunday school and tract society and also editor of the *Christliche Botschafter*. In 1863, Escher was elected bishop, a role in which he remained for thirty-seven years. He was also responsible for the mission to Europe and Japan. Karl Heinz Voigt, "Johann Jacob Escher," in *BBKL*, vol. 15 (1999), columns 528–37.

25. The first Sunday school of The Evangelical Association was held in 1860 in Plochingen. The United Brethren also had Sunday schools, but there are no dates for their beginning.

26. According to *Christliche Botschafter* in the United States, it was named *Evangelischer Botschafter*. It was published weekly from 1864 onward.

27. *Tractathaus* of the MEC in Bremen in 1850; *Christliches Verlagshaus* of the EA in Nürttingen (later Stuttgart) in 1871. Name and circumstances of the UB publishing house in Zeitz are unknown.

28. After uniting with the seminary of The Methodist Church in 1968, the seminary remains in Reutlingen. Following state acknowledgment, its name changed in 2008 to *Theologische Hochschule Reutlingen, staatlich anerkannte Fachhochschule der Evangelisch-methodistischen Kirche* (Reutlingen School of Theology, A United Methodist–related Institution of Higher Education).

29. *Bethesdaverein für allgemeine Krankenpflege zu Elberfeld.* The *Diakoniewerk Bethesda* still exists with several branches in Germany and Switzerland.

30. Georg Christian Heinrich Bischoff (1829–85) was a member of a pietistic Lutheran society in Naila, Franconia. His brother immigrated to the United States and wrote letters about his conversion. Bischoff followed his brother in 1867, became a member and contributor of the United Brethren, was ordained in 1869, and was sent as a missionary to Germany. He evangelized unremittingly until he died in an accident. Bischoff was the founder of the United Brethren in Christ in Germany.

31. John Nuelson, *Geschichte des Methodismus von den Anfängen bis zur Gegenwart* (Bremen: Bremer Traktathaus, 1929), 683.

32. Milton Wright, the editor of the *Telescope-Messenger*, reported in this periodical on Dec. 18, 1872: "The board has desired for some time to reenforce the mission; but it seemed impossible to secure efficient missionaries to send to Germany, owing to the fact that our work among the foreign German in this country is also in need for more labourers. But this want of the German mission is now to be supplied."

33. Ibid,. 682.

34. Patrick Streiff, *Der Methodismus in Europa im 19. und 20. Jahrhundert* (Stuttgart: 2003), 108 [EmK Geschichte. Monografien, vol. 50].

35. Dorothea Sackmann and Ulrike Knöller, "Erste Zusammenkünfte von Vertretern der drei Gemeinschaften methodistischen Ursprungs in Deutschland, Sitzungsprotokolle 1881–85," *EmK Geschichte. Quellen-Studien-Mitteilungen* 28, no. 2 (2007): 83–86.

36. Schuler, *Die Evangelische Gemeinschaft*, 141–59.

37. These and the following statistics are taken from the minutes of the sixth European Central Conference of The Evangelical Association in 1946 (*Tagung der Europäischen Zentralkonferenz der Evangelischen Gemeinschaft*, 1946). The data differ from those that Steven O'Malley took from church periodicals (O'Malley, *On the Journey Home*, 40).

38. Schuler, *Die Evangelische Gemeinschaft*, 187–209.

39. O'Malley, *On the Journey Home*, 37.

40. Journal and records of the Board of Missions and the Executive

Committee, Feb. 6 (Dayton, Ohio: Center for EUB Heritage, United Theological Seminary, 1947), 14.

41. This embarrassing situation and development are described by Andrea Strübind, *Freikirchen und Ökumene.* In *Kirchliche Zeitgeschichte 6, 1993, Heft 1: Die Rolle der Kirchen im gesellschaftlichen und politischen Umbruch in Mittel-und Osteuropa,* 187–210. Also, the history of the *Hilfswerk der Evangelischen Kirchen* is explored in Johannes Michael Wischnath, *Kirche in Aktion. Das Evangelische Hilfswerk 1945–57 und sein Verhältnis zur Inneren Mission* (Göttingen: 1986) [Arbeiten zur Kirchlichen Zeitgeschichte, Reihe B: Darstellungen. 14].

42. The main reason to found this organization was to speak in a collective voice as free churches as a counterpart to the former state churches.

43. The complicated organizational structure of the different relief organizations and their goals and practices are described in Schuler, *Die Evangelische Gemeinschaft,* 222–62.

44. See ibid., 231. This is also recorded in the minutes of the Seventh Central Conference in 1950, 19.

45. There were also transport problems because of American harbor strikes in 1946 and the collective German guilt after the awful discoveries in German concentration camps.

46. This problem exists to this day because *evangelisch* is always identified as the main Protestant church.

47. O'Malley, *On the Journey Home,* 25.

48. Journal and record of the Board of Missions and the Executive Committee, June 1947, 70.

49. See Schuler, *Die Evangelische Gemeinschaft,* 246–62. The sources (files, minutes, correspondences) are filed in the Central Archives, Reutlingen, Germany.

50. Richard Leger (1884–1957) was an Evangelical Association minister (1924–51), superintendent and member of the parish council (1927–54), chairman of the EA's public corporation in Württemberg, member of the trustees of the Bethesda deaconesses and the publishing house in Stuttgart, and chief executive officer of the *Hilfswerk der Evangelischen Gemeinschaft.*

51. Report about the *Hilfswerk 1946–50,* in Minutes of the Central Conference (1950), 25 (translation).

52. See statistics in Schuler, *Die Evangelische Gemeinschaft,* 370–72.

53. See ibid., 263–85.

11. "True Holiness" as Social Practice in the Evangelical and United Brethren Traditions

1. In the Evangelical United Brethren tradition, social practice was regarded as a function of "true holiness" or the fruit of sanctification. This

doctrine is expressed in Article XI—Sanctification and Christian Perfection in *The Confession of Faith of The Evangelical United Brethren Church*. See *The Book of Discipline of The United Methodist Church, 2008* (Nashville: The United Methodist Publishing House), 69–70. See also "Sanctification," in *The Evangelical United Brethren Church: What We Believe* (Dayton, Ohio: Board of Christian Education, 1956), 13–14.

2. Roberta Schaeffer, *The Story of Red Bird Mission—Its Beginnings and Growth* (Beverly, Ky.: Red Bird Mission of The United Methodist Church, 1980), 1.

3. F. Ernest Stoeffler, *The Rise of Evangelical Pietism* (Leiden: E. J. Brill, 1965), 202–3, 205–6.

4. John J. Stoudt, ed., *Devotions and Prayers of Johann Arndt* (Grand Rapids: Baker Book House, 1958), 40.

5. Stoeffler, *Rise of Evangelical Pietism*, 230–34.

6. F. Ernest Stoeffler, *German Pietism during the Eighteenth Century* (Leiden: E. J. Brill, 1973), ix–x.

7. J. Steven O'Malley, *Early German-American Evangelicalism: Pietist Sources on Discipleship and Sanctification* (Lanham, Md.: Scarecrow Press, 1995), 3, 8.

8. *The Book of Discipline of The United Methodist Church, 2008*, 69–70.

9. For more on the organization and content of the Confession of Faith, see the chapter by Jason E. Vickers in this volume.

10. Millard J. Miller and Raymond M. Veh, eds., *My Church Faces Union* (Dayton, Ohio: Otterbein Press, 1944), 42.

11. Ibid., 62–63.

12. J. Bruce Behney and Paul H. Eller, *The History of The Evangelical United Brethren Church* (Nashville: Abingdon Press, 1979), 348–49, 307–8.

13. *Year of Programs for Local Societies, 1933–34* (Dayton, Ohio: Women's Missionary Association Literature Department, 1933), 1–6.

14. Behney and Eller, *History of The Evangelical United Brethren Church*, 376–77.

15. *Selected Materials Relating to the Merger of The Evangelical United Brethren and The Methodist Churches and the Uniting Conference of The United Methodist Church, April 23, 1968* (Lake Junaluska, N.C.: General Council on Ministries, 1993), 132.

16. D. T. Gregory, ed., *Christian Service* (Dayton, Ohio: Otterbein Press, 1948), 12.

17. Ibid., 11.

18. Cawley H. Stine, ed., *Our Church and Christian Social Action* (Dayton, Ohio: Otterbein Press, 1956), 61–63.

19. "Blue Book of Reports and Memorials to the 38th General Conference," 46, quoted in Stine, *Our Church and Christian Social Action*, 61–62.

20. Floyd L. Fulk, "The Former Evangelical United Brethren Church in the Southeastern States: A Paper" read at the Annual Meeting of the Southeastern Jurisdiction Methodist Historical Society, now to be known as the S.E.J. Commission on Archives and History—in session at Lake Junaluska, N.C., July 9-11, 1968, 4–5.

21. Warren J. Hartman, *Growing Together in Christian Fellowship, Camper's Book* (Dayton, Ohio: Otterbein Press, 1955), 11.

22. Stine, *Our Church and Christian Social Action*, 4, 58–59, 61, 64–65.

23. George Frey, "The Church and Race," in Raymond M. Veh, ed., *Penetration for Transformation* (Dayton, Ohio: EUB Board of Publication, 1967), 75–76.

24. Personal conversation between the author and Dr. Charles Brown.

25. Arthur C. Core, "Ponderings on Pietism: The Relevancy of Pietism Today," *Telescope-Messenger* 128, no. 14 (July 7, 1962): 8.

26. Stoudt, ed., *Devotions and Prayers of Johann Arndt*, 35.

12. Women in the Pietist Heritage of Methodism

1. I will use the term *Pietist women* to refer to the women associated with and contributing to The Evangelical United Brethren Church and its predecessor bodies.

2. See in particular, Clifford W. Towlson, *Moravian and Methodist* (London: Epworth Press, 1957); Martin Schmidt, *John Wesley: A Theological Biography*, 2 vols. in 3 pts. (New York: Abingdon Press, 1962–73); Howard Snyder, *The Radical Wesley* (Downers Grove, Ill.: InterVarsity Press, 1980); and the more recent analysis of Kenneth Collins, "John Wesley's Critical Appropriation of Early German Pietism," http://wesley.nnu.edu/wesleyan_theology/theojrnl/26-30/27.3.htm.

3. W. Reginald Ward and Richard P. Heitzenrater, *The Works of John Wesley*, vol. 21, *Journal and Diaries, IV, 1755–1765* (Nashville: Abingdon Press, 1992), 495. See my discussion of this influential circle in "An Early Methodist Community of Women," *Methodist History* 38, no. 4 (July 2000): 219–30.

4. The full title of the work is *Pietas Hallensis: or, A Public Demonstration of the Footsteps of a Divine Being yet in the World: in an historical narrative of the Orphan House and other charitable institutions at Glaucha near Halle in Saxony*, trans. A. W. Boehm (London, 1705).

5. See the depiction of Spener and Francke's Pietism in F. Ernest Stoeffler, *German Pietism during the Eighteenth Century* (Leiden: E. J. Brill, 1973), 55.

6. J. Bruce Behney and Paul H. Eller, *The History of The Evangelical United Brethren Church*, ed. Kenneth W. Krueger (Nashville: Abingdon Press, 1979), 118. See also the several other essays in this book that explore this theme.

7. With regard to the five major stages that Sklar identified in relation to the writing of women's religious history in the United States—namely, collecting facts about women, applying a feminist critique that asks questions about the limiting circumstances of women's lives, articulating a "female culture" proactively, exploring the diversity of women's experience, and providing synthetic and larger interpretations—scholarship with regard to EUB women has hardly moved beyond the first phase. See Kathryn Kish Sklar, "The Last Fifteen Years: Historians' Changing Views of American Women in Religion and Society," in *Women in New Worlds: Historical Perspectives on the Wesleyan Tradition*, vol. 1, ed. Hilah F. Thomas and Rosemary Skinner Keller (Nashville: Abingdon Press, 1981), 48–65.

8. Elaine Magalis, *Conduct Becoming to a Woman: Bolted Doors and Burgeoning Missions* (Cincinnati: Women's Division, Board of Global Ministries, The United Methodist Church, 1973).

9. Jean Miller Schmidt, *Grace Sufficient: A History of Women in American Methodism* (Nashville: Abingdon Press, 1999).

10. Donald K. Gorrell, "'A New Impulse': Progress in Lay Leadership and Service by Women of the United Brethren in Christ and The Evangelical Association," in *Women in New Worlds*, ed. Thomas and Keller, 1:233–45. Prof. Gorrell's concern to retrieve the story of the women dates back to a research seminar he taught in 1978, "Women in the United Methodist Heritage," at United Theological Seminary. "It quickly became obvious," he recalls, "that women had a larger place in the historical records than earlier historians had indicated and that apparently historians had been responsible for distorting the picture." Donald K. Gorrell, "Introduction," in *Woman's Rightful Place: Women in United Methodist History*, ed. Donald K. Gorrell (Dayton, Ohio: United Theological Seminary, 1980), 7.

11. James E. Will, "The Ordination of Women—The Development in the Church of the United Brethren in Christ," in *Woman's Rightful Place*, ed. Gorrell, 27–40. His essay was reprinted with only minor changes in Thomas and Keller, *Women in New Worlds*, 2:290–99. Cf. Donald K. Gorrell, "Ordination of Women by the United Brethren in Christ, 1889," *Methodist History* 18, no. 2 (Jan. 1980): 136–43. Two studies have enhanced the narrative of women's ordination: Jonathan Cooney, "Maintaining the Tradition: Women Elders and the Ordination of Women in The Evangelical United Brethren Church," *Methodist History* 27, no. 4 (Oct. 1988): 25–35, and Daryl M. Elliott, "The United Brethren General Conference of 1889 and the Ordination of Women," *Methodist History* 28, no. 2 (Jan. 1990): 143–46. See also J. Michael Mansfield and Donald K. Gorrell, "The First Female United Methodist Elder," *Telescope-Messenger* 5, no. 2 (Summer 1995): 2–3, and Barbara B. Troxell, "Ordination of Women in the United Methodist Tradition," *Methodist History* 37, no. 2

(Jan. 1999): 119–30. Patricia J. Thompson provides the most current rendering of the scholarship to date in *Courageous Past—Bold Future: The Journey toward Full Clergy Rights for Women in The United Methodist Church* (Nashville: General Board of Higher Education and Ministry, 2006).

12. Identified in some sources as Sister Copeland.

13. On the life and work of Lydia Sexton, see *Autobiography of Lydia Sexton: The Story of Her Life through a Period of over Seventy-two Years, from 1799 to 1872* (Dayton, Ohio: UB Publishing House, 1882). Cf. Sarah D. Brooks Blair, comp., *The Evangelical United Brethren Church: A Historical Sampler* (Nashville: The United Methodist Publishing House, 2000), 40–41, and Julia Dagenais, "The Last Years of Lydia Sexton," *Telescope-Messenger* 7, no. 2 (Summer 1997): 3–4.

14. Julia Dagenais, "A Sisterhood of Preachers," *Telescope-Messenger* 11, no. 1 (Winter 2001): 3.

15. Much of the following information is drawn from the exhibit "Women in Ministry: The Role of United Biblical Seminary," United Theological Seminary, October 2006–January 2007. Hospitality extended to women in other institutions of higher learning such as Otterbein College also reinforced the elevated place and role of women in the church. Women comprised nearly one-third of the first class admitted to Otterbein, this institution being only "the second American school to enroll women on the college level on equal standing with men." Henry Garst, *History of Otterbein University* (Dayton, Ohio: UB Publishing House, 1907), 79. See also Behney and Eller, *History of The Evangelical United Brethren Church*, 176.

16. See Mansfield and Gorrell, "First Female United Methodist Elder," 2–3.

17. *Proceedings of the Twentieth General Conference of the United Brethren in Christ* (Dayton, Ohio: UB Publishing House, 1889), 52–53.

18. See Will, "The Ordination of Women," 32, 38–39.

19. Thompson, *Courageous Past—Bold Future*, 17.

20. Elliott, "1889 and the Ordination of Women."

21. Quoted in ibid., 45.

22. Cynthia S. Meyer, "'Doing the Master's Work, However Homely': The Image of Women in the Church of the United Brethren in Christ, 1872–1875," unpublished paper, see 9–11.

23. Will, "The Ordination of Women," 296.

24. Cooney, "Maintaining the Tradition," 25–35. Pat Thompson includes a lengthy discussion of the conversations that revolved around the question of women's ordination at the time of merger in her analysis of women elders in the EUB tradition. The conclusion that she draws, based in large measure on interviews with contemporaries of these events, is that "the EUB Church left to the annual conferences the decision

as to whether or not to ordain women, depending upon the inclinations of those with the authority to make such decisions. Consequently, some conferences ordained women; others did not." Thompson, *Courageous Past—Bold Future*, 66–67.

25. Cooney, "Maintaining the Tradition," 26–27.

26. Ibid., 31. Cooney offered four potential explanations for the continuation of this practice. The ordinations may reflect the ambiguous state of the EUB *Discipline*, the weakness of the union itself, the social and theological flux of the period, or the effectiveness of the female pastors and the potency of the tradition (32). One district superintendent whom he interviewed indicated that the "advancement of women to the order of elder...occurred because of two conditions. First, the church could not deny that the women's call to the ministry was valid. Second, their 'willingness to serve the most menial appointments was commendable'" (31).

27. Dana Lee Robert, *American Women in Mission: A Social History of Their Thought and Practice* (Macon, Ga.: Mercer University Press, 1996), 129. Cf. Patricia Hill, *The World Their Household: The American Woman's Foreign Mission Movement and Cultural Transformation, 1870–1920* (Ann Arbor: University of Michigan Press, 1985).

28. Rosemary Skinner Keller, "Women and the Nature of Ministry in the United Methodist Tradition," *Methodist History* 22, no. 2 (Jan. 1984): 108.

29. Audrie E. Reber, *Women United for Mission: A History of the Women's Society of World Service of The Evangelical United Brethren Church, 1946–68* (Dayton, Ohio: Otterbein Press, 1969), 17.

30. Jean Miller Schmidt, "The Present State of United Methodist Historical Study," *Methodist History* 28, no. 2 (Jan. 1990): 111.

31. More materials are available on this topic than any other related to women in the EUB heritage. Much of the historical material was authored by women who held important positions of leadership in the movement. For information on the WMS of The Evangelical Association, see Mrs. H. Bennett, *Her Story: History of the Woman's Missionary Society of The Evangelical Association* (Cleveland: Mattill and Lamb, 1903); Paul Himmel Eller, *History of Evangelical Missions* (Harrisburg, Pa.: Evangelical Press, 1942); Mrs. S. J. Gamertsfelder and Sarah E. Snyder, *The Abiding Past; or, Fifty Years with the Woman's Missionary Society of The Evangelical Church, 1884–1934* (Harrisburg, Pa.: Woman's Missionary Society of The Evangelical Church, 1934); P. W. Raidabaugh, *History of the Woman's Missionary Society of The Evangelical Association* (Cleveland: Thomas and Mattill, 1887), and Mrs. John S. Stamm, *Twelve More Years of the Abiding Past, 1934–46* (Cleveland: Publishing House of The Evangelical Church, 1946). For information on the WMA of the United Brethren, see Lillian R. Harford and Alice E. Bell, *History of the Women's Missionary Association of the United*

Brethren in Christ (Dayton, Ohio: UB Publishing House, 1921); *History of the Woman's Missionary Society of the United Brethren in Christ* (Dayton, Ohio: UB Publishing House, 1910); Mary R. Hough, *Faith that Achieved: A History of the Women's Missionary Association of the Church of the United Brethren in Christ, 1872–1946* (Women's Society of World Service, Evangelical United Brethren Church, 1958); Justina Lorenz Showers et al., *Missions at Home and Abroad* (Dayton, Ohio: Home Mission and Church Extension Society and Foreign Mission Society of the United Brethren in Christ, 1935); M. M. Titus, "History of the Woman's Missionary Association" (unpublished manuscript); and "U[nited]. B[rethren].—Woman's Missionary Association: Articles dealing with women's work copied from denominational periodicals, 1872–1881" (bound typescript, United Theological Seminary). For information on the WMS of the United Evangelical Church, see Estella Hartzler Steinmetz, ed., *Reminiscences: Record of 25 Years Progress in the Woman's Missionary Society of the United Evangelical Church* (Harrisburg, Pa.: Publishing House of the United Evangelical Church, 1910). For a study of the WSWS of The EUB Church, see Reber, *Women United for Mission*. Among the many contemporary critical studies, the most important include Hill, *The World Their Household*; J. Steven O'Malley, *On the Journey Home: The History of Mission of The Evangelical United Brethren Church, 1946–68* (New York: General Board of Global Ministries, The United Methodist Church, 2003); and *Stir into Flame: The Story of Women in Mission* (Baltimore: Baltimore Conference, United Methodist Women, 1991).

32. Mary McLanachan, "A Record of Constant Outreach: The Women's Missionary Association," http://gbgm-umc.org/umw/history/record1.html, quoting from *The Abiding Past*. In the Evangelical tradition, a similar association of women commenced as early as 1839 in Philadelphia, but this local project was short-lived and never expanded to a churchwide movement until much later in the century. See Reber, *Women United for Mission*, 9.

33. Benjamin H. Niebel and Homer H. Dubs, *Evangelical Missions* (Harrisburg, Pa.: Home and Foreign Missionary Society of the United Evangelical Church, 1919), 106–7.

34. See W. E. Musgrave, *The Church of the United Brethren in Christ: Teachings and Progress*, rev. ed. (Huntington, Ind.: Department of Education, Church of the United Brethren in Christ, 1956), 69.

35. In Magalis, *Conduct Becoming to a Woman*, 26, quoting from *Religious Telescope*, Oct. 13, 1875.

36. Ibid., quoting from *Religious Telescope*, Nov. 24, 1875.

37. See Reber, *Women United for Mission*, 12.

38. Ibid., 13.

39. Gorrell, "A New Impulse," 242.

40. Ibid., 237.

41. Keller, "Women and the Nature of Ministry," 110.

42. *Women's Evangel* (Jan. 1882): 2.

43. For the evolution of these various periodicals through subsequent unions and mergers, see the timeline in the appendix of this volume.

44. Magalis, *Conduct Becoming to a Woman*, 35.

45. Dana L. Robert, ed., *Gospel Bearers—Gender Barriers: Missionary Women of the Twentieth Century* (Maryknoll, N.Y.: Orbis Books, 2002), 7.

46. See Lois Olsen, *Contentment Is Great Gain: A Missionary Midwife in Sierra Leone* (Milwaukee: Leone Press, 1996).

47. For a general discussion of the deaconess movement, see Jane Marie Bancroft, *Deaconesses in Europe and Their Lessons for America* (Charleston, S.C.: BiblioBazaar, 2007), which includes the chapter "Deaconesses in German Methodism," and Mary Agnes Dougherty, *My Calling to Fulfill: Deaconesses in the United Methodist Tradition* (New York: Women's Division, General Board of Global Ministries, 1997). On the specific role of deaconesses within the Pietist heritage of Methodism, see Dee Dee Hefner, *Called to Serve: A Survey of the Deaconess and Home Missionary Movements in the Former Evangelical United Brethren Traditions* (Espanola, N.M.: published by author, 1976) and Phil Ware, "The Deaconess Work," in Papers on the Ministry of The Evangelical United Brethren Church, comp. Arthur C. Core, unpublished papers, United Theological Seminary.

48. Behney and Eller, *History of The Evangelical United Brethren Church*, 234.

49. See the excellent history of the Women's Society of World Service, Reber, *Women United for Mission*.

50. See the vignettes of some of these women in *They Went out Not Knowing: An Encyclopedia of One Hundred Women in Mission* (New York: Women's Division, General Board of Global Ministries, 1986).

51. Reber, *Women United for Mission*, 14.

52. See Gorrell, "A New Impulse," 242–44. In addition to the general histories of the denominations, the only serious attempt to delineate the issues related to laity rights for women in the EUB heritage is Karen Heetderks Strong, "Ecclesiastical Suffrage: The First Women Participants at General Conference in the Antecedents of The United Methodist Church," *Methodist History* 25, no. 1 (Oct. 1986): 29–33.

53. According to Behney and Eller, "In 1895 Mrs. Hartman from the St. John's parish in Oregon was acclaimed as 'the first female member of an annual conference.'" *History of The Evangelical United Brethren Church*, 285.

54. Ibid., 243.

55. Karen Strong's research indicates that the Methodist Protestant Church was the first of the predecessor bodies to seat women at General Conference, only one year before the United Brethren action. See Strong, "Ecclesiastical Suffrage," 29.

56. Quoted in Schmidt, *Grace Sufficient*, 227. Despite the clear affirmation of women by the hierarchy of the church, the fact that misogynist attitudes continued to surface is evidenced by the apologetic articles published in the twentieth century by the *Quarterly Review* of the United Brethren in Christ with titles such as "The Place of Women in the United Brethren Church" (1902), "Women in the General Conference" (1904), and "Shall Women Be Delegates to General Conference?" (1904).

57. Keller, "Women and the Nature of Ministry," 107.

58. Ada Marie Krecker, *The Beautiful Life of Mrs. Elizabeth Krecker* (Harrisburg, Pa.: Woman's Missionary Society of the United Evangelical Church, 1905), 151–52.

59. On the life and legacy of Sarah Dickey, see Helen Griffith, *Dauntless in Mississippi: The Life of Sarah A. Dickey, 1838–1904* (Northhampton, Mass.: Metcalf, 1965); Sarah Ann Dickey, "Education of Colored Girls in the South," *United Brethren Review* 9, no. 2 (March–April 1898): 181–82; Helen Griffith, "Sarah Ann Dickey," in *Notable American Women 1607–1950: A Biographical Dictionary*, vol. 1, ed. Edward T. James and Janet Wilson James (Cambridge, Mass.: Belknap Press of Harvard University Press, 1971), 473–75; and Center for the Evangelical United Brethren Heritage, Archives (Dayton, Ohio: United Theological Seminary), vertical file.

60. Magalis, *Conduct Becoming to a Woman*, 82.

61. Griffith, "Sarah Ann Dickey," 473.

62. In 1905 her daughter, Ada Marie, produced a hagiographical account of her labors titled *The Beautiful Life of Mrs. Elizabeth Krecker*, which includes some of her memorable addresses. In addition to this now rare biographical study, the fragments of her unusually busy life must be garnered from records of the Women's Missionary Society, the Woman's Home and Foreign Missionary Society (its successor in the United Evangelical Church), and other denominational records.

63. Krecker, *Beautiful Life*, 20–21.

64. Ibid., 84.

65. Ibid., 93.

66. Ibid., 112.

67. On the life and legacy of Susan Bauernfeind, see Lowell Messerschmidt, *Bauern-Sensei: The Story of Susan Bauernfeind, Pioneer Missionary to Japan* (Lima, Ohio: Fairway Press, 1991); Lowell and Betty Messerschmidt, "Susan Bauernfeind: Pioneer Missionary to Japan for The Evangelical Church," *Telescope-Messenger* 2, no. 1 (Winter 1992): 1–3; Susan Bauernfeind, *Wayside Sowing: An Illustrated Story of the Work in Mukijima, Tokyo* (Cleveland: Woman's Missionary Association of The Evangelical Association, n.d.); Susan Bauernfeind Papers, Center for the Evangelical United Brethren Heritage, United Theological Seminary, Archive HC3; and records of the Susan Bauernfeind Memorial Church, 1951, United Methodist Archives, Drew University.

68. Thompson, *They Went out Not Knowing*, 12.
69. Messerschmidt, "Susan Bauernfeind," 2.
70. Ibid.
71. Barbara Troxell and Patricia Farris, "One Eye on the Past, One Eye on the Future: Women's Contributions to Renewal of The United Methodist Church," *Quarterly Review* 18, no. 1 (Spring 1998): 47.
72. Krecker, *Beautiful Life*, 152.
73. Bauernfeind Papers, uncataloged material.
74. Reber, *Women United for Mission*, 33.
75. Krecker, *Beautiful Life*, 157.
76. Mrs. J. Hal Smith, *The Radiant Life of Vera B. Blinn* (Dayton, Ohio: Otterbein Press, 1921), 86.
77. Marion L. Baker, "'Her Story' Out of 'The Abiding Past,'" http://gbgm-umc.org/umw/history/herstory1.html, quoting from Gamertsfelder and Snyder, *The Abiding Past*.
78. Krecker, *Beautiful Life*, 164.
79. Ibid., 159–61.
80. Bauernfeind Papers.
81. Ibid.
82. Krecker, *Beautiful Life*, 200–201.
83. The prayer of Frances Schneider, quoted in Reber, *Women United in Mission*, 132. The prayer has been adapted for corporate use.

Afterword: The Evangelical United Brethren Tradition and the Future of United Methodism

1. I owe this term to Douglas M. Koskela, *Ecclesiality and Ecumenism: Yves Congar and the Road to Unity* (Milwaukee, Wis.: Marquette University Press, 2008). This whole study is of great assistance in tackling the broader theological issues that are important for the subject matter of this chapter.

2. It has been a particular pleasure to read through A. W. Drury, *History of the Church of the United Brethren in Christ*, rev. ed. (Dayton, Ohio: UB Publishing House, 1931), and Raymond W. Albright, *A History of The Evangelical Church* (Harrisburg, Pa.: Evangelical Press, 1942). It is a great pity that J. J. Esher's three-volume *Christliche Theologie* (Cleveland: Publishing House of The Evangelical Association, 1901) is not only virtually impossible to find but unavailable in English translation.

3. For an illuminating discussion of the meaning and history of Pietism, see K. James Stein's excellent chapter in this volume.

4. Note that this is not a comprehensive list of all that would need to be covered.

5. Taking the whole sweep of the tradition seriously would have shown the complexity of reception and development.

6. Even so, I have no desire to eliminate this strain from the dialogue within United Methodism. We need diversity, not unanimity, in our political theologies, and the Mennonite strain can rightly act as a leaven in the whole tradition.

7. The doctrine of the Christian life features prominently in many chapters in this volume, including those by Stein, Inbody, Naumann, and Vickers.

8. The relevant priorities are eliminating killer diseases (malaria and HIV) and working with poor and marginalized people. The other priorities are planting new congregations and developing lay and clergy leadership. It is astonishing that none of these take up the mission statement of the church, making disciples for the transformation of the world, much less the salvation of souls.

9. We can live with the current mission statement, of course, for it captures vital elements of the work of mission. However, we should not be complacent about the danger of this change becoming one more excuse to dodge two crucial considerations that are likely to be overlooked. First, there is no sign that there is any intention of operationalizing this mission statement. The heavy lifting currently is on the proposed restructuring of United Methodism and in the four priorities adopted at the General Conference of 2008. Second, the current mission statement may imply that we take personal conversion and salvation seriously, but there is no guarantee that it will do so. The more likely option is that the current mission statement will be the occasion for systematic evasion.

10. This handy phrase was invented by Randy Maddox to capture certain aspects of the work of grace in the human agent, but it has become something of an empty slogan of late that bypasses the deeper elements that Maddox sought to capture originally. See Randy L. Maddox, *Responsible Grace: John Wesley's Practical Theology* (Nashville: Kingswood Books, 1994), 19.

11. I have explored this thesis with respect to Christian perfection in "Christian Perfection," in William J. Abraham and James E. Kirby, eds., *The Oxford Handbook of Methodist Studies* (Oxford: Oxford University Press, 2009).

12. Thomas Bowman, *The Great Salvation* (Cleveland: Publishing House of The Evangelical Association, 1909).

13. Ibid., 52.

14. I suspect that the tradition may have overdosed on these themes and in its weariness opted for a simplistic rendering of them conceptually and experientially. This development may well have led to a rejection of them as unrealistic and intellectually offensive. This is the impression I have gained from many conversations in Texas.

15. The exception that proves the rule is the fine attempt to come to

terms with the doctrine of Christian perfection by Stephen W. Mansker, *A Perfect Love: Understanding John Wesley's* A Plain Account of Christian Perfection (Nashville: Discipleship Resources, 2003).

16. For an introduction to the Confession of Faith that highlights its pneumatological orientation and catechetical value, see the chapter by Jason E. Vickers in this volume.

17. The irony of the first names of Wolff and Kant is dramatic in the wake of this development.

18. To be fair to Outler, he did change his mind toward the end of his life, but this is not widely known. I show this in an unpublished paper, "United Methodism, Ecclesiology, and Ecumenism," presented at the Outler Conference, Southern Methodist University, January 2008.

19. I know this from personal conversation with Outler in Seattle in the late 1970s.

20. It is a pipe dream to think that we can reach agreement on theological method, much less expect the whole church to sign on to it. It is canonical doctrine of the kind enshrined in the Articles of Religion and Confession of Faith that we need, not canonical epistemology.

21. The landmark treatment of this topic is Ellen Charry, *By the Renewing of Your Minds: The Pastoral Function of Christian Doctrine* (New York: Oxford University Press, 1999).

22. My local church, Highland Park United Methodist Church in Dallas, has developed a splendid relationship with the Evangelical Methodist Church in Costa Rica to build an orphanage in San Jose. The amount of labor and money spent on this is remarkable.

23. I know this from firsthand experience in Kazakhstan and Nepal.

24. For a good example of how The Evangelical United Brethren Church attended to the full range of mission work, see the chapter by Ulrike Schuler in this volume.

CONTRIBUTORS

William J. Abraham is Albert Cook Outler Professor of Wesley Studies and Altshuler Distinguished Teaching Professor at Perkins School of Theology, Southern Methodist University, Dallas, Texas. He is coeditor (with James E. Kirby) of *The Oxford Handbook of Methodist Studies* (2009) and the author of *Wesley for Armchair Theologians* (2007) and *Aldersgate and Athens: John Wesley and the Foundations of Christian Belief* (2010).

Paul W. Chilcote is Professor of Historical Theology and Wesleyan Studies at Ashland Theological Seminary in Ohio. Author of fifteen books and many scholarly articles, he has published extensively in Wesleyan studies, including several volumes related to early Methodist women, among them *She Offered Them Christ* (1993), *Her Own Story* (2001), and *Early Methodist Spirituality* (2007).

Wendy J. Deichmann Edwards is President and Associate Professor of History and Theology at United Theological Seminary, Dayton, Ohio. She is the author of several articles and coeditor (with Carolyn DeSwarte Gifford) of *Gender and the Social Gospel* (2003).

Tyron Inbody is Professor of Theology Emeritus at United Theological Seminary, Dayton, Ohio. He is the author of more than forty articles and several books, including *The Constructive Theology of Bernard Meland: Postliberal Empirical Realism* (1995), *The Transforming God: An Interpretation of Suffering and Evil* (1997), *The Many Faces of Christology* (2002), and *The Faith of the Christian Church: An Introduction to Theology* (2005).

James E. Kirby is Professor of Church History Emeritus at Perkins School of Theology, Southern Methodist University, Dallas, Texas. He is the author of numerous articles and books, including *The*

Methodists (1996) (with Russell E. Richey and Kenneth Rowe), *The Episcopacy in American Methodism* (2000), and *Brother Will: A Biography of William C. Martin* (2000) and co-editor (with William J. Abraham) of *The Oxford Handbook of Methodist Studies* (2009).

Scott Kisker is Associate Professor of the History of Christianity at Wesley Theological Seminary, Washington, D.C. He is the author of *Foundation for Revival: Anthony Horneck, the Religious Societies, and the Rise of an Anglican Pietism* (2007), *Mainline or Methodist: Recovering Our Evangelistic Mission* (2008), and (with Elaine Heath) *Longing for Spring: A New Vision for Wesleyan Community* (2009).

Kendall McCabe is Professor of Evangelization in the Heisel Chair at United Theological Seminary in Dayton, Ohio, where he has previously served as Professor of Homiletics and Worship and as Academic Dean.

William Naumann is Emeritus Professor of Religious Studies, North Central College, Naperville, Illinois. He also taught at Fukuoka Jo Gakuin College in Japan (1991–95), and he is the author of *Theology and German-American Evangelicalism: The Role of Theology in the Church of the United Brethren in Christ and The Evangelical Association* (1966).

J. Steven O'Malley is John T. Seamands Professor of Methodist Holiness History, Asbury Theological Seminary, and Director, Center for the Study of World Christian Revitalization Movements, a research center funded by the Henry Luce Foundation in Wilmore, Kentucky. He is the author of numerous articles and books, including *On the Journey Home: The History of Mission of The Evangelical United Brethren Church* (2003), *Early German-American Evangelicalism: Pietist Sources on Discipleship and Sanctification* (1995), and *Pilgrimage of Faith: The Legacy of the Otterbeins* (1973).

Kenneth E. Rowe is Emeritus Professor of Church History and Methodist Librarian at Drew University in Madison, New Jersey. He is the author and editor of several books, including *United Methodism at Forty* (2008) and *The Methodist Experience in America* (2000 and 2010).

CONTRIBUTORS

Ulrike Schuler is Professor of Church History, Methodism, and Ecumenism at the Reutlingen School of Theology, a UMC-related theological faculty in Germany. As Director of the Commission on the History of The United Methodist Church in the German-speaking areas (Germany, Austria, Switzerland), she oversees the publication of the *EmK Geschichte. Quellen-Studien-Mitteilungen* (historical journal), as well as the *EmK Geschichte. Monografien*. She is President of the Historical Commission of the Methodist Church's European Council.

K. James Stein is a senior scholar in Church History at Garrett Evangelical Theological Seminary in Evanston, Illinois, where he was a faculty member for thirty-six years. He served as Dean and President of the former Evangelical Theological Seminary in Naperville, Illinois, prior to its 1974 merger with Garrett Theological Seminary. He is the author of *Philipp Jakob Spener: Pietist Patriarch* (1986), *Great Devotional Classics Study Guide* (1989), and *Faith Stories of the Protestant Reformers: Spiritual Guides for the 21st Century* (2000), as well as numerous articles concerning Pietism and the former Evangelical United Brethren Church.

Jason E. Vickers is Associate Professor of Theology and Wesleyan Studies and Director of the Center for EUB Heritage, United Theological Seminary, Dayton, Ohio. He is the author of *Invocation and Assent: The Making and Remaking of Trinitarian Theology* (2008) and *Wesley: A Guide for the Perplexed* (2009) and coeditor (with Randy L. Maddox) of *The Cambridge Companion to John Wesley* (2009).

Index

Abbott, Benjamin, 29
Abraham, William J., 163
Adam/Christ Typology, 58
Africa, 64, 69
African Church, 31
Age of Reason, 7
Age of the Spirit, 64, 67
Ahlstrom, Sydney, 100
Aisenryo Orphanage, 207
Albright Brethren, 35
Albright College, 206
Albright, Jacob, 10–11, 14, 37–44, 45–49, 52–53, 70–72, 91, 93, 95–96, 106, 180, 225
Albright, Raymond W., 11
Albright's People (*Albrechtsleute*), 39, 46, 49, 67, 70
Alleine, Joseph, 97
Allentown, Pennsylvania, 38, 47
Alsace-Lorraine, 168
Amana Colonies, 68
America, 9, 19, 24, 29, 46
Amsterdam, 72
Anabaptist, 60, 88
  theology, 77
Anglicanism, 77
annual conference, 31, 33, 40, 42
Antietam Creek, 26, 28, 31
anti-Gnostic Christology, 58
Apocalypse of John, 62
Apostles' Creed, 40, 45, 158
Arian controversy, 110

Aristotelian Orthodoxy, 59
Arndt, Johann, 5–6, 95, 97, 181–82
Arnold, Gottfried, 61,65
Arnold, Valentine, 9
Articles of Faith, 11, 71–72, 103, 151, 153
Articles of Religion, 43, 50, 80, 90, 109–10, 112, 114–26, 221–22
Asbury, Francis (Bishop), 4, 24–25, 28, 30–37, 41-8, 51–53, 89–91, 96
Asbury/Philadelphia Conference, 43
Asia, 64
Association (*Gemeinschaft*), 15–16, 37–38, 49, 65
The Association of Reformed Congregations in Maryland, 28
assurance, 10, 14, 24, 26, 39, 76-77, 81, 94, 99, 169
Aurand, Dietrich, 31

Babylon, 62
Baltimore, 10, 15, 28, 30
Baltimore Church, 28
Baltimore MEC Conference, 33
Bangor, Pennsylvania, 38
baptism, 13, 27, 50, 68, 76, 87, 111, 130, 152–53, 157–58, 161
baptismal confession of faith, 158
baptismal regeneration, 13, 87
  of fire, 68
  in the Spirit, 64, 68–69, 71–73
Baptists, 19, 152
Barto, Pennsylvania, 38

Index

Batdorf, L. J., 196
Bauernfeind, Susan, 201, 207–12
Baulus, Valentine, 35
Baxter, Richard, 97
Beatty, C. B., 194
Becker, George, 41
Becker, Samuel, 40
Beeken, Emily, 199
Beissel, Johann Conrad, 19
Bemesderfer, James, 11
Bengel, Albrecht, 59
Berks County, Pennsylvania, 38
Berleburg, 63
Berleburg Bible, 63, 65–66
Bethesda, 171
Bethesda Deaconess Society, 174
Biederwold, William, 103
Bischoff, Christian, 168
bishop, 22, 29, 32, 41, 47–48, 68, 71, 87, 89–90, 103
Bishop Coke, 44
Bishop Epp, 185
Bishop Hostetter, 22
Blinn, Vera, 210
Bloesch, Donald, 6
Board of Christian Social Action, 183
Board of Missions, 199–200
Board of Ordained Ministry, 110
Board of Public Morals, 183
Boehm, Henry, 20, 22, 29–31, 43–44, 48
Boehm, Jacob, 20, 62
Boehm, Martin, 9–10, 14–16, 20–24, 26–27, 29–34, 36, 42, 47, 65, 67, 69, 77, 85, 88, 180
Boehm's Chapel, 31, 34
Bohemian Brethren, 60
Book of Common Prayer, 151, 160
Book of Concord (1580), 4
Bosanquet, Mary, 192
Boston University, 188
Bowman, Fay, 160
Bowman, Thomas (Bishop), 220–21
Brandenburg, 8
Brewer, Mattie, 202
Broske, Conrad, 61
Brown, Charles, 188

Brown, Dale, 6
Brown, Hezekiah, 44
Bucks County, Pennsylvania, 38
Bushnell, Horace, 104

Caldwell, Charles, 205
Calvin, John, 4
Calvinism, 5–6, 10, 79, 154
Camissard rebellion, 64
Carl, J. S., 64–65
Catholic mysticism, 5, 10, 13
catholicity, 52
Chalcedonian definition, 127
Children's Membership Record, 157–58
Christ, 7, 14, 22, 26, 32, 50–52, 59, 66–70, 73, 94, 155, 160, 181, 190
Christendom, 62–64
Christian Perfection, 43–45, 61, 68, 71, 85, 99, 119, 129, 131–32, 182, 189
Chrysostom, John, 110
Cincinnati, Ohio, 52
Civil War, 99, 194
class meeting, 15, 26, 28-9, 33–34, 36, 38–39, 53, 81, 141, 167
Clemens, Louisa, 194
Clewell, T. G., 99
Coalbrookdale Iron Works, 38
Cocceius, Johannes, 58, 60, 62, 67
Cocceain hermeneutic, 59, 67
Collect for Purity, 50, 153
collegia pietatis, 15, 60
Comenius, John, 60
Commission of Christian Social Action, 184
Committee on Ritual, 158, 160
Confession of Faith, 11, 36, 79, 87, 90, 109–35, 152, 182, 221–22
  in catechesis, 110
  in worship, 110
consecration, 50, 87, 157, 201
continental Pietism, 12, 20, 36, 88, 191
conversion, 76, 84, 94, 178
  experience, 13, 77, 79–80
Cook, Joseph, 100–102
Cooney, Jonathan, 196
Cooperative for American Remittance

to Europe (CARE), 173
Core, Arthur C., 189
Course of Study, 97, 100, 104
Courtland, L., 194
Crider, Martin, 30

Dallas, 69
Danish-Halle mission, 9
Davies, Isaac, 11
Day, Emeline, 198
deaconess, 168, 174, 194, 201
deaconess societies, 203
Dedication, 50, 157–59
  of Infants without Baptism, 158
de Marsay, Hector, 66
Der Christliche Botschafter, 65
Dickey, Sarah, 201, 204–5, 210
Dickins, John, 45
Dickins/Dreisbach catechism, 45
Dillenburg, Nassau, 24
doctrine, 80
  of Christian and Property, 133
  of Christian perfection, 71, 85, 99
  of the Church, 129
  of civil government, 133
  of entire sanctification, 68, 71–72, 85
  of eternal damnation, 133
  of the fall, 22
  of God, 127
  of good works, 132
  of grace, 14
  of the Holy Spirit, 128
  of Jesus Christ, 127
  of the judgment and the future state, 133
  of justification and regeneration, 131
  of justification by grace, 6
  of the Lord's Day, 133
  of original sin, 83
  of predestination, 29
  of the priesthood of all believers, 154
  of public worship, 133
  of reconciliation in Christ, 131
  of repentance, 80
  of the Sacraments, 87, 115–16, 121–23, 129–30
  of sanctification and justification, 43, 132
  of Scripture, 128
  of Sin and Free Will, 14, 131
  of total depravity, 82–84, 89
Dreisbach, John, 40, 42, 45, 47–49, 94, 96, 99
Drury, A. W., 23–24, 31, 79–80, 152
Dry Valley, Union County, 49
Dubs, C. Newton, 104
Dubs, Homer H., 198
Dubs, Rudolph (Bishop), 104–5
Dunkers, 19, 22, 24, 27, 31, 36
Dutch Methodists, 38, 40

East Prussia, 168, 170
Easter, 41
Eby, Henry, 42
ecclesiology, 85–86, 89, 91, 128, 135
ecumenism, 16–17, 36, 81, 105, 163, 178, 202
Edwards, Jonathan, 97
Eller, Paul, 40
Elliot, Daryl, 195
Elliott, Maggie, 195
English Reformation, 111
Ephrata, 20, 25–26
Erneuerung (renewal or sanctification), 8
Ernst, John, 30
Escher, Johann Jacob (Bishop), 68, 71, 168
EUB Department of World Mission, 174
The Evangelical Association in Germany, 168
The Evangelical Church, 10
Evangelical General Conference, 11
Evangelical General Conference of 1843, 51
The Evangelical Messenger, 47
Evangelical School of Theology, 104, 106
Evangelical Theological Seminary, 188
Evangelical Youth Fellowship, 177

INDEX

Evangelical's *Book of Doctrine and Discipline* (1809), 68
Evangelische Gesmeinschaft, 171–73, 175, 176
evangelism, 163–65, 176, 219
Evanston, Illinois, 72
experiential religion, 21, 25–26, 77, 149

faith, 203, 211, 213
Farley, Edward, 6
Farris, Patricia, 208
Federal Council of Churches, 17, 82, 102, 185
Federal Republic of Germany, 177
Federal theology, 60, 67
filioque clause, 128
Finney, Charles, 154
First Great Awakening, 20, 22–23, 26, 36
Fletcher, John, 94, 97, 220
footwashing, 67, 150
Formula of Concord (1577), 4
Francke, August Hermann, 8–9, 12–14, 192
Frankfurt, 5, 19, 60
Frederick IV of Denmark, 9
Frederick Wilhelm I, 9
Frederick, Maryland, 26, 28
Free Church Federation, 172
Freetown, 69
Fry, Jacob, 40
fundamentalism, 103, 105–6

Gaebelein, A. C., 103
Gamertsfelter, S. J., 79, 102, 104–5, 216
Garrett Biblical Institute, 103–4
Geeting, George Adam, 26, 30–31
Gemeinschaft (Fellowship), 15–16
General Christian Social Action Committee, 186
General Conference, 34, 49, 51, 53, 86–87, 89, 91, 98, 103, 157, 159, 165, 167–68, 184, 186, 189, 194–96, 203
General Rules, 45
German Baptists, 19
German Calvinism, 10

German Conference of the MEC, 47
German Democratic Republic, 177
German Evangelical Reformed Church, 28
German Methodist Church, 46, 48–49
German Philadelphian societies, 63
German Pietism, 5, 7, 37, 43, 52, 80, 149, 192
German rationalism, 100
German Reformation, 77
German Reformed Church, 27, 36, 180
  in America, 20
  in Baltimore, 27
German Reformed Pietists, 58–59, 65, 88, 90
Germantown, 19–20, 26
Germany, 9, 19, 24, 27, 165–78
Gesinger, Jacob, 31
Glossbrenner, J. J., 70
Goins, Minnie Jackson, 195
Golgotha, 51
Gorrell, Donald, 193, 200, 202
Gray, James, 103
Great Meetings, 23, 26–27, 31, 33, 60
Greensburg, Ohio, 99
Griffith, Helen, 205
Grosch, Christopher, 30
grosse Versammlung (a big meeting), 10, 23, 38, 67
Gruber, Eberhard Ludwig, 64, 68
Gruber, Jacob, 48

Halle University, 8–9, 59, 64
Hammer, W. H., 201–2
Hangen, Ammon, 105
Harper, William Rainey, 102
Harrisburg, Pennsylvania, 41
Hartzler, H. B., 103
Hartzler, Jacob, 103
Haug, Johann Friedrich, 63
Haumersen, Irene, 203
Haven, Joseph, 100
heart religion, 5, 23, 76, 94
Heck Lectures, 216
Heidelberg Catechism, 10, 59, 63, 77, 79–80, 83, 88

INDEX

Herborn Academy, 9, 59, 62, 192
Herborn School of Reformed Pietism, 57
Hershey, John, 31
Heussi, Karl, 5
higher criticism, 100, 102–3
Hoffman, Lizzie, 198
holiness, 64, 66, 84–85, 95, 131, 161, 164, 183, 188–89, 218, 224
Holland, 58, 72
Holy Catholic Church, 40
Holy Communion, 50, 160
Holy Spirit, 14, 26–27, 38, 68, 72–73, 77, 97, 114–20, 127–28, 130–35, 182, 189, 217, 226
Horch, Heinrich, 62–63
Houtz, Anthony, 11, 93
Huelster, Anton, 100, 102

Iliff School of Theology, 104
Industrial Revolution, 166–67
infant baptism, 87–88, 151, 158–59
infant dedication, 87, 156–57, 159
Inspirationists, 67–68, 72
International Council of Religious Education, 102
Iowa, 68
Irenaeus, 58

Jacoby, Ludwig Sigismund, 168
James, William, 76
Jansenism, 5
Japan, 206
Jesus Christ, 6, 13, 15, 50, 64, 107, 154, 161, 163, 171, 182–85, 214
Job, Rueben (Bishop), 14
Johnstown, Pennsylvania, 69
Josephus, 97
Juniata County, Pennsylvania, 38
justification, 10, 84, 182
justifying grace, 220
justifying love, 21

Kant, Immanuel, 100, 217, 222
Kantian intuitionism, 78
Keagy, Nancy, 21

Keller, Rosemary, 196, 203
Kemp, Peter, 31
Kentucky, 179
Kimmel, G. B., 106
Kingdom Advance Program, 171, 173–74
Kingdom of God, 164
Kingdom Service Fund of the Evangelical Association, 171
Kleinfeltersville, Pennsylvania, 40
Kohl, Manfred, 7
Kramer, Lois, 208
Krecker, Elizabeth, 200–201, 203, 205–12
Krecker, Frederick, 206
Krum, Henry, 31
Kurz, Sebastian, 167
Kutztown, Pennsylvania, 47

Lancaster, Pennsylvania, 10, 20, 23–26, 30, 41–42, 47, 67, 206
Landeskirche, 7, 61, 165, 170
Lane, S. A., 196
Last Supper, 153, 160
Latvia, 168
Lawrence, John, 15
Leade, Jane, 62
Lebanon, Pennsylvania, 30, 42
Leger, Richard, 176
Lehigh County, Pennsylvania, 38
Lehman, Adam, 30–31
Leisser, Samuel, 40
Lewisburg, Pennsylvania, 49
liberal Protestantism, 78
liberal theology, 78–79, 167
liberation theology, 218
Lichtes Leute, 67
Lindberg, Carl, 3
Link, Conrad, 168
Long, Joseph (Bishop), 97
Long's barn, 10, 16, 26, 67
Lord's Prayer, 45
Lord's Supper, 8, 40, 50, 130, 152–53, 159–61
Lorenz, Edmund S., 156
Lotze, Rudolph, 102

Index

Love Feast, 31, 67
Luther, Martin, 4
Lutheran, 4, 6, 11, 26, 37, 67
Lutheran Augsburg Confession, 43

Macarius, 61
Macartney, Clarence, 103
Mack, Alexander, 19
Magalis, Elaine, 193
Marburg Bible, 62
Maryland, 20, 27, 32, 75
Mather, Cotton, 9
Mathews, Shailer, 102, 104
Mayer, Abraham, 32
McLanachan, Mary, 198, 201
Mennonist Society, 20, 29
Mennonites, 9, 16, 19–23, 26–27, 30, 36–37, 77, 85, 88–89, 180
Middletown, Pennsylvania, 42
Mifflin, Pennsylvania, 38
Miller, George, 39, 41–45, 71, 95–96
Miller, Roy D., 185
Mills, John S. (Bishop), 69–70
mission society, 165
missionary societies, 197
Mississippi Basin, 65
Moody Bible Institute, 103
Moravian(s), 15, 19, 24, 30, 36, 68, 192
Mount Hermon Female Seminary, 205
Mount Holyoke Female Seminary, 205
Mueller, Reuben (Bishop), 17

Naila, Franconia, 168
Nassau, 9
National Council of Churches, 17
Neidigs Leute, 67
Neitz, Solomon, 99
Nelson, James, 45
Ness, John, 151–52
Netherlands, 20, 24
New Berlin, Pennsylvania, 14, 51
new birth, 13–14, 26, 76, 87, 164, 220–21
New Jersey, 20, 38
New Jerusalem, 63, 66, 69
New Lights, 22–23, 26
New Measures, 154

New Prophets, 64, 67–68
New Theology, 100, 103
New Virginia, 22, 27
New York, 20, 24
Newcomer, Christian (Bishop), 15, 30–31, 35
Nicene Creed, 110, 112
Niebel, Benjamin, 198
1908 Social Creed of the Federal Council of Churches, 183
Niswonger, Ella, 183, 194–95, 202
North-Western College, 100
Northampton County, Pennsylvania, 38

Oberlin College, 104, 154
Old Otterbein Church, 15
O'Malley, J. Steven, 9, 16, 25, 37–38, 44, 53, 84, 166, 173, 181
Ontario, 65
Opheral, Charity, 194
ordinances, 152–53
ordination, viii, 152, 196
  of women, 183, 193, 195–96, 198, 202
ordo salutis, 220
original sin, 102
orthopathy, 76, 164
Oslo conference, 173
Otterbein, George, 10
Otterbein, Johann Daniel, 10
Otterbein, Philip William, 4, 9–16, 24, 26–28, 30–36, 42, 47, 57, 60, 65–69, 77, 79–81, 83–85, 88–91, 180, 192, 225
Otterbein Press, 187
Outler, Albert, 145, 215, 217, 222

Pastorius, Franz Daniel, 19
Pearl Harbor, 211
Pennsylvania, 9–11, 20, 26–27, 38, 47, 57, 60, 65, 67, 71, 75, 93, 99, 166
Pennsylvania German Methodists, 46
Pentecost, 26, 30, 58, 64, 67–69, 71
Pentecost Meetings, 67
Pentecostal, 68
Perkins, Mellie, 201

Index

Pfrimmer, George, 31
Philadelphia, 19–20, 24, 47, 62
Philadelphian hermeneutic, 66
philosophy, 100
Pipe Creek, 26, 28
Pittsburgh, 47
pneumatology, 128, 134–35
Pottsville, Pennsylvania, 38
prayer, 203, 208–9, 213
Prayer for Pardon, 50
Prayer of Consecration, 153
Prayer of Humble Access, 50
Prepatory Membership Roll, 158
Presbyterianism, 86
prevenient grace, 220
Prussia mission, 166
Pseudo-Macarius, 61
purgatory, 111
Puritanism, 6

Quakerism, 5
Quakertown, Pennsylvania, 38
Queen Anne of England, 20

radical Pietists, 58, 60–66, 69
Rall, H. F., 104
Ramist Theology, 60
Rauschenbusch, Walter, 104
Reading, Pennsylvania, 38, 44, 46–47
rebaptism, 87, 151
Reber, Audrie, 197, 199, 201, 209
Red Bird Mission, 179–80
Reformation, 4–5, 20, 63, 79, 154, 156, 163, 166–67, 178
Reformed Church, 9–10, 37, 77
Reformed Church in Germany, 24
Regeneration, 77, 83, 182
Reitz, Johann Heinrich, 61
religious affections, 94
religious empiricism, 6
renewed Pentecost, 58 ,68–69 ,72
responsible grace, 220
Reutlingen Seminary, 168, 174
Revolutionary War, 60
Rhineland, 58, 72
Riegel, Adam, 11, 93

Ritschl, Albrecht, 102
Robert, Dana, 197, 200
Rock, Johann Friedrich, 64
Romer, Dr. Ignaz, 42, 44
Runyon, Theodore, 164
Ryan, Sarah, 192
Ryland, Brother William, 35

Sabbatarianism, 8
Sabbath, 19, 21, 23, 31, 34, 133, 183, 185
Sacraments, 84, 86–87, 150, 152–54, 160, 170
Sage, Esther Balmer, 194
salvation, 21, 32, 46, 71, 76–77, 84, 87, 190, 219
salvation history (*Heilsgeschichte*), 58–59, 62, 67
Sam's Creek, 28, 30
sanctification, 6, 10–11, 26, 51, 68, 72, 77, 84–85, 89, 182, 188–89
sanctifying grace, 220
Sanctus, 50, 153
Satan, 26
satisfaction theory of atonement, 131
Sattler, Gary, 8
Saxons, 80
Saxony, 192
Schaeffer, Roberta, 179–80
Schlatter, Michael, 20, 24
Schleiermacher, Friedrich, 79, 217
Schmidt, Jean Miller, 193, 197
Schneider, Francis, 213
scholastic theologies, 61
scholastic theology, 99
Schramm, Johann Henry, 9
Schutz, Johann Jakob, 19
Schuylkill County, Pennsylvania, 38
Schwarzenau Brethren, 19
Schwope, Benedict, 4, 26, 28, 30
Scofield, C. I., 103
Scottish common sense realism, 78, 100, 102
Second Great Awakening, 76
1792 Methodist Communion rite, 50
Sexton, Lydia, 194
Seybert, Johannes, 65, 68, 94, 97

Index

Sheldon, H. C., 104
Showers, Justina Lorenz, 201
Sierra Leone Conference of United Methodism, 69
Simpson, A. B., 103
sin, 26, 32, 66, 71, 76–77, 83–84, 94–95
slavery, 182–83, 185–86
Social Creed of 1909, 82
social gospel, 105–6, 183
social justice, 184, 189, 219
Social Service Commission, 183
society, 165
Society of the Inspired, 64
sola scriptura, 78
Song of Songs, 62
Spayth, Henry, 20, 22, 24–25, 27
Spener, Philipp Jakob, 4–8, 12–14, 19, 59–60, 181
Spreng, Minerva Strawman, 199, 201, 206, 210
Stahlschmidt, Christian, 65
Stamm, John (Bishop), 17, 106, 182
state churches (*Landeskirchen*), 7, 61, 165, 170
Stauffacher, C. H. (Bishop), 182
Staves, S. J., 202
Steinacker, Peter, 7
Stevens City, Virginia, 30
Stevens, George, 104
Stoeffler, Ernest, 3, 6, 181
Strawbridge, Robert, 26, 30
Stukenberg, Edward, 203
Stuttgart, 71
Stuttgart Publishing House, 174
Stuttgart-Bonlanden, 167
substitutionary atonement, 105
Sunday, Billy, 103
Sursum corda, 50
Susquehanna River, 38, 47, 49
Swiss Reformed Church, 20
Switzerland, 9, 19, 168, 172, 174
Synder, David, 32
systematic theology, 68

temperance, 183, 185
Terry, Milton, 72, 103
Tersteegen, Gerhard, 65, 72
Teutonic, 80
theosis, 132
Third Reich, 170
Thirty Years War, 5
Thirty-nine Articles of Religion, 80, 90, 151
Thompson, Maggie, 194
Thompson, Patricia, 195, 207
Tokyo Bible School, 207
Torrey, R. A., 103
Tranquebar, India, 9
transubstantiation, 111
Tremont Temple, 100
Trotter, Mel, 103
Troxel, Abraham, 30–31
Troxell, Barbara, 208
Tubingen, Germany, 7, 64
Tulpehocken, 10, 25
Twenty-five Articles of Religion, 43, 80, 109–35

Union Biblical Institute, 72, 100, 152, 194, 206
The United Brethren mission in Germany, 168
United Theological Seminary, 152, 187–88, 216
universal atonement, 79
University of Chicago, 102, 106

Virgin Mary, 127
Virginia, 23
Virginia Preachers, 23, 27
Vitringa, Campegius, 59–60
Vogelbach, Jacob, 94
von Zinzendorf, Nikolaus (Count), 15

Walter, John, 39–40, 42, 46, 94, 96
war, 134
Ward, Reginald, 72
Watson, Richard, 97, 220
Weidner, Henry, 30
Weimar Republic, 170
Wert, Newell, 106
Wesley, Charles, 152

Wesley, John, 13, 39, 44–45, 50, 52, 61, 111, 133, 151–54, 160, 163, 165, 189, 192, 217–18, 223, 225
Wesleyan quadrilateral, 222
Wesleyan revivalism, 88
West African Colony, 69
Wetterau district, 64
Whatcoat, Richard (MEC Bishop), 31
Whateley, Richard, 100
Whitfield, George, 22
Wichern, Johann Hinrich, 167
Wicke, Lloyd (Bishop), 69
Wiedergeburt (the new birth), 8
Will, Jim, 195–96
Willett, Herbert, 102
Wilson, Robert Dick, 103
Wittgenstein, 63–64
Wolff, Christian, 222
Woman's Home and Foreign Missionary Society, 200, 206
Women's Missionary Association, 198, 200
Women's Missionary Association of the EA, 207
Women's Missionary Association of the UBC, 183
Women's Missionary Society, 200, 202, 206, 208
World Council of Churches, 17
World War I, 170, 198
World War II, 170, 172, 211
Wright, Milton (Bishop), 69–70
Wurttemberg, 59, 67, 168, 170

Yale Divinity School, 149, 188
York, 10, 26–27
Yost, Ella, 199, 201

Zwingli, Ulrich, 4

www.ingramcontent.com/pod-product-compliance
Lightning Source LLC
Chambersburg PA
CBHW011139290426
44108CB00020B/2684